The
'I Wills' of Christ

The
'I Wills' of Christ

Thoughts on some of the passages
in which the words 'I will' are used by
our Lord Jesus Christ

PHILIP BENNETT POWER

THE BANNER OF TRUTH TRUST

THE BANNER OF TRUTH TRUST
3 Murrayfield Road, Edinburgh, EH 12 6EL
PO Box 621, Carlisle, Pennsylvania 17013, USA

★

First published 1862
First Banner of Truth edition 1984
ISBN 0 85151 429 4

★

Reproduced, printed and bound in Great Britain by
Hazell Watson & Viney Limited,
Member of the BPCC Group,
Aylesbury, Bucks

PREFACE.

HE following pages do not pretend to exhaust the subject of the "I wills" of Christ. Those which are to be found in the messages to the Churches in the commencement of the Revelation, and which are here left untouched, would be abundantly sufficient for a volume. The author has taken but one here and there, and woven them together so as to present the reader with a picture of the Lord's gracious work upon a soul. The book might have been, with tolerable accuracy, entitled "The history of a soul exemplified in the 'I wills' of Christ."

We have the sinner presented to us as *invited;* then on his acceptance of the invitation, as being *received;* then as being *healed;* then made a *confessor of Christ;* then a *worker for Christ;* then as *comforted of Christ* in life's struggles; then as being *placed wholly at Christ's disposal;* then as attaining to the highest of all points of sanctification, viz., *the subjection of the will;* and finally as being *received to glory* to be with Jesus where He is.

Experience has shewn the author the great value of illustration both in writing and preaching; he has, therefore, gathered together many facts with which to illustrate the truths in the following pages. Some of the extracts it was impossible to shorten, as by so doing, the spiritual *processes,* in which consist their value, would have been lost; they would have been worthless if more condensed. Some of these extracts have been printed in smaller type so as to save space.

The author is deeply thankful to Almighty God, for the blessing which He has vouchsafed to very many of the readers of his book, to which this is a companion, viz., "The 'I Wills' of the Psalms;" and he earnestly prays that a like blessing may be vouchsafed to the readers of this book. Having heard Christ's "I will" of invitation, may they hear also His "I will" of glorification, and finally be with Him for ever, where He is.

Christ Church Parsonage,
Worthing, October, 1862.

CONTENTS.

The "I Will" of Invitation.

The "I Will" of Reception.

The "I Will" of Healing.

The "I Will" of Confession.

The "I Will" of Service.

The "I Will" of Comfort.

The "I Will" of Disposal.

The "I Will" of Subjection.

The "I Will" of Glorification.

The preciousness of family gatherings—Solemn thoughts connected with them—The family gathering of the redeemed—Efforts now being made therefor—The prominent position which this "I will" occupied in the mind of Christ—Jesus, a man of the future as well as the present—The future of Christ's people before Him

The "I Will" of Invitation.

Matthew xi, 28—30.

MATTHEW xi, 28.

"Come unto me, all ye that labour and are heavy laden, and I will give you rest."

⟶⊸◇⊶⟵

"REST!" Rest! this weary world, and all therein, are seeking rest! It may be that men little know what their hearts, in deepest truth, are craving, but in all cases, it is Rest.

For rest, the warrior draws his sword—for rest, the merchant toils behind his desk; for rest, the sailor ploughs the waves—for rest, the shepherd tarries by his flock; for rest, the young man mingles in the dance—for rest, the widow weeps in misery alone; the heart is full of craving; and hither and thither does it turn for rest. 'Tis true, heart-cravings are not alike in all; this one seeks rest in honour, and this in wealth; this in love, and this in hate; some would find it in grasping all things, and some only in being let alone; but so it is, that ever since man departed from his God, whether he be found in solitude or in a crowd, probe to the very *bottom* of his heart-longings and exertions, and he will be found to be in pursuit of *rest*.

And where will he find it? It is a part of earth's
curse, that in some form or other it is ever claiming the
sweat of the brow, throwing forth thorns and thistles,
and that it can afford to man no rest. "Arise ye and
depart, for this is not your rest," is the voice which
flowers and fruit, as well as thistle and thorn have for
all the sons of men. "In us," say all created things,
"when used, even to the uttermost, man finds no abiding
rest. There *remaineth* a rest for the *people of God.*"
And for *them*, there is also a present rest; amid earth's
turmoil, the shaking of its thrones, and principalities,
and powers, there appears ONE with soft and gentle voice
and look, who proclaims Himself a King—the Prince of
peace—the Giver of rest to all who will be the subjects
of His kingdom, which was not of this world, but from
above. Oh, let it be observed, how distinctly Jesus
declared that His kingdom was not of this world, for
that if it were, then would His servants have fought,
securing it by earthly toil and strife. It would have
been easy for Him to muster under His banner all the
Jews from Dan even unto Beersheba; and the history of
the siege of Jerusalem shews us, how desperately they
would have fought. Had Jesus undertaken at that time
to restore the kingdom unto Israel; and had He been
willing to assume the headship of it to Himself, the
country would have rushed to arms, and there is little
doubt but that it would have been freed.

This repudiation of earthly sovereignty we find all
through the life of Christ, and incidentally it comes
before us here.

Had Jesus been an earthly Sovereign, about to set
up an earthly kingdom and an earthly court, He would

have attracted to Himself such as would have conduced to His earthly honour, to His profit, to the stability of His throne. The monarchs of this world try to attract to their courts those who are famous for learning, wisdom, and art; they like to be surrounded by the influential and the rich; but the blessed Jesus tried to attract to Himself the wretched, the outcast, and the sad; from such were to be drawn the noblest courtiers for a spiritual throne. This is what we find Jesus doing here; yea, this is what He is doing even now; still saying, as He did of old, "Come unto me, all ye that labour and are heavy laden, and I will give you rest." Christ proposes Himself as an object of attraction now; He will be one of repulsion hereafter, when He utters those tremendous words, "Depart, ye cursed, into everlasting fire, prepared for the devil and his angels." It is an awful thought; He must necessarily be so; there is no such thing as Christ's mere toleration of anyone hereafter; the mighty power that is in Him must act; those who rejected Him, and would not be drawn by Him, shall not be able to abide with Him; Christ must then exercise a throwing-off power; it will be no longer, "Come unto me all ye that labour and are heavy laden;" but "Depart into the land of unrest for ever, to labour, and to be heavy laden evermore."

May no reader of this book ever hear such words as those; rather may each have rest in Jesus here; and finally enter into the rest which remaineth for the people of God.

Let us first of all see (1.) WHO THE LABOURERS AND HEAVY LADEN ARE; (2.) then we shall see WHO HELPS THEM; and (3.) lastly, WHAT IS THEIR REST.

"All ye that labour and are heavy laden" embraces a wide field indeed. This voice passes over the troubled waves of human life wherever they are surging; it is the only voice that can say, "Peace, be still!" And where, in the world, do we find any rest apart from the hearing and yielding obedience to this voice? Nowhere! man is ever being urged on in the hope of obtaining satisfaction; he always has, as he thinks, a point in which he will obtain rest; but when he reaches that point, he finds that there is unrest on the crest of the wave, as well as in the trough of the sea: that man never continueth in one stay; he finds that the utmost he has done, is to surmount one of the many hills that are around—the fancied rest is further—ever further on;—he must gird up his loins and climb again. Oh! with what weary, heated spirits are men seeking after rest; and the bustle and toil of life seem such that they have no ears for hearing the meek and lowly voice of Jesus, saying "Come unto ME, and I will give you rest,"—not always rest *from* earthly toil, but rest *in* earthly toil; calm repose, even though the ship in which you sail be tossed about upon the waves. Adam entered upon unrest when he hid himself in the trees of the garden, from the presence of the Lord; and he transmitted that unrest to us. Rest can only be had in restoration, and that is what Jesus offers.—"I will give you rest." *

* Cain, as a rejecter of atonement by blood, and a persecutor unto death, of the one by whom such atonement was held and acted upon, is presented to us, as put into a position of permanent unrest. "Behold thou hast driven me out this day from the face of the earth, and from thy face shall I be hid; and I shall be as a fugitive and a vagabond upon the earth; and it shall come to pass that everyone that findeth

Who are the labourers here invited by the Lord?
Stier says,* that " κοπιῶντες (kopiontes) the 'labourers' is
subject to a necessary *restriction,* and connects itself
with πεφορτισμένοι (pephortismenoi) the 'heavy laden,' as
τῷ πνεύματι (to pneumati) 'in spirit,' does with πτωχοὶ
(ptokoi) 'poor,' in the Sermon on the Mount.   It means
not here, according to its usual meaning elsewhere, those
who labour simply, and strain their energies, for such
vehement personal labour and exertion, as long as it is
fruitlessly put forth, effectually hinders from coming to
the only source of re-invigoration; but it means, according to the proper and original idea of the word, those
who are *exhausted* and spent; who, pressed down by
their burden, can bear it no longer.   Though He may
call all, yet is His call heard only by those who feel their
burden, and would be freed from it: this is the mediatorial link between the offer and acceptance of salvation."
We agree to this; but between the 'labouring' and the
'heavy laden,' we think we see a distinction—possibly
two classes; it may be that in the labour and the
oppression of the burden, we have two phases of the
same misery.   We shall speak of the labouring and the
heavy laden separately; alas! the combination of them
both is only too easily within our reach.

And, first: some there are who are labouring after
God's peace; they want justification; the consciousness

me shall slay me."   Cain's doom, in its fearful, typical aspect was not
thus to be cut short.   "And the Lord set a mark upon Cain, *lest* any
finding him should slay him."   We subsequently find Cain building a
city—an attempt, perhaps, to invalidate the curse; in which he,
doubtless, never could succeed.

* Stier on the "Words of Christ."

of pardon; they have attained to a knowledge of need; they are, and must be, restless until that need be supplied. The history of the Church of God is full of instances of the hard labour of His people, while they were endeavouring after rest; and ere they found it in His Son.

Let us look at a few of these instances; nothing appeals so forcibly to the mind as cases of actual experience. In the appendix the reader will find the hard struggling of Martin Luther, and David Brainerd. The processes of their minds during their earnest search after rest are of so much importance that we have given their experiences at some length; many who think it strange concerning the fiery trial with which they are tried, will find that as regards intensity and duration it has been gone through by others before them. The unwritten lives of the great majority of God's people, who have departed in peace, would tell us like tales of struggling and labouring if they were unfolded to our view; after a storm has come the calm. Let us look, however, at the records which we possess of the struggles of some of God's people.

Simeon's account of himself is this. He says:—

"It was but the third day after my arrival at college, that I understood I should be expected shortly to attend the Lord's Supper. Without a moment's loss of time, I bought the 'Whole Duty of Man,' (the only religious book I had ever heard of,) and began to read it with great diligence; at the same time calling my ways to remembrance, and crying to God for mercy; and so earnest was I in these exercises, that within three weeks I made myself quite ill with reading, fasting, and prayer.

I next procured 'Kettlewell on the Sacrament,' but I remember that it required more of me than I could bear, and, therefore, I procured 'Wilson on the Lord's Supper,' which seemed to be more moderate in its requirements. I continued with unabated earnestness to search out, and mourn over the numberless iniquities of my former life ; and so greatly was my mind oppressed with the weight of them, that I frequently looked upon the dogs with envy; wishing, if it were possible, that I could be blessed with their mortality, and they be cursed with my immortality in my stead. I set myself immediately to undo all my former sins, as far as I could ; and did it in some instances which required great self-denial, my distress of mind continued for about three months, and well might it have continued for years, but God began at last to smile upon me, and to give me a hope of acceptance with Him. The circumstances attendant on this were very peculiar. My efforts to remedy my former misdeeds had been steadily pursued, and in comparison of approving myself to God in this matter, I made no account of shame, or loss, or anything in the world. In proportion as I proceeded in this work, I felt somewhat of hope springing up in my mind ; but it was an indistinct kind of hope, founded on God's mercy to real penitents. But as I was reading 'Wilson on the Lord's Supper,' I met with an expression to this effect: 'That the Jews knew what they did, when they transferred their sin to the head of their offering.' The thought rushed into my mind, What! may I transfer all my guilt to another? Has God provided an offering for me, that I may lay my sins on His head ? Then, God willing, I will not bear them on my own soul one moment longer. Accordingly

I sought to lay my sins upon the sacred head of Jesus; and on the Wednesday began to have a hope of mercy; on the Thursday that hope increased; on the Friday and Saturday it became more strong; and on the Sunday morning, (Easter Day,) I awoke with those words upon my heart and lips, 'Jesus Christ is risen to-day! Hallelujah!' From that hour peace flowed in rich abundance into my soul."*

Hewitson again, speaking of his conversion, says:— "I am sure of this, that *for a long, long time*, I have been deceiving myself and making myself miserable every day, through ignorance of the free, glorious gospel, while I imagined that I clearly understood its gracious character. For long the painful feeling still preyed upon my mind, that I must do some good works myself, or God would not accept me in Christ Jesus; and my misery was, that while Satan thus blinded my eyes, I found myself unable to do the good works that I would. Now I see that the gospel is quite different—that it is free, and full, and wholly of grace."

And if we go back to the early history of the Church, the confessions of St. Augustine will supply another striking example.

The house he lodged in had a little garden, in which he could always reckon on finding a quiet retreat. "Thither," says he, "the tumult of my breast hurried me, where no man might hinder the hot contention wherein I had engaged with myself. What said I not against myself? With what scourges of condemnation lashed I not my soul, that it might follow me striving to

* See Carus' "Memoirs of Simeon."

go after Thee! . . . . Thus soul-sick was I, and tormented, accusing myself much more severely than my wont, rolling and turning me in my chain."

For *ten years* had he been groping after Christ, but all his struggles only left him more guilty and more self-condemned. "I cast myself down," says he, "I know not how, under a certain fig-tree, giving full vent to my tears; and to this purpose spake I unto Thee;—'How long, Lord, wilt Thou be angry? for ever? How long? how long? to-morrow, and to-morrow? Why not now? why not now?'" Augustine was still speaking and weeping in the most bitter contrition of his heart, when suddenly, there fell upon his ear from a neighbouring house, a voice, as of a boy or girl chanting and oft repeating—"Take up and read! take up and read!" Checking the torrent of his tears, he arose, interpreting it to be no other than a command from God, to open the book and read the first chapter he should find. He snatched the volume of St. Paul, which he had brought with him to the garden, opened it, and his eye fell on that Scripture—"Put ye on the Lord Jesus Christ, and make not provision for the flesh, to fulfil the lusts thereof." "No further would I read," says he; "nor needed I; for instantly, at the end of this sentence, by a light as it were of serenity infused into my heart, all the darkness of doubt vanished away; I felt it scatter, and descried the dawning day. . . . .

"How hast thou loved us, Father, delivering up thy only Son for us ungodly! Well may my hope be strong through such an intercessor; else I should despair. Many and great are my diseases, Thy medicine larger still! . . . Terrified with my sins, and the weight

of my misery, I was desponding, but thou encouragest
me, saying, 'Christ died for all, that they which live
should not henceforth live unto themselves, but to Him
who died for them and rose again.' So I cast all my
care on Thee, Lord, that I may live—not with doubting,
but with assured confidence do I love Thee, O Lord!
Thou art my King; reign absolute in my heart!" And
some years after this, we find him saying: "No want of
deserving on my part, not even the lowest and most
mortifying thoughts of my vileness and unworthiness, nor
the highest and most enlarged notions of the excellence
of the bliss in heaven, can cast me down from this high
tower of hope."*

Many a long century had passed away, when a boy
at Oxford, Charles Wesley by name, "began to be concerned about the conscientious improvement of his time,
which had before been lost in idle diversion, and commenced diligently to observe the *method* of study prescribed by the statutes of the University. Others joined
him, forming a little society, distinguished by observance
of the method of study, and of the sacramental observances and means of grace. A thing so extraordinary
in that day as serious attention to study and religious
worship, even on the part of a handful of boys, could
not pass without observation and ridicule, and young
Wesley and his friends, from their regard to the method
of study, soon went by the slang epithet of the 'Methodists.' John Wesley, who was five years older than
Charles, now four years a serious and devout clergyman

* See "Milner's Church History," Vol. II ; and "Memoirs of St.
Augustine," by Rev. J. Baillie.

of the Church of England, at this time returned to Oxford as a tutor, and joining the little society of 'Methodists,' became a master-spirit among them. Their earnestness and austerity in religion deepened to a wonderful extent, and exhibited itself in unbounded self-denials, charities, fastings, prayers, and labours, in all which they found no spiritual peace, yet persevered in spite of opposition, defamation, and contempt.

" Four or five years had thus passed over the heads of these young devotees, when an indigent student entered as a *servitor*, defraying his college expenses by performing menial offices in the rooms of the wealthier young men in the university. This was George Whitefield, then eighteen years of age, both by nature and grace marked as the greatest beyond comparison of those among whom he moved as a menial. He was strongly attracted towards the Wesleys and their associates, by their earnest religious life, but from the poverty of his station dared not intrude himself upon their notice. But having been named to Charles Wesley by a poor woman whom he had employed on an errand of charity, he was sought out, and introduced to the little brotherhood, of which he became one of the most zealous members. It was among their rules, for example, frequently 'to interrogate themselves whether they had been simple and recollected, whether they had always prayed with fervour, on Monday, Wednesday, Friday, Saturday noon; if they had used a collect at nine, twelve, and three o'clock; duly meditated on Sunday, from three to four, on Thomas à Kempis; mused on Wednesday and Friday, from twelve to one, on the Passion,' etc. 'I now began,' says Whitefield, 'like them,

to live by rule, and to pick up every fragment of my
time, that not a moment of it might be lost. Like them,
having no weekly sacrament at our college, although the
rubric required it, I received it every Sunday at Christ
Church. I joined with them in keeping the Stations, by
fasting Wednesdays and Fridays, and left no means
unused which I thought would lead me nearer to Christ.
By degrees I began to leave off eating fruits and such
like, and gave the money I usually spent in that way to
the poor. Afterwards I chose the worst sort of food,
though my place furnished me with variety. My apparel
was mean. I thought it unbecoming a penitent to have
his hair powdered. I wore woollen gloves, a patched
gown, and dirty shoes. It was now suggested to me
that Jesus Christ was among the wild beasts when He
was tempted, and that I ought to follow His example ;
and being willing, as I thought, to imitate Jesus Christ,
after supper I went into Christ Church walk, near our
college, and continued in silent prayer nearly two hours,
sometimes lying on my face, sometimes kneeling upon my
knees. The night being stormy, gave me awful thoughts
of the day of judgment. The next day I repeated the
same exercise at the same place. After this the holy
season of Lent came on, which our friends kept very
strictly, eating no flesh during the six weeks, except on
Saturdays and Sundays. I abstained frequently on
Saturdays also, and ate nothing on the other days
(except Sunday) but sage tea without sugar, and coarse
bread. I constantly walked out in the cold mornings
till one part of my hands was quite black.'

"This truly Romish course of penance and austerity
finally exhausted nature, and threw him into an alarm-

ing illness which lasted seven weeks. This sickness Whitefield calls, in his journal, 'a glorious visitation.' The constant brotherly attentions of his fellow-ascetics, the Wesleys, with their maxims and citations, were ineffectual now to comfort or direct his mind. His course of externals, with the energy of the natural man which had much to do in prompting and sustaining it, was effectually broken up, and his thoughts communed with his own heart and the word of God. He spent much of his time in reading the Greek Testament, and in prayer. He gained more clear, truthful, and affecting views of his own sinfulness, and saw how hopeless was the effort to remove a sense of guilt by religious observances. 'One day,' he informs us, 'perceiving an uncommon drought and noisome clamminess in my mouth, and using things to allay my thirst but in vain, it was suggested to me that when Jesus Christ cried out '*I thirst*,' His sufferings were near over. Upon this I threw myself on the bed and cried out, *I thirst, I thirst!* Soon after I perceived my load to go off; a spirit of mourning was taken from me; and I knew what it was truly to rejoice in the Lord. When I said those words, *I thirst, I thirst,* my soul was in agony; I thirsted for a clear discovery of my pardon through Jesus Christ, and the seal of the Spirit. I was at the same time enabled to look up with faith to the glorious Lord Jesus as dying for sinners, and for some time I could not avoid singing psalms wherever I was."

These are but specimens of a vast multitude who are labouring after peace and rest; could we see all who are thus toiling, we should have to look upon hundreds of thousands; and very fearful indeed would be the anguish

revealed.   Were all the various forms of toil embodied
before our eyes, we should be surprised at the different
loads under which men are struggling in their efforts to
get peace.

And here will be a fitting place to say a word or two
with reference to what is popularly known as "the
revival" in the present day.   I quite believe that there
are seasons when there are special manifestations of God's
Spirit; and at such seasons I am quite prepared to look
for something beyond the experience of what we might
call "ordinary times."   I fully believe that people may
be what is popularly called "stricken;" and that the
peace of God may be obtained in a moment of time.
But, whilst holding all this, I cannot but object to the
violence of many who are known as "revival preachers"
(alas! that we are not all known as revival preachers!)
and who in too many instances deal with indiscriminat-
ing force.

It is true that there is but the one panacea for all
human guilt and woe, and that is the blood of Christ.
The "Come unto ME" is the only hope; but we say,
this mighty truth may be abused as well as used.   Yes!
unthinking, unconscience-stricken men may be carried as
it were off their legs by the torrent of the preacher's
energy; and be swept down the stream of the prevailing
enthusiasm, without being able to give a reason for the
desire that is within them.   We shall never be surprised
at hearing that some who were thought to be savingly
affected at the time of a revival have fallen off; we
firmly believe that a sufficient number will remain as a
solid increase to the church of God, to prove that the
revival was no myth.   It has been well observed, that

the proportion of awakenings to conversions, is much the same as of blossoms to fruit. Who disbelieves in the existence or value of the fruit, because it has swelled, and ripened, from amid a quantity of blossoms which have come to nought?

We believe, we say, that there will be fallings off, and we believe that amongst these will be found many, who had so to speak, only been revived by man—galvanized, but not vivified. They heard a formula about "finding peace in Christ;" but they knew not that they were at war with God—they heard about "rest in Christ," but they knew not that they were heavy laden; they heard of His being a physician, but they knew not that they were sick—they knew not that they "were wretched, and miserable, and poor, and blind, and naked;" they thought that they had need of nothing; they needed to be counselled to buy of Him gold, tried in the fire, that they might be rich; and white raiment, that they might be clothed; and that the shame of their nakedness do not appear, and to anoint that eyes with eye-salve that they might see: Rev. iv, 17, 18.

There seems to be a crude and sweeping way of dealing with all souls alike, as though because there were but the one disease and the one remedy, therefore all should be treated in exactly the same way. We believe fully in the oneness of the disease and of the remedy; but we believe also in diversities of mental constitutions; and in processes of the Holy Ghost. It is possible that we may be met with the statement that conscience and faith—the two great elements in conversion—are independent of the mental constitution; and that, whatever a man's mental constitution may be, he can be converted, if his conscience be smitten, and his faith be stirred—we firmly believe it—we hold that but scant intelligence is *necessary* to salvation;* but at the same time, when there is a mental constitution it will work; it will show its peculiarities; it has often to be carried through certain ¡processes; and we cannot agree to ignore this method of the Spirit's dealing, because by a *speedy* act of faith, so many have, thank God, found peace.

The tendency, in the present day, is to undervalue such spiritual work as is not rapid; and to think that souls must be converted as with the speed of a lightning flash.

It would be sad indeed for the church of God, if there were none who could sympathize with the labouring soul, with its difficulties, its struggles, its burdens, and its tears; if there were none skilled to enter into

---

* "I have seen Jesus," said a poor imbecile, who for many years had been the terror of his neighbourhood, but who under the Divine influence had become a mild and gentle creature. "I have seen Jesus," was his only reply to those who inquired what had induced a change so wonderful. And as the years passed on, and the love of Jesus showed itself in his every act, this single testimony to the power of the cross, won many a stouter heart to yield to the blessed Redeemer.

"Does Jesus love foolish boy?" asked an idiotic lad of the superintendent of the Idiotic Asylum at Essex Hall. On being told that He did, the poor child could hardly contain himself for joy. "Jesus love, Jesus love me," he cried, "nobody love foolish boy before;" and as his time passed on, the consciousness of the love of Jesus made even the lack lustre eye and grinning face of the boy to assume a look of intelligence, and his struggles to subdue the evil propensities of his wayward nature, showed that grace had indeed found a lodgment in his heart.—*Revival Incidents.*

the intricacies, and peculiarities of different minds; such as deal thus with souls are also true evangelists; with the most professed revivalists, they cry of Jesus, "Come unto ME;" but with Him also, they note the 'labour' and the burden of the soul. These men have to do with souls, which are like Israel in the desert; often skirting the promised land, and then doubling wearily away, yet entering in at last. It is through much tribulation that many enter into the kingdom of God; not perhaps the tribulation of outward suffering, but that of mental conflict.

It is not true, that the simple display of the great truth of free justification by the blood of Jesus, will at all times bring peace to the soul *at once;* there may be obstacles to the reception of that truth, which require to be cleared away; there may be processes of the Spirit required for doing that great work; and this must not be forgotten in the present day, when so many think that the chief truth to be insisted on is, that "the kingdom of heaven suffereth violence, and the violent take it by force."

But whilst we thus plead for patience with labouring souls, and for skill rather than violence in their treatment, we state our full belief in the truth, that the way to deal with sinners is to set before them a *present* Saviour; it is the privilege of every Christian to say to the labouring soul, not, 'Jesus *will* forgive you,' but 'Jesus *does* forgive you.' There is amazing power in a present salvation; as long as we preach, 'Jesus *will* forgive you;' we leave the soul with little or nothing to grasp. Why should we say, "He *will* forgive you?" Is it when He sheds more blood? Jesus will never die

again. Ah! you know that. Well! is it when He has
more love to you? Why should He ever love you
better than He does now? What reason have you for
thinking that He will ever do so? Oh no! you don't
expect that Jesus's love to you will come in some wonderful way; you think He loves the poor sinner now.

Well then; is it when you are better than you are?
Ah! even at the best, must we not be imperfect still?

But is it, when you have repented more? what a
common thought this is; as if repentance could ever
make us worthy; as if there were a certain point, on the
attainment of which Jesus would meet us, and pour over
us His blood.

The sinner must be told that there is not a particle
of hindrance in Christ; but at the same time we must
endeavour to remove the hindrances which lie in himself; there is often, as it were, a laying on of the hand,
and a saying, "brother Saul," before the scales fall from
the eyes.

But there are other labourers besides those who are
seeking for pardon—for justification before God. There
are labourers *after sanctification*—after personal holiness
—after riddance of the power of the old Adam; and to
such, as well as to those who are seeking after salvation,
Christ gives this great invitation; to such He promises,
with this great "I will."

It is highly possible for a man, after having found
justifying rest in Christ, to enter upon a state of deep
need as regards sanctifying rest. We think we shall not
go far wrong, if we say, that this has been the experience of almost every believer that has ever lived.

We may quote one instance by way of example; it is that of Sarah Martin, a well-known name in the roll of God's most earnest labourers.

"In the autumn of 1810, I was led by my most merciful God to examine the great subject in earnest; and I became convinced, not only of the truth of Divine revelation, but also that my own crime in having rejected it, embodied guilt capable of every possible manifestation, when not held back by God himself. By the light of the Divine majesty, and by His law, I saw myself condemned, and I felt the justice of my condemnation; for not only had I violated that righteous and holy law, but I had added to it contempt of the blessed gospel, and rejection of the Son of God. And yet such was the pity of my God, and such His tenderness to me, that in the immediate disclosure of these my circumstances, He showed to me, as in the same glance, the mediator Jesus Christ, my Saviour, and forgiveness through Him.

"For twelve months after this, my satisfaction was incomplete, and my happiness was held back, not knowing the extent of the promise, 'If thou return to the Almighty, thou shalt be built up:' Job. xxii, 23; therefore with strong confidence in my own imaginary power, and supposing all the while that God required it of me, I sought to advance, less by receiving from the fulness of Jesus, than by providing something to bring. To this end I sought to satisfy my thirst for religious knowledge, by reading theological works. The Bible was indeed read formally, a few chapters daily, but not honoured as the supreme source of divine knowledge; whilst my first expectation of advance was from religious books, to the reading of which late and early hours were devoted:

and of every sermon I heard, I wrote an outline afterwards.

"About the close of this year, I became increasingly
bowed down in spirit with heavy disappointment, toiling
hard and reaping no fruit; for in full acknowledgment
and wonder at God's power, in the change which he had
wrought in my thoughts, principles, and habits, I had yet
believed that it was required of me to take a distinct
part in carrying forward the work of religion in my own
life: nor was I made happy, until, in Divine compassion,
the Almighty removed my error, by making it known to
me, that to uphold and prosper Divine life in principle,
and in its fruits, was His sovereign prerogative, as exclu-
sively belonging to the Holy Spirit, as the first movement of the soul from spiritual death; and that in the
plan of the salvation of a sinner, according to his eternal
wisdom and purpose, was comprehended all I needed for
persevering advance in godliness, as to knowledge and
obedience. These happy views were suddenly opened
to me whilst reading the ninth and eleventh of Romans.
There, seeing salvation, not in its commencement only,
but from first to last, to be entirely of grace, I was made
free; and looking upon a once crucified, but now glorified
Saviour, with no more power of my own than the praying thief had upon the cross, I also found peace. The
declaration of Jesus Christ, 'It is finished,' was enough,
and I was graciously given to understand, that contrition,
love, and holiness, are the fruits of the Spirit, produced
in a believer when looking unto Jesus. I read the
chapters referred to much. On one memorable day, the
words, 'It is not of him that willeth, nor of him that
runneth, but of God that showeth mercy,' were as

heavenly music to my heart; for whilst experience had shown my utter destitution before God, I rejoiced to see my eternal salvation secure on the ground of God's free and sovereign mercy, and realized the blessed promise, 'Thou shalt forget thy misery, and remember it as waters that pass away:' Job xi, 16. The high assurance, that Christ was mine, and with Him 'all things,' has never been withdrawn; but in all I have been called to resist, or conquer, or endure, or suffer, it has been a light from God not to be obscured, an ocean of comfort from the rock of my strength."

If we look a little at the circumstances of a man thus delivered from the load of guilt, we shall easily understand how it is that he enters upon a course of subsequent labour. When a sinner finds peace in the blood of Christ, he becomes a new man; old things are passed away, all things have become new; he is now a *forgiven* man; an *illumined* man; and he becomes also pre-eminently an *assaulted* man. Here are three sources of labour; and in each of them the soul can find no rest except in Christ.

For be it observed, that the forgiveness of sins brings with it the impulses of love; the sap, flowing out of the stem of the vine into the branches, makes them shoot and bud; and man starts forward into a new set of activities; he feels he must be "doing" for Christ. Now this new-born activity has to exert itself in the midst of old enemies and many obstacles. We must remember that the work of sanctification is progressive; the Canaanite is still in the land; and forasmuch as we cannot keep quiet, owing to the impulse of love, we have all our work made as hard as possible to us by our

old enemies. Then commences hard toil; at one moment we are like men carrying a heavy load through a
ploughed field; at another we are like those who have to
elbow and push their way through a rude crowd; and
yet, but a little while, and we are like the night-watchers,
who have to guard a treasure from the midnight thief
Now, we seem to have dropped some good thing, and we
have to stoop down and look for it; now, we see some
good thing a little farther on, and we have to try to
attain to it; and thus, we labour, sometimes all day and
all night long too.

Be it remembered that the Christian is an *illumined*
man; the light gradually dawning upon his heart and
conscience, reveals to him how much has to be purged
out, what heights are to be attained; and as the light is
ever growing stronger, so is it ever revealing more evil
to be shunned, more holiness to be attained; and the soul
responds to the teaching, and at each fresh light a fresh
struggle begins.

We must also bear in mind, that a soul, thus circum-
stanced, becomes especially *assaulted*. The strong man
armed, who used to keep his goods in safety, will not
see them taken away from him tamely. Why should
he? I often think how unreasonable Christians are to
expect quiet from Satan! If men are going to take
away our property, we try to hinder them; why should
not the devil do the same? And so his assaults gather
especially round the believer, just as the moths and
insects of the night gather especially around the light.

All this being the case, can we be surprised, that
many a believer is found labouring—labouring after
holiness of character—after obedience—after spiritual

attainment—after perfect freedom from the presence of,
it may be, some particular sin? He is delighting in the
law of God after the inward man, but he sees another
law in his members, warring against the law of his
mind, and bringing him into captivity to the law of sin,
which is in his members. [Rom. vii, 22, 23.]

To such an one the promise of Christ applies; to
him is the invitation given, "Come unto Me, all ye that
labour and are heavy laden, and I will give you rest."
And in truth there is a need that this should be pointed
out to many in the Church of God. After having received Christ, they seem to lose Christ; they forget
what the Apostle has written in 1 Cor. i, 30. "But of
Him are ye in Christ Jesus, who, of God, is made unto
us wisdom, and righteousness, and *sanctification*, and
redemption." Yes, we are forgetting oftentimes that
Christ is our sanctification, as well as our justification;
and we are terrified as to what appearance we shall hereafter make, even though our sins have been forgiven us,
so that we are secured from the danger of being lost.

Dear reader, I know well that the believer is called
to labour; that Scripture is full of imagery, which shows
Him as one, all whose energies are called forth; I know
he is a warrior, [1 Tim. vi, 12] and a racer, [Heb. xii, 1]
and a workman; [2 Tim. ii, 15] still, it is his privilege
to have a quiet mind in Christ; we may be peaceful in
our toil; we may be working, striving, in the full assurance that we are "accepted in the Beloved."

We are very apt to lose ourselves in spiritual toil; we
may easily be led away from Christ, while earnestly engaged in it; we may become so absorbed in the work, as
to forget for Whom it is being done. And of this Satan
will take immediate advantage; he will decoy us by

holy things away from Christ; he will make us to be
so taken up with our work, that we forget Him. We
may thus be led far away from Jesus; we shall in all
probability be induced to look at frames, and feelings,
and advancement in sanctification, as having something
to do with our being saved; our short-comings will be
suggested to us as causes of doubt, as to whether we are
the Lord's at all; and then, perhaps, will ensue a long,
weary wandering back again, to find our first great
spring and principle of hope—our Lord upon His cross.
Is it not well known to every Christian, that one of
Satan's grandest aims is, to fix the eye on self?—to
divert the eye *from* "self," when a man is living in sin,
so that he may not know his vileness—to fix it *upon*
self when he has escaped from the power of sin, so that
he may be brought into a state either of self-righteousness or despair. Let us be upon our guard; whatever
we have to do, let us do it as in the presence of our
Lord—of the One who said, "Come unto me." Thus,
and thus only in the great work of Christian life, can
we have rest. Yes, every day let us say, "Return unto
thy rest, O my soul, for the Lord hath dealt bountifully
with thee:" Psalm cxvi, 7. Let us continually cast our
eyes around, so that on no account the cross be allowed
to be out of sight; and whatever may be our improvement in character, and *moral* meetness for heaven, let
our single hope of the possession of the "beauty of
holiness," be in the possession of the One perfect in all
holiness, even Jesus Christ Himself.

And now, a word for those who might be described
as the *heavy laden*.

We must be permitted to look at them as a class by

themselves. No doubt, as we have already seen, the 'labouring ones' are, in many instances, the 'heavy laden;' but it does not of necessity follow, that all the 'heavy laden' are 'labourers.' No! there is sometimes in the human breast such a crushing weight of unforgiven sin, such a realized consciousness of impotence; it may be, also, such a sense of the rejection of former calls, that the heart refuses to try; the weight is so heavy as to crush and paralize all hope.

Now Christ Jesus is prepared to deal with such a case as this: as He is ready to set at rest the labouring one, so is He ready to stimulate the energies of the one utterly bowed down; He will take man in every phase of his need; and thus there shall doubtless be, throughout eternity, varied specimens of his power.

I feel quite prepared to preach the full grace of Jesus to such an afflicted soul as this; let there be but a consciousness of sin, and a heavy suffering under it, and then, I believe, that although there be paralysis, still there is life; that this is a salvable creature; that he may be, so to speak, brought to Jesus, like the palsied man, borne of the four. Moral consciousness is of inestimable price.

The best way to deal with such, is to show them that there is hope. Hope will make them lift up their eyes, and they shall see that there is a cross; then it may be that they will see that there is One hanging thereon; then, as they look, perhaps, they will try to drag themselves to Him who says, "Come unto me, all ye that labour and are heavy laden, and I will give you rest!"

As in this work it is our aim to influence the mind

of the reader by facts, as well as by statements of truth,
let us here consider the case of a desperate offender,
who sought Christ, and found Him, laden though he
was with guilt. The story is from the man's own pen,
and the reader will be gratified by being informed, that
the subject of it has been for a considerable time a
faithful minister of the Gospel.

I have seen the lives of men painted in dark colours. I
have heard the preacher denounce the vices of human nature.
I have read the pages of God's Word; but all fall short in
depicting my career. All these seem, when compared to my
awful course, as fair and bright spots of virtue. I drank in
iniquity with greediness. How can I express myself in language sufficiently strong to mark my horror and loathing
indignation of my crimes? If I were to attempt a recapitu-
lation of the wickedness to which I was at this time prone,
the vicious would themselves turn pale at the sight, and
wonder that I had not long ago paid for these iniquities in a
hell of torment. At this time I began to be passionately
fond of plays. The theatres, the casino, and places which it
were a shame even to mention, were now my continual
resort.

With the money that I had won by raffling I commenced
a scene of the most sickening debauchery. Living with the
most abandoned persons, I now became a wretch revolting to
myself; all thoughts of my position as a man seemed fled; I
was truly a brute, unfit to die, and yet unfit to live.

A wretched sickness overtook me; my tongue was like
a burning fire; bloated from drink, suffering the keenest
anguish on account of my state, neglected by my companions,
I lay upon a bed in a low public-house in Hereford; at last I
crawled to the coach and went home, a distance of about
fourteen miles. In this weak and painful state I acted the

part of a guard, removing the luggage and putting the slipper on when we came to a hill. I was entirely destitute of means to pay the coach fare.

When I arrived at home, heart-broken, my grandmother spoke to me about my conduct; this I could not brook, there I could not stop, what was I to do? I had made up differences with my intended wife, and I determined to go over to L— and lodge at her father's house (he being an innkeeper.) I went there and my sickness increased, my health now rapidly declined; God only knows what agony of mind I suffered! Fiends in the bottomless pit could endure no more. Stretched upon a bed, I lay there emaciated, the wreck of my former self: my God, what evils sin has brought upon the world! Shame covered me; the remembrance of a happy home—the recollections of good advice and rejected counsels pressed upon me; with burning thirst, with blood-shot eyes, with fever raging in my system, I determined to make an application of leeches; I obtained some—I went to bed and put them on, and from the pain and exhaustion I fainted. Never shall I forget the next morning—there I lay weltering in my blood! For weeks I continued in this state of suffering, while my wants were daily supplied by her who afterwards became my wife. Time will never efface the remembrance of the kindness shown to me. If God had not thus provided for my necessities I must have died uncared for and forgotten. I now found myself a little better, and determined to go home; like the returning prodigal I entered under the roof, where, in early life, I had been trained in ways of piety. I went to bed, and for weeks and weeks I was under the care of a skilful surgeon. Slowly my abused health returned, but with shame and confusion I must confess it, immediately I was well, I again began, though not to such an extent, my course of sin. During all my illness I never had a thought of eternity; I had no religious impressions;

callous and indifferent I marched on towards the pit. At this time I became very fond of races—betting was my hobby —the public-house my habitation. My mind had become unfitted for anything; the powers of memory seemed to have fled; drunkards and low companions were my constant attendants.

At this time some tight-rope dancers and singers were in the town of L—, performing at a public-house. I became quickly acquainted with them, and used, upon a Sabbath evening, to go and practice walking upon a tight rope. I went with this low and abominable set on a short tour, but their life soon disgusted me, and I determined upon going again to London. In a short time I arrived there and obtained a situation; for a time I was steady, but again the pent-up fire of an unconverted heart burst forth, and I, to my lasting disgrace, became worse than ever. I seemed to be like a brute beast that had no redeeming quality. I never by any chance went inside a place of worship, nor read a book; although in all the establishments in which I lived in London there were libraries, yet these had no attractions for me. My evenings were spent amongst other young men at smoke rooms. Here, for the most part, young men resort, who take their turns in the chair: while toasts and songs, the most obscene, are the order of the evening. These public-houses are so many cesspools, diffusing abroad an unwholesome and destructive pestilence, alike deadly in their influence upon both body and soul. Thank God, great and glorious efforts have of late been made. The Young Men's Christian Association, and the Early Closing Society, have conferred boons of incalculable good upon the young men of London and the provinces. God grant that they may estimate these blessings with thankful gratitude, and evince by their attendance and cordial support, the interest they take in these noble efforts for their temporal and spiritual good.

I now became entirely reckless; I drank again freely, and gradually glided into the vortex of crime, deeper, if possible, than before. One Sunday evening, I well remember the day, it was the height of summer—the people were cheerfully wending their way round the little lakes made in St. James's Park, and I only, of all the race of human beings, seemed miserable. Stretched upon the grass, ruminating upon the dark and vile deeds of my eventful life, I determined upon enlisting for a soldier: I went down a narrow street below the Horse Guards, and entering a low public-house, soon got into conversation with a soldier; he quickly told me of the privileges of a soldier's life, the chances of promotion, the great advantage an education would give me, and it was agreed I should enlist. I went upstairs into an empty room, pulled off my shoes, and was measured by the standard. I came down, but after some further conversation, I declined being enlisted.

I now determined upon returning home, but what course to take I did not know. A plan soon struck me which was the most dreadful and diabolical ever invented by a human being. The cholera was very bad in London, and I thought I would pretend to be ill. What, if God had made that real which to me was pretence! I must have for ever felt the gnawing of the worm that dieth not, and the fire that is never quenched. The rich man's fearful experience would have been mine—his bitter wail, "I am tormented in this flame," would have been echoed by me. But mercy triumphed over wrath: Christ had love—free boundless love in store for me. I feigned illness—the doctor was sent for—I managed to deceive him; he ordered immediately warm fomentations, and mustard plasters; in a short time I pretended to be delirious. One of the masters of the establishment came to my room, and looking at me he said, "Poor fellow." This abominable assumed illness lasted for a few days, when I got

well enough to go home. It was about the month of August,
1849 ; a great many races were about this time, and I spent
most of my time in going about from place to place.

At this time, the autumn of 1849, I had made up my
mind to be married. I consulted my grandmother, and she
gave her consent reluctantly, because she thought we were too
young. However at last she promised to give us up the
spirit business. We were not long in arranging matters, and
on ——, we were married at W—, by a faithful and devoted
clergyman, the Rev. R. D—. He gave me and my dear wife
counsel, which, if it had been received, would have tended to
sweeten life ; but, alas ! all good counsel I rashly disregarded,
judging it the height of impudence for a clergyman, or any
one else, to concern himself about me. My wife and I went
to London, at which place, like most new married couples,
who are not overstocked with money, we spent most of what
we had in seeing sights. After staying here about three
weeks, we returned to W—, and from thence to L—, at
which place we arrived in May, 1850, with £1 in gold, and
some odd coppers. This was all we had to begin business.
My grandmother left us about £10 worth of stock, and with a
small quantity of spirits of each sort, we began. Fortune,
often fickle, smiled upon us. Indeed, we were supported in a
marvellous manner. I, who had before been desperately
wicked, became apparently steady. We had by this time
turned ourselves round, and I began to feel that I had been
in the house too much. So I regularly went out to other
public-houses, and soon became a complete drunkard. I now
used my wife in the most brutal manner. For the most
trifling thing, I would strike her and pour upon her the most
disgusting epithets. I played frequently at cards, and used
to raffle a great deal with dice. The races round about I
regularly attended, almost habitually coming home drunk.
At other times my friends found me fighting. Religion, alas,

I utterly repudiated. My course was now a black one. I was the transcript of the Infernal One. I became a more dreadful swearer than ever, and embraced the lowest dregs of scepticism. I would pray for a fresh baptism of the spirit of God, every time the following fiendish circumstances occur to my mind. It is to me a matter of astonishment that God did not now sweep me in a moment from the earth, for crimes such as mine never could have been paralleled. Eternal thanks to God the Father and to Christ the Son, that I was spared as a monument of eternal mercy. May my sins continually appear more disgusting, and may I perceive more than ever the infinite condescension that has stooped from heights celestial to lay hold upon a miserable wretch like me.

I used to delight in sullying the character, and heaping the most obscene epithets upon the blessed Redeemer's name. I laughed at the monstrous absurdity, as I called it, of Christ being equal with the Father, or of His being born of the Virgin. Not only in L—, but in W—, did I, in drunken fits, attempt to defame and blacken the character of the Righteous One. But what were the internal feelings of my mind? Did I believe, in the depths of my heart, what I said? No! No! I *wished* there was no God. It was the "child of my wish." I was a coward, and I believe that men do not really believe in what is called infidelity. They want it to be so; but they are afraid, in the face of the Bible, to deny the great truths there propounded.

My tongue, at this period of my existence, was the conveyer of the most horrible blasphemies. One night in my bed-room I was swearing dreadfully, and my dearest wife begged of me to desist. "Tom," she said, "the Lord will strike you dead." So hardened and insane was I in my wickedness, that this amused me wonderfully. I said, "Who is the Lord?" and then followed the most glaring profanity ever uttered by mortal lips. I defied, with bitter imprecations, the Lord to hurt me. I cursed God, and heaped oath after oath upon the Deity. I swore till I trembled; cold, icy sweat rested on my brow, and I sank down exhausted in this maddened and excited state. My dear wife has since told me that she thought the room shook. That night's tragedy now appears before me; but God spared me. He who saw me did not cut me down. Mercy had interposed between the culprit and the Judge.

About this time, the autumn of 1850, my wife went home to the funeral of her dear father, and upon her return we went to church. I had not been there for a long time. Mr. R— preached a most searching sermon; I well remember it, it was on the Depravity of Man. I gnashed my teeth, and having no one on whom to vent my anger, I turned to my poor wife, although suffering deeply from the calamity which robbed her of her parent, and being at the time near her confinement, impelled by the most savage ferocity, I kicked her downstairs. Such conduct I cannot recall without horror, but it magnifies the grace of God, which has reached even me.

I had a great love for races, and in the June following I went to T— races. I had not been long on the course before I began fighting, and was near being placed in the hands of the police. Some friends took me away, and I am at a loss to conceive how I got home that night. My dear wife, terrified at my appearance when I returned, went to her room and locked the door against me, requesting me to sleep in another room. This I refused to do, and upon another denial, I broke a panel out of the door, and crawled in on my hands and knees. I went to a large mirror, and beholding my face swelled in it, my indignation was hurled at the glass, which I broke with my fist in a thousand pieces. When I went from home my wife never knew whether I should return drunk or sober. For the most trivial opposition to my will I would throw the tea things behind the fire, break the silver spoons in pieces, tear up dresses and shawls, no matter what they cost. At one time I would break all the glasses I could come near, turn the taps of the spirits on and let the contents of the cask run all about; sometimes I would drink perhaps half a pint of neat brandy, and this was attended with oaths and blasphemings; at another time I would threaten to destroy myself, and bind a handkerchief round my neck till suffocation had almost released me of life; my affrighted wife would tear it from my neck, and thus often become the saviour of my life.

All this time the Lord had given me no harrowing affliction. I had despised His goodness, rejected all His love, but now a heavy domestic bereavement was about to come upon me, which called into action all the sensibility of which my depraved nature was capable. I had an only daughter, called Maria; she was about two years old, the pet of my heart. Often, when I have come home and brutally used my poor wife, until the briny tears issued from her swollen eyes, and made their course down her careworn cheeks, would this darling child scramble upon her mother's lap, and pulling up her little pinafore, would say, in sweetest accents, as she wiped away the tears, " Don't cry, mamma," and then turning her little face to me, would say, while tiny anger mounted in her little face, "Ah! naughty papa to make poor mamma cry." Often would she become the little peace-maker, and prevail upon us both to be reconciled. I did love this little child with an idolatrous affection, but my Heavenly Father chose to remove her from me.

One Saturday evening in March, 1853—I well remember the day—while sitting in a public-house, my servant, with the child in her arms, came to request me to come home; I told the girl I should come immediately. My dear little

child looked up in my face as if to say "Come now." Late
in the evening I went home drunk, and on the Monday
following the child was taken ill. I was out on this day also,
drinking, so that my wife could not render the child the
necessary attention. On the Wednesday the dear little
sufferer was taken away from such an inhuman parent ; and
at the same hour as on the previous Saturday I was intoxi-
cated in the public-house, the next Saturday, (March 27th,
1853,) I stood beside the grave of this, my dearest lamb. I
shall never forget that day. Dark and melancholy gloom sat
upon my brow ; the only hope and comfort of my dear wife
was fled. Night after night as we retired to rest, between its
death and burial, would my poor wife and I enter into the
little room where she lay silent in all the sweet composure of
the sleep of death, upon a sofa, with her golden ringlets resting on her snowy brow. Beside her cold form I used to
stand, and press with all the madness of disappointed hope
my darling child. Good God ! what I felt as I would lift
her little curls, and hold within my grasp her tiny hand.
The Lord took her and transplanted her into a more genial
soil, where, through countless ages she will sing the triumphs
of Immanuel ; and perhaps she is now the guardian angel
which hovers about our domestic hearth, where, thank God,
the sounds of prayer and praise arise, instead of the disgusting ones of blasphemy.

About this time (1853) there came into the town of ——
a missionary of the name of Mr. G. O—, a layman of the
Church of England, who caused a great stir by his preaching.
He was supported by a Mr. G. S—, and one or two other members of the Established Church. This I considered an
excellent subject for ridicule. I circulated the most ridiculous
tales about these good men ; and often would I keep the cus-
tomers in my smoking room in roars of laughter while I told
of these religious saints. If any person preached the gospel

in the street, it was a source of high gratification to me, to go and make a noise. I had the greatest contempt for religion. I considered every man a hypocrite that professed it. Mr. O— now began to be the talk of the town; various opinions were given respecting him. My wife went to hear him; she did not like him at all, he was so plain; but she thought, "If I can get Tom to go, I think he would be impressed." My curiosity was excited, and three or four of us went together. The place where he preached was in the National School Room—a very large building, capable of holding 600 persons. The subject of his address was "The wise and the foolish virgins." The characters were drawn with a masterly hand; and I was not long in perceiving that I was amongst the foolish virgins. I felt riveted to the place. I turned one way, then another. I wanted to go: yet I wanted to stay. I did stay out the prayer meeting; and went home impressed with the solemn conviction that, if I continued in my career of wickedness, I must perish eternally. I determined I would alter my course; I made up my mind to leave off excessive drinking, swearing, and all my former habits.

There was one thing especially that gave me great uneasiness: that was, that my house had always been kept open on the Sabbath. I saw it was wrong; but my wife at first did not like to give it up. At last she gave way; and we closed our shop upon the Sunday. This was the signal for opposition. Now taunts, threats, and sneers were unscrupulously heaped upon me. Anonymous letters, threatening a withdrawal of custom, were among the many means devised to retard my onward course. Everything was done to block up my way; but it was the Lord's work; and blessed be His holy name, He did not give me up in despair. At this time I was beset with numerous temptations. Knowing nothing of the way of salvation, I was endeavouring to get justified by my works, but no peace came. No matter how particular I

was over my conduct, no relief came: my burden continued
to oppress me. At last, not being yet established on the
Rock of Ages, I grieve to say I gave way. The railway
between Shrewsbury and Hereford (upon which Mr. O—
laboured as missionary) was to be opened in December, 1853.
A grand demonstration was to be made; coal was to be given
to the poor; and a large dinner and ball was to celebrate the
affair. So great a power did the devil exercise over me, that
I went to a draper in the town on Sunday, and bought my
wife's ball dress. Yet, after this strange infatuation, the
same evening I went to hear Mr. O— preach. He delivered a
most impressive address upon the hand appearing upon the
wall, when Belshazzar was feasting with his nobles, and worshipping the gods of gold and silver. This sunk deeply into
my heart, although it did not produce the desired effect. On
the Monday I went to the dinner, and sung a song which I
had composed for the occasion. I went with my wife to the
ball; but, whilst gliding through the mazy dance, I expected
to see the hand appear, writing in letters of blood, "Mene,
Mene, Tekel, Upharsin." Often did I lift my eyes with
anxious fear to the sides of the room; but wine banished the
impression.

Not satisfied with going to the ball at L—, we must go
to the one at H— on the following day, held at the Shire
Hall. After staying in H— a day or two, we returned
home, though not before it could be said of me "that the dog
had returned to his vomit again, and the sow that was
washed to her wallowing in the mire." I gave way to drink,
and, in a state of beastly intoxication, came home to my
house in L—.

The next morning I felt at enmity with myself. I was
ashamed of my conduct, and I felt as if I could not face the
light of day. True is that Scripture which saith, "men love
darkness rather than light, because their deeds are evil."

Many laughed at me and derided my profession. I was almost induced to give up all, but He who had begun a good work in my soul, and who had promised to carry it "on to the day of Jesus Christ," proved how faithful He was. I went again to hear Mr. O—, he continually preached upon the necessity of believers knowing their sins were forgiven. I could not understand this. I could not see how salvation could be obtained simply by faith. I was told to believe in Christ, but I could not tell how: my mourning was great; I was truly miserable; I wandered about day and night. My load grew intolerable; week after week did I groan on account of my state; I longed for peace; I wrestled for peace.

Night and day did I seek for the comfort which flows from a settled dependence upon Jesus. I imagined I must see something. In the dead of night I used to search under the curtains of the bed. I had the idea that Christ must manifest himself personally to me, and that I must not rest until I had ocular proof. Sometimes I would twinkle my eyes while in prayer, and the dazzling rays of the candle would shed its light across my vision. Then I would think He is coming now! and, like a drowning man, I would cling in despair to the hope that this was what I wanted. But peace dawned not upon my soul, I felt truly wretched; others said they were happy; but I was a forlorn wanderer. I talked to everybody; but no sympathy could I get. At this time I gave out the hymns, and prayed publicly in meetings. I was not ashamed to confess the Lord, yet I could not call him mine.

At last, one night, I went home determined to find Christ if possible; I went upstairs into a spare bedroom, and there I prostrated myself before God, and poured out my soul with tears and strong cries, to Him whose ears are opened to every poor sinner's request. After being a long time upon my knees, I asked myself the simple question, what am I praying for ? Salvation. Who came to purchase salvation for me ? Christ. Instantly light dawned into my soul, my burden fled, and I was enabled to rejoice ; and by casting my poor naked soul upon Christ's finished work, "I did, yea and *I will* rejoice." I sprang upon my feet, and ran up to my wife's room, to tell her the joyful news. I almost frightened her into fits, for she was near her confinement. Next morning I went down to my old brewhouse, and began to pray. I had doubts thus early of the reality of my conversion, I fancied I was deceived, but I got upon my knees and I looked up to Christ, and prayed that God would give me a clearer evidence of my acceptance ; when all at once my heart seemed to be on fire ; my very soul seemed to be consumed with burning love ; the most delightful joy overcame me ; I said is this excitement ? I stayed from praying out loud, and calmly looked up to Christ. Yet still the fire seemed to envelop my soul. It was truly the " Spirit of burning ;" never before, nor since, have I experienced such a glorious feeling in my soul. It was past all expression. I now felt satisfied that " God, for Christ's sake, had pardoned all my sins."

I now became decided for Christ. I cared not for rebuke. I had that within which enabled me to bear up against all the darts of the enemy. It may be truly said, that the grace of God was sufficient for me. I was soon counted mad. The cold shoulder from my friends I had now to endure, despised and forsaken by old companions, yet I cheerfully endured all these things ; and in all my seasons of depression it was my chief joy to be enabled, though deserted and spoken evil of, to retire to my closet, and, throwing myself upon my knees, to look up, and with the consciousness of God's presence, and in full dependence upon Him, to say, " My Father."

When we read a case like this, need any heavy laden man despair? Need we despair, who desire to draw sinners to Christ out of the very deepest pits? Not so! the great "I will" of Jesus meets all the need, does all the work; He speaks it still, "I will give you rest."

And oh! dear readers, if there be indeed any necessity for urging upon you this coming to your Lord, let me beseech you by the earnestness of Christ. Was He in earnest to save, and shall not we be in earnest to be saved? Did He even sweat blood in the fearful hour of His agony, and drain the cup to its dregs, rather than that it should pass from Him, and with it the salvation of a ruined world? Then let it be seen that this bread of life has not been given to the dogs, or this pearl of great price been cast before swine. No! but let the multitude of toil-worn and heavy-laden men, who respond to this invitation of their Lord, show that they are alive to their best interests, that they appreciate the deeds of the mount, the garden, and the cross; that they are of the number of those upon whom the torch of wisdom has thrown its brightest beam, and upon whom the might of celestial strength has been unmistakably brought to bear.

Let our own necessities, which press upon us from every side, urge us nearer and nearer to the Christ, until we have touched Him, and felt, by the benefit which we ourselves have received, that virtue has gone out of Him. Let us think of the glory of the results, and let that, as with a hand of light, beckon us onward to the cross. No longer shall we be poor, pitiful cowards, always in bondage unto death; but our load having been removed, we shall spring upwards in our expecta-

tion of everlasting life. No more shall "the judgment"
and "eternity" be words rendered awful by the fear of
impending torment, but we shall learn to weave their
cyphers into our hopes; no more shall we be the victims
of a low task-master, who hastes us to fulfil our daily
task of unreasonable toil; but we shall be the servants
of the Most High God, and children of the Heavenly
Father, the citizens of the celestial city, and the heirs of
eternal glory.

If any reader of these lines is delaying, let him remember that time is speeding on; and that if this work
be not done now, it may never be done at all. While
graves are being dug, and years are rushing past, almost
as quickly as the lightning flash athwart the sky, is this
a time to be careless, to slumber, and to sleep?

Remember that hell is up in arms to oppose you; that
heavy yokes are being forged there to bind you, each
year, more surely to your ruin. Remember that what a
spiritual power puts on, that can a spiritual power alone
take off; and that the bonds of Satan can be severed
only by the Christ.

The rememberance of this, if sanctified by the Holy
Ghost, will bring you to the cross, where your burden
shall be rolled from your shoulders; and where, from
having been the slaves of sin, you shall be numbered
amongst the freedmen of the Lord; and if numbered
amongst the freedmen of the Lord, yours shall be the
freedman's privileges—privileges, not of necessity received all at once, but secured to you nevertheless.

"I will give you rest," says Jesus; and that promise,
like every promise of the Lord, comprehends all that we
require in the depth of our need; all that in the height

of His fulness He can give. "I will give thee rest" from the fear of condemnation. Thy life shall not be a going onward to the place of execution; thou shalt not have always before thee the vision of the sword; thou shalt not always labour under the depression of thy knowledge of thyself; thou shalt be refreshed in thy ·knowledge of Me; thou shalt know that thy condemnation is behind, and not before thee; a thing passed and not to come; one destroyed, and not one waiting to be developed. "I will give thee rest" from thy wearying search after happiness. Hither and thither hast thou sought it, now in life's shady paths, and now in its summer highways; like the prodigal thou didst go out from the presence of thy Father, not knowing that with Him and Him alone, thou could'st find rest: lo! I restore thee to thy Father, and to my Father; and to that house in which only there is happiness, in which only can be rest.

I will give thee rest from all thy vague longings— the swayings to and fro of thy thoughts, and thy affections seeking the great centre-point of rest. I am the heart's peace, its satisfaction, and its abiding joy—in me thou shalt have rest.

I will give thee rest in realization of thy future goal. Earth has no goal which the heart of man can reach, and on attaining it find rest. Ever onward must it travel, toil-worn and foot-sore; attaining to the summit of each barren crag, only to see that there are barren crags above it still; in Me thou shalt see the assured inheritance, the blood-bought home, the "rest that remaineth for the people of God."

The substance of such words as these are spoken in

this great promise—they are spoken, dear reader, to
thee. If thou hast wrought hard, yet done naught;
travelled far, yet attained to naught; striven hard, yet
gained naught; run swiftly, and yet won naught—
naught save weariness and disappointment; naught
save earth's sweat, and toil, and dust: lo! here thou
findest one who hath wrought, and travelled, and
striven, and run for thee; and wheresoever He finds
thee now; softly and solemnly drop His refreshing
words upon thine ear, "Come unto me all ye that
labour, and are heavy laden, and *I will* give you rest."

The "I Will" of Reception.

John vi, 37.

"Him that cometh to Me I will in no wise cast out."

�⟩

NO grander, no lovelier sight could we desire to see, than that of the multitude of those who have been saved through the mighty influence of this verse. Millions upon millions are now in joy unutterable, who in the power of this single sentence sprang upwards from the dust, with a new light in their dull despairing eye; with a fresh hope in their withered hearts; with the belief that they could be saved, that they were privileged to grasp the cross on earth, the crown in heaven.

If the imagination be overwhelmed at the thought of this multitude, arrayed in light ineffable; the wonder is increased at the revelation of the materials of which it is composed. These are they that have come out of great tribulation, and made white their robes in the blood of the Lamb. Here are desperate offenders; some, whose hands had been reddened by their brother's blood;

some, whose lips had been the mouthpiece of the Evil
One for all blasphemy; some, who had been ringleaders
of all assaults upon the faith; well known were they to
the angels; well known to their fellow men as desperate
characters, beyond all human reach, all human hope; no
common truth would have had power to lift them, in the
day when they were struck by the Holy Ghost to the
earth, and when their sins leaped demon-like upon them,
to strangle the faintest expectation which might have
risen in their hearts, of there being a chance for such as
they; when lo! for them, in their low estate, mercy provided in this "no wise" a cord long enough to reach
them in their low abyss, and strong enough to bear their
weight; a cord, not to bind, but to deliver; they grasped
it; they were drawn forth into light and life; and they
were saved.

In that glorious crowd, are doubtless some, who were
peculiarly buffeted of the devil; he sifted them like
wheat; he tried with mighty strokes to beat them down
from the cross, and with cunning arguments to reason
them out of hope; many a time did he almost cast them
into despair, and break their hearts; and it seemed as
though it needed but the finishing stroke, and then they
were his own; when lo! he was met and foiled—not by
mighty arguments; not by extraordinary revelations;
but by these simple words; the Spirit shone upon the
"no wise" of Christ; the poor afflicted soul beheld the
vast circumference of its sweep; the sinner saw that it
embraced himself; he also clung tight; and though he
was dragged through many waters, and buffeted by
doubts and fears, still he held on, until at last, he was
landed safe upon the heavenly shore.

Here also, in this glorious crowd, there will be found many *upon whom other texts appeared to fail;* but in this one they found life. The positiveness, the simplicity of this declaration, became the means of their salvation. It may be, that they put other truths away from them, as being too high for their understandings; perhaps they hedged them round with so many limitations that they thought they could never come up to all these requirements and demands; but this struck home to them as the very one that suited their case; they learned to understand all other Scriptures by this; they entered into the various mysteries of truth through this plain homely door; they themselves learned in no wise to deny their Lord, but to be stedfast and immovable for Him; because He would in no wise be shaken in, or beaten off from, His love to them.

Oh! what desperation of faith was seen in some, as they clutched this truth with a dying grasp; their destiny for eternity hanging upon a word; oh! what calm composure was seen in others, as for long days and nights of weariness, they lay expecting from hour to hour their summons into the presence of the King. No fears, no anxious thoughts had they; they rested on a message from above; they knew in whom they believed; they remembered that these words came from One who could not mistake or lie; and conscious on their part that they had simply come to Christ, all sinful as they were; they had peace in the consciousness that He would never send them away.

"For all I have preached, or written," said Mr. James Durham, "there is but one Scripture I can remember, or dare grip to; tell me, if I dare lay the weight of my salvation upon it, '*Him that cometh to me, I will in no wise cast out ?*' His friend replied, 'You may indeed depend upon it, though you had a thousand salvations at hazard.' A gleam of joy lighted up the soul of the dying saint, under the radiance of which he was ushered into the glory and brightness of eternity."

"I have no hope in what I have been or done," said Dr. Doddridge on his dying bed, "Yet I am full of confidence; and this is my confidence, there is a hope set before me. I have fled, I still fly for refuge to that hope. In Him I trust, in Him I have strong consolation; and shall assuredly be accepted in this beloved of my soul."

The Rev. Richard Baxter, when near the close of his course, exclaimed, "I have pains; there is no arguing against sense; but I have peace, I *have* peace." "You are now drawing near your long desired home," said one; "I believe, I believe," was his reply. When asked, "How are you?" he promptly answered, "ALMOST WELL!" To a friend who entered the chamber he said, "I thank you, I thank you, for coming." Then fixing his eyes upon him he added, "The Lord teach you how to die!" These were his last words.

The Rev. Robert Bruce, having lived to a venerable old age, one morning after breakfasting with his family, reclined awhile in his chair, silently meditating. Suddenly he spoke, "Daughter, hark! doth not my master call me." Asking for his Bible, he perceived that his eyes were dim, and that he could no longer read its precious words. "Find for me," said he, "the eighth chapter of Romans, and lay my finger on the passage; 'I am persuaded that neither death nor life, nor angels, nor principalities, nor powers, nor things present, nor things to come, nor height, nor depth, nor any other creature, shall be able to separate us from the love of God, which is in Christ Jesus our Lord.' Now is my finger placed upon these blessed words?" Being assured that it was, he said, "Then God bless you, God bless you all, dear children: I have refreshed myself with you this morning, and shall be at the banquet of my Saviour, ere it is night." And thus he died.

"During seven weeks of Romaine's severe suffering, a fretful or murmuring expression never escaped his lips; but often would he say, 'How good is God to me! What entertainments and comforts does He give me! Oh, what a prospect of glory and immortality is before me! He is my God, through life, through death, and to eternity.' When inquiries were made how he felt, his general reply was, 'As well as I expect to be this side heaven.' To a brother minister he said; 'I do not repent of one word that I have printed or preached on faith in Jesus, for I now feel the blessed comforts of that precious doctrine.' 'I have lived,' said he to another, 'to experience all I have spoken, and all I have written, and I bless God for it.' Afterwards he observed, 'I knew the doctrines I preached to be truths, but now, I experience them to be blessings.' As he lay waiting for his dismission, the friend in whose house he was, said to him, 'I hope, sir, you now find the salvation of Jesus inestimably precious to you.' 'Yes, he replied with a feeble voice, 'He is precious to my soul. 'More precious than rubies,' said his friend. He caught the word, and completed the Scriptural idea, 'and all that can be desired is not comparable to Him.'"

The one great truth is all powerful everywhere.

There was once a caravan crossing to the north of India, and numbering in its company a godly and devoted missionary. As it passed along, a poor old man was overcome by the heat and labours of the journey, and sinking down was left to perish on the road. The missionary saw him, and kneeling down at his side, when the rest had passed along, whispered into his ear, "Brother, what is your hope?" The dying man raised himself a little to reply, and with a great effort succeeded in answering, "The blood of Jesus Christ cleanseth from all sin!" and immediately expired with the effort. The missionary was greatly astonished at the answer, and in the calm and peaceful appearance of the man, he felt assured he had died in Christ. How, or where, he thought, could this man, seemingly a heathen, have got this hope? And as he thought of it, he observed a piece of paper grasped tightly in the hand of the corpse, which he succeeded in getting out. What do you think was his surprise and delight, when he found it was a single leaf of the Bible, containing the first chapter of the first Epistle of John, in which these words occur! On that page the man had found the gospel.

And what this verse has done, it yet can do; it can repeat its triumphs; it can descend into the abyss, and bring up more souls; it can enter the arena of conflicts, doubts, and fears, and calm more troubled hearts; it can smooth more dying pillows, and gild the horizon of more closing days. If you, dear reader, have not yet found rest and peace in Christ, may these words now give them to you; and if you have, then take these words into your lips, and evangelize with them the vilest of the vile; go everywhere; go to everyone; go with mighty hope ; go with a consciousness of superhuman power; go in the strength of this great declaration of your Lord ; see in every sinner a soul that may be saved ; and proclaim your Saviour in his own great words, "Him that cometh to Me I will in no wise cast out!"

And now, to look a little more closely into these words ; observe how

Our Lord deals with the individual. In all individuality there is a concentration of power. The sinner has here this special advantage, that he need not look upon himself merely as *one of a class,* but as *an individual.*

It is precisely thus that Jesus wishes to deal with the poor sinner : He wishes to take him in his individual wretchedness, depravity, and fears, and to apply Himself to them all. We know that men often hide themselves in their "class ;" a threat or a promise may belong to their class, and yet not to them ; many an one says, "yes ! that promise is for sinners, but not for me."

Now, here Jesus seems to take poor sinners individually ; it is as though he called us all aside, one by one, and said, "I have something to say unto thee, and to thee, and thee ;" it is true, when we come to compare notes, we shall find that He has perhaps said exactly the same to each of us, "Him that cometh to Me I will in no wise cast out ;" but each heart will have heard the word with power, saying, "'twas said to *me,* to *me.*"

And oh ! what a comfort it is, that the Saviour enters into our individuality ; into each one's need, each one's position, each one's hopes and fears. When deep solemnities of eternal things are realized, we never can content ourselves with generalities; we feel, *I* must be saved, or *I* must be lost; we think but little of ourselves in our position as belonging to a class. Jesus meets us in our need. Jesus says, "I come to *thee* that *thy* interests may be secured, that *thy* soul may be saved. And hence we are warranted in our hours of deep-felt personal necessity in coming to Christ, even though we have not deep knowledge of the abstract nature of sin; though ours be only simple (and perhaps very imperfect) knowledge of *our own* sin. Ever so little knowledge of our own personal necessity is more to the point, than ever so much knowledge of necessity in general. Jesus wants an individual sufferer to apply to Him; one smarting, sorrowing, fearing; and him He "will not cast out."

And now, what is contained in this promise to the individual sinner? If Jesus cast him out, what will it be out *from*? what will it be out *to*?

Jesus will not cast out the poor sinner *from the place of safety he seeks.* Mark that panting, sweating man, who rushes along with almost unearthly speed; his nostrils are dilated, his eyes are bloodshot, and the veins stand out like knotted cords upon his brow; on, on he bounds, as though he had winged feet; as though to win this race were life; and to lose this race were death. And, in truth, it is a race of life or death; this is the man that has killed his neighbour unawares; and behind him, bounding after him with eager face and vengeful arm, is the avenger of blood; there is but little distance between them; let that be but overpast; and then, with one fatal leap, the avenger springs upon his prey, and his sword is crimsoned with his blood. On, on they speed; the man upon whose hands are the stains of his neighbour's blood nears the gate of the city of refuge, and inside that gate are eager eyes watching the event of this race for life; thence come inspiring shouts; there are ready arms to pull in the runner, if he should fall exhausted upon the threshold, ere he takes the last spring which will put him far beyond the avenger's reach. Whose are these eager eyes, these ready arms? They belong to men who have themselves found refuge in the city; and can we imagine for a moment that with an iron grasp these watchers would seize the new-come refugee and throw him out to the avenger, that he might wreak his vengeance, and shed the still boiling blood upon the ground? Oh no! they never would cast him out; and shall they thus receive to refuge one who comes to their city to save the life of the body; and shall Jesus cast out one that comes to him to save the life of the soul? Not so! Jesus will never cast out from the place of safety the one who speeds to it to save his life; well does He know the dread importance of this race: well does He know the value of the soul; He has no arm outstretched to dash us back upon the sword point of the avenger; He has an arm outstretched to draw us in to Himself; never did those who crowded the gate of the city of refuge receive another escaped one, added to their company, with such pleasure, as Jesus receives another added to His. He sees an individual imperiled; He sees him rush for his life; He feels him touch Himself, the portal of life; He accepts, He shields, He saves; the avenger of blood in vain demands his prey; the voice of Jesus sends him disappointed and empty

away, "Him that cometh to Me I will in no wise
cast out."

Nor will Jesus cast out the sinner *from the position
he thus takes up.* We cannot come to Jesus without
taking up a high position; indeed so high a one, that
if it entered into a sinner's sober calculations, he would
in all probability be alarmed, and shrink back from
coming to Christ at all.

None can come to Christ savingly, without entering
into union with Him. Jesus knows that; and knowing it, still gives the poor sinner the full guarantee his
trembling soul desires. It has often happened, that the
men who have come to Christ to be saved, and who in
this act, have had their sin and unworthiness before
them, have thought of tarrying there, never dreaming of
advancing into fellowship with their Lord. They did
not know what being 'received' or 'saved' involved;
and when pressed on by the impulses of divine life, they
thought, 'it is presumption in me to expect this.' The
courtier who is invited to the public reception of his
sovereign, could not be surprised if he were turned out,
should he be found intruding into the private apartments
of the royal family; to be a member of the court is one
thing, to be a member of the family is another. It is to
belong to this latter, that all are destined who come to
Jesus; He gives them, as it were, the keys of the private
chambers of His heart; He will never turn them out if
they venture there. Oh! that we were less satisfied
with the outer courts of safety; Oh! that we ventured
into the inner chamber of His love; for what, dear
reader, have we been saved? Is it merely to remain

unslain? Is our bare life to form the highest trophy of
the blood of Christ? Is this all that is to be said of the
saints, "The devil could not *kill* them?" Can that evil
One mock us and say, "Aha! Christ has you, but He
will never make much of you—try to get into closer
communion with Him, and you'll soon see that He will
resent the liberty, and send you away." The little promise before us rescues us from this; it penetrates beyond
the outer courts of atonement, into the inner sanctuary
of communion. Make bold, dear reader, to enter into
Christ; remember that you are "accepted in the Beloved,"—not only "pardoned," but "accepted;" not only
received into life, but into sonship; when the prodigal
returned, the fatted calf was killed. Let us go deep
into Christ; He will in no wise cast out.

And if Jesus were to cast us out, what would He cast
us *to?* To rest upon our own resources; and that, He
knows well, would be our death. In Him is life, and
out of Him is death; if Christ cast us out, or repel us,
He deliberately hands us over to ruin. The enemies of
our soul are hard by, ready to pounce upon us, and make
an end of us, the moment they ascertain that He will
have nothing to do with us. Can we imagine the
blessed Jesus thus deliberately thrusting any earnest
soul into the very jaws of death? Can we imagine His
deliberately giving the devil such a terrible and eternal
triumph as this? Oh! if Jesus were to cast out a single
soul that came to Him, in repentance and belief; I can
well believe that that soul would henceforth be the
greatest phenomenon of the land of perdition—the
strangest curiosity of hell. All would understand how

the murderer and adulterer fell into the land of woe;
how the impenitent and the unbelieving dropped into
the lake of fire; but how came this man there? Who
can solve the riddle of his being damned? There is
not a devil that would not look upon him with wonder;
the arch-fiend himself would confess, that this man's
being lost, was a greater mystery than all others being
saved; the devil's choicest treasure would be this
rejected soul.

And cannot we well imagine the use he would make
of it; how he would make himself master of all the
circumstances of its rejection; how he would chronicle
carefully all its sighs and tears; its timid trial; and its
fierce repulse; and then, how he would go forth to poor
perishing sinners, and tell them, that 'he knew for a fact,
that Jesus did not receive everyone that came to Him.'
There is no instance on record of Christ's having done
this; if there were, we can easily understand how the
Evil One would be continually bringing it up, preaching
all sorts of sermons upon it, writing all sorts of treatises
upon it; that would be his favourite subject; he would
always preface it with "it is written;" he would give
out the text very plainly, much more so than some
ministers give out their texts; so that everyone might
know where exactly to turn in the sacred volume, and
find out for himself the fact, that Jesus sent a poor distressed and believing man empty away. Blessed be God,
the great enemy of souls can shew no rejection of anyone
in need, on the part of Christ. 'Tis true, he could, even
at the worst, point to but this single case: but this one
would do for him; "what has been," he would say,
"may be; 'tis true, this is the first, but perhaps it is

not the last; what happened to another, may happen to you; so, in your vaunted promise, you have no ground for hope."

Oh! how Satan would work that *possibility* of our being lost; no matter how strongly we insisted upon the *improbability* of it, he would pertinaciously work the *possibility*, whispering continually into our ears, "But you *may* be; you *may* be!"

Thanks be to God, we may meet him, dear reader, in the power of these words, "him," and "in no wise;" sovereign grace has made this proclamation for poor sinners; we may live on it; we may die on it! "Brother, brother," said the Rev. Legh Richmond when he was dying, "strong evidences, nothing but strong evidences will do at such an hour as this. I have looked here, and looked there for them—all have failed me; and so I cast myself on the sovereign, free, and full grace of God in the covenant by Jesus Christ; and there, brother, (looking at me with a smile of tranquillity quite indescribable) *there*, I have found peace." Even so; the free grace of the promise, is just our only hope.*

What a blessed thought it is, that Jesus will "in no

---

* It is said that in his last hours, Bishop Butler, when conversing with his chaplain on those subjects, which could then alone be interesting, thus expressed his uneasiness,—"Though I have tried to avoid sin, and to please God to the utmost of my power; yet, from being conscious of my constant weakness, I am afraid to die." "My lord," said his chaplain, "you forget that Jesus Christ is a Saviour." "True," replied the Bishop; "but how shall I know that He is a Saviour for me?" "My lord, it is written, '*Him that cometh to Me, I will in no wise cast out.*'" "True," said the Bishop, "and I have read that Scripture a thousand times, but I never felt its full value till this moment—stop there, for now I die happy."

wise" cast out the one who comes to Him. The figure
used here is a litotes—*où μή*—two negatives, equal to
"In no wise"—"No! No!" Such words falling from
the lips of Jesus, who was "the way, the *truth*, and the
life," are of inexpressible importance to us. It is as
though Jesus said, "Such a thing is not even to be
spoken about; it does not come within even the range of
possibility much less probability; under no circumstances
could such an event take place." We know that circumstances often prove too strong for the sternest resolutions
of men; but Jesus is above all circumstances; nothing
but a deliberate act of His will would make Him hand
over the poor sinner to his ruin; and the whole testimony of His promises, His life, His cross secure to us
His will.

"What!" says Satan, "will He not cast you out
when He finds how feeble your faith is?" "*où μή*"—
"No! No!"

"Will He not send you off when He has had a close
sight of you, and sees how horribly bad you are?"
"*où μή*"—"No! No!"

"Will He not say that He will have no more to do
with you, when He finds how hard it is to make anything out of you?" "*où μή*"—"No! No!"

"Will He not get tired of you, and say, I'll look for
more promising subjects on which to work?" "*où μή*"
—"No! No!"

"No! No!" We will enter into no further argument
with Satan than this: we will meet him with Scripture,
after the example of our Lord: whatever cogitations
and reasonings we may have in our own minds, there is
no need of our enlarging upon them to him: "No! No!"
is quite enough; He will "in no wise" cast us out.

And in truth, though we do not enter upon them with Satan, we know of many considerations why the Lord Jesus will not cast us out.

Christ's own feelings engage Him not to do this dreadful deed. See how tenderness marks all His words to the poor, weak, and sorrowful ones; and could He ever bring Himself to send them away; after having raised their hopes, and invited them to come? Did He not weep over Jerusalem? Did He not mourn over the sheep who were without a shepherd? Did He not love the young man who came unto Him? Did He not say that He would not break the bruised reed, or quench the smoking flax; and that He did not come to condemn the world, but to save? Christ would do a violence to His own feelings, if He turned the poor trusting sinner off. Yes! where would His love for souls be, when He did this dreadful deed? How could He fashion His lips to pronounce the awful words? How could He look sternly, and coldly, upon the poor creature, that stood before Him, ready to see life in His smile, and death in His frown? Surely all, all would be changed, if Jesus could do this; this must be a different Jesus from the one who used to speak lovingly to, and look lovingly on, sinners when He was upon the earth; His heart must have been changed at His ascension, but we know that it was not; Jesus is "the same yesterday, to-day, and for ever;" and His very feelings are part of our guarantee for life.

But we can understand how Jesus would say, "*Common justice forbids my doing this;* I have pledged my word to the sinner; I have induced him to venture all on me; I have declared, that 'he that believeth shall be

saved;' I have stripped the poor sinner of every other
plea; I have left him nothing to hope for from himself;
I must perform to him my word."

And then, would not Jesus also say, "*the whole tenor
of my life and death forbids this.* Did I not die, 'the
just for the unjust to bring sinners unto God?' Was it
not for carrying out this great design that I lived and
died? To what purpose have I lived and died, if I am
to cast out any who come to me for life?"

We cannot imagine the Lord Jesus Christ frustrating
the design of His own life and death; deliberately
making void the bloody sweat in Gethsemane, and the
bitter agonies of Calvary; we cannot imagine His
coming short of the full fruition of His sufferings, which
He must do, if He reject a single soul, really willing to
be saved in His own way. Christ's life and death have
a price in His own eyes, as well as in those of the
Father, and of a soul.

And would not *the whole counsel and will of the
Father be overthrown,* if Jesus cast out any poor believing
soul? What was the counsel and will of the Father but
this, that there should be a highway made for sinners to
come back to Himself; that whosoever believed should
be saved; that He Himself should be honoured, and
glorified, in the freeness of the terms, in the eternal life
of those by whom they were accepted; in whom but
sinners is that counsel to be carried out? and how is it
to be carried out, but by their being certainly received?
All, all conspire to secure the safety of the man that
comes; a multitude of reasons, not one of which can be
gainsaid, all confirm to us the word, "Him that cometh
to Me, I will in no wise cast out."

Let none be deterred by *considerations of old slights;* Jesus will never mention them. Where was He so slighted as in Jerusalem? And yet when He sent forth His apostles to evangelize the world, He said, "beginning at Jerusalem."

Let none be deterred by *considerations of present sinfulness.* Jesus knows your nature; He came "not to call the righteous but sinners to repentance;" He takes you, in your poor sinful nature, just as you are; and will gradually make you what He would have you be. *Leave it to Him,* by His Spirit, to make you what He would have you be; you can no more sanctify, than you can justify yourself; with present sinfulness, and present sins, just come to Him.

Behold the universality of Christ's cures on earth; whom did He ever send away unhealed? Not one; were any closed eyes left unopened? were any deaf ears left unstopped? was any arm left shrivelled? was any foot allowed to halt? who was sent away unfed? who uncleansed? not one! they gathered to Him in crowds; they came to Him one by one; and He helped, and blessed them all. And shall it ever be said, that He did all this for the body, but that He leaves undone the greater work for the soul? Shall it be said, 'He never sent anyone away unhealed in the flesh, He did send some one away unhealed in the soul?' Oh no! we rise from the less to the greater; from the body to the soul; and we hear the voice proclaiming for man's higher needs,

"Him that cometh to Me, I will in no wise cast out."

The "I Will" of Healing.

MATTHEW viii, 2—3.

MATTHEW viii, 2, 3.   (Mark i, 41.   Luke v, 13.)

"And, behold, there came a leper and worshipped Him, saying, Lord,
  if thou wilt, thou canst make me clean.   And Jesus put forth
  His hand, and touched him, saying, I will; be thou clean.   And
  immediately his leprosy was cleansed."

UR earthly friends do not like our putting
them on very difficult tasks; they are not
willing that we should throw heavy responsibility upon them.   But herein is Jesus, the
"friend that sticketh closer than a brother"—"the friend
of publicans and sinners"—different from all other friends,
and superior to them; He is willing to undertake the
most difficult tasks for us; He does not shrink from any
amount of responsibility.   The darker our sky, the more
luminously does His friendship shine; so that the believer
may well triumph in his Lord, and cry, "This is my beloved, and this is my friend, O daughters of Jerusalem:"
Cant. v, 16.   If any doubt the Saviour's willingness to
undertake a heavy responsibility, or a difficult task, on
behalf of a poor sinner; let him hear that one great invitation which embraces every form of misery, and every
one bending beneath its load, "Come unto me, all ye that
labour and are heavy laden, and I will give you rest."

(Matt. xi, 28.) There is no task too hard for the One
who is able to save a world.

Many were the difficult tasks upon which the Lord
Jesus Christ was put, during His sojourn amongst men ;
the blind were brought to Him, to receive their sight ;
the dumb to be made to speak ; and the deaf to hear ;
all manner of sicknesses were proposed to Him for cure ;
He refused not one ; with a rich, free, powerful hand He
cured them all.   Do not all these mighty deeds unite in
common   testimony,   and say ; "Poor, laden, stricken
sinner ; Jesus Christ, who did all these wonderful works,
is the Saviour for thee ?"

And here we have Christ allowing Himself to be
put on a most difficult task, even the cure of a leper ;
the task was beyond all human power ; the man Christ
Jesus was the only One who could accomplish it ; and
so we find Him throwing open His sympathies to this
poor afflicted creature ; and that, with the certainty that
He did not raise any hope, which by and bye He would
be constrained to disappoint.   O blessed thought !
Jesus never raises any false hope, Jesus never dis-
appoints.

Now, let us think for a while over this wonderful
cure of the leper ; let us dwell upon his "if thou wilt,"
and upon the Lord Jesus Christ's " I will;" and may the
Holy Spirit enable us to gather up some blessed teachings
for ourselves.

Our Lord had been preaching and healing, through
Galilee ; and was now returning to Capernaum. Strength
had flowed from His word, and healing from His touch,
in His progress from place to place ; and His steps had
left prints of light wherever they fell, whether on the

road way, the hamlet, or the town; for in every place men sought Him, and healing by Him, and found all that they desired. And now that Jesus is returning, mercy must mark His incoming even as it did His outgoing; and so this poor leper is found in His path; his measure of faith no doubt imperfect, but the love of Jesus, beyond all measure, perfect; and according to the perfection that is in Christ, the man finds his cure.

"It may be," as Kitto says, "that the lepers had heard of Christ; that they had seen Him afar off; that they had talked to each other of His great doings, in their isolated communities; and as they recounted the wonders of mercy He had wrought, that they shook their sad heads, and remarked one to another, that He had not yet cured a leper; and asked, who since the days of Elisha had ever heard of a leper being cured? But there was one poor man who suffered a ray of hope to enter into his heart; and being entered, he nourished it, until it grew into faith. The more he thought upon the miraculous cures of which he had heard, the more he felt that in the prophet of Galilee dwelt a power such as the world had not before known; and which it were idle to limit to leprosy. Yes! He *could* cure him, but *would* He do so? Would He deign even to look upon an object so loathsome and so vile? Would He not rather, as scores of famous teachers and learned doctors had done, warn him from His path as a pollution? The poor leper may be forgiven this doubt; for his affliction had not allowed him to enter the cities in which Jesus taught, or to mix in the crowds that saw His miracles. He had not, therefore, been able to witness the divine compassion, that so

often beamed from the Saviour's eyes; or to hear the
tender gentleness of those tones in which He spoke to
the cast down and the miserable. Well, then, Jesus
could doubtless heal him; and it remained to be seen if
He were willing. He could at least try. He lost nothing,
nothing, alas! but hope, if he were repelled: he gained
much if he were accepted. This concluded, there remained yet the difficulty of getting access to His presence. He could not go into any town to seek Him; nor
could he, to approach Him, enter the crowds by which
He was usually in public surrounded. There was but
one course; and this was, to wait upon the road leading
to Capernaum, when the return of Jesus was expected;
and to accost Him, as He went by with His disciples.
He went; he waited; and doubt not that his unleprous
heart beat in audible throbs, when he at length beheld
the near approach of One who might deliver him from
the horrible bondage in which he had lain so long. He
advanced towards our Lord as He came nigh, and laying
his head low in the dust before Him, he cried, 'Lord, if
Thou wilt, Thou canst make me clean.' Oh! the agoniz-
ing suspense of the moment that followed! But it was
not protracted. A replying voice, that went at once to
his heart, and filled it with rapture, said, 'I will;' and
our Saviour, moved with deep compassion, put forth His
hand and touched him—him, whom no unleprous hand
had touched for years; and the same voice, which never
left the memory more, said to him, 'Be thou clean!' At
that word a change passed over him, he felt new blood
tingle through his veins, he felt the flush of healthy life
in all his tainted members; he knew that the leprosy had
passed from him, and he stood up, cleansed, enfranchised,

restored to his family and friends, and to all the blessings of social life." *

This description, sufficiently graphic, may give us a correct account of exactly how this leper came into the immediate presence of the Lord; enough for us that he is now there; our teaching is to be from what subsequently happens.

The leper, having thrown himself into a position of lowliest reverence, worshipping Jesus, addresses Him at once upon the subject of his misery; his address was short; none of the three evangelists, by whom the narrative is given, tells us of his having said anything more than the one sentence which we are considering now—"Lord, if Thou wilt, Thou canst make me clean." We are glad that the leper's petition is so concentrated; perhaps it would not have so much teaching for us if it had been more diffused.

" If Thou wilt."

The whole onus is here thrown on Jesus; the man says, " I am miserable, I am ready, and Thou art able;" one thing only was wanting, and about that the leper was not altogether sure—it was Jesus' will; and so he challenged that; this was a happy word—it secured the cure. Let us examine, in something of order, what this leper did, when he thus threw himself upon the will of Jesus.

In the first place, *he deeply touched the sympathies of Christ.* Saint Mark, with one of those little touches peculiar to himself, tells us, that Jesus was "moved with compassion;" there was a spring in the Saviour's mind which the word of supplication touched; a fountain, the

* Kitto's "Life and Death of our Lord," p. 262.

waters of which it unsealed; a fire, which it caused to
glow; the leper threw himself upon the innermost
tenderness of Christ's nature; and the whole being of
our Lord answered to the touch. There was no question
of *power* to be solved or proved; the method of the
appeal left no room for argument; the leper's words, as
they passed into the depths of Christ's loving nature,
which alone was invoked, cut a passage for themselves,
through which the healing waters could flow; the
response was instant—"if Thou wilt"—"I will."

And bear in mind, dear reader, that Jesus still has
sympathies; He is "the same yesterday, and to-day, and
for ever;" in Him there is "no variableness or shadow of
turning;" we also must appeal to the sympathies of our
Lord. In Heb. iv, 15, we are told, that "we have not a
high priest which cannot be touched with the feeling of
our infirmities;" O no, such a hard and stern high-
priest would be of little use to us, who are in circumstances to need sympathy continually. For, setting
apart for a moment such deep need as this of the leper
—fundamental need, touching even life itself—is not our
daily life full of little needs, of needs which have more
to do with sympathy than anything else? Have we not,
insensibly it may be, still continuously, to fall back upon
the sympathies of those who are around us? Are we not
dependent for our comfort rather upon their *will* than
their power—upon the tenderness of sympathetic feeling
rather than the display of great resources and strength?
Sympathy is the heart's load-stone, silent, mysterious,
all-powerful, attracting to it all forms of misery, and
imparting to it its very self; and such is the sympathy
in the heart of Jesus.

And do not be afraid, dear reader, to make a claim upon these sympathies of Jesus, because you think that your present case is not one of such deep importance as the leper's. Life is made up of little things; and if Jesus cannot sympathize with us in little things, then, instead of living ever close to Him, and ever in communion with Him, we must spend the greatest part of our life away from Him. · Jesus looks at things, not in their abstract, but in their relative importance—in the precise relationship which they bear to His people. A little scratch, at which a surgeon would laugh, may be productive of great suffering to persons of some constitutions; Jesus, the great Physician will take the constitution into account, and give His sympathies, not according to appearances, but according to our need; He "seeth not as man seeth;" He is "of quick understanding in the fear of the Lord, and shall not judge after the sight of His eyes, neither reprove after the hearing of His ears:" Isa. xi, 3. Was not Jesus touched with sympathy at that wedding feast, at Cana of Galilee, when His mother said to Him, "they have no wine?" Yes, He was; then He felt how the bridegroom would be put to shame at such scant provision, on this, the day when every one brought forth his best; then he felt how the pleasure of this, one of life's brightest and most joyous days, would be marred, if threadbare poverty were thus rudely and unexpectedly to intrude; there was no absolute need for Jesus to show His power; no harm, so far as we can see, would have ensued from there being too little wine; but Christ's sympathy was touched; far was it from Him to wish to see a cloud float across the horizon of this short passing day of earthly bliss; He was at that festive board

a sympathetic guest ; and so, He turned their water into
wine ; such wine as man had never drunk before.

Surely this sympathetic Saviour is the very one for
us ; and what are we but foolish neglecters of the mighty
power, which Jesus Himself has put into our hands, if
we fail to use this sympathy of our Lord ?   In giving us
access to His sympathy, Jesus has bared to us the very
secret of His being ; He has privileged us to pass beyond
all outer courts into the very holy place itself. Be not
afraid, then, dear friend, to appeal to the sympathies of
your Lord ; the relationship of sympathy admits of all
sorts of little things ; rather be afraid of stripping yourself by unbelief of this privilege ; for if you throw
aside this privilege ; if you view it just as a piece of
sentimentality, and nothing else, what ground will you
go upon when you come to Christ for help ? Will you
come upon His justice, and power, and so forth ?   No ;
you will feel the disproportion between your little wants,
and these vast attributes ; and the consequence will be,
that you will keep many of your necessities from Him,
you will try to bear many of your trials unbefriended and
alone ; heaven's choice gift will have been left unused,
and you have been left unblest.

In thus touching the great spring of Jesus' sympathy,
we must observe, *The Confession, and the painful display
of human infirmity, made by this poor leper.* All this
was brought before Jesus in the one word "clean."
"Thou canst make me clean."   The man was in a state
of living death ; "unclean life" was his portion. Those
who wish to know what leprosy really was, can refer to
the note at the end of this volume, in which they will
find it pictured with appalling minuteness ; it is sufficient

for us here to consider that this poor man led *a burdened life; a suffering life;* and *one of conscious misery:* all this was surely enough to make him an earnest suitor for the blessings which Christ could give.

"Burdened life!" We hear men sometimes say, "My life is a burden to me;" the leper, surely, might pre-eminently have said this; morning by morning he awoke to the realization of misery; night by night he lay down without a hope; his life dragged wearily along, and there was no spring in his existence, nothing but the heavy, even crushing of his daily burden of disease. If there be any of us leading such a burdened life as this; what can we do better than come with it before Jesus, and say, "If thou wilt, thou canst" take this load off my soul? His own blessed words seem peculiarly to invite us to do this. He says, "Come unto me, all ye that labour and are heavy laden, and I will give you rest." Our blessed Lord might be truly said, in many respects, to have led a burdened life Himself; how could He have "borne our griefs, and carried our sorrows," (Is. liii, 4,) without feeling the pressure of the load? Let us look at the absence of sympathy, at the perverseness even of His own disciples, at His physical sufferings, His long watchings, and all, in fact, that goes to make up the history of His life amongst men, on earth; and how is it possible to think of that life, otherwise than as a burdened one? All who are thus suffering may come to Jesus, and make use of this "if thou wilt;" if you have to say with Job, "I am a burden to myself:" chap. vii, 20; or with the psalmist, "Mine iniquities are gone over mine head: as an heavy burden, they are too heavy for me:" Ps. xxxviii, 4; or with the apostle, "We that are

in this tabernacle do groan, being burdened :" 2 Cor. **v**,
4; Jesus meets you all with His offer, " Come unto me
all ye that are heavy laden; my yoke is easy, my
burden is light." And let us suppose, for a moment,
that your chief trouble is only this sense of being burdened; that deep depression is the characteristic of your
whole spiritual system; that you have no great external
sores to exhibit; oh! do not think that Jesus will not
enter into this form of misery. He knows what depression is; in Gethsemane He "began to be sore amazed,
and to be very heavy," His soul was " exceeding sorrowful unto death :" Mark xiv, 33, 34. And when you,
dear reader, plead your burden, He will remember His
burden, and will do for you whatever your case requires.

The like may be said of *suffering*. This poor leper
had something more than his dead weight of misery to
contend with; he felt the corroding influence of the
leprosy eat into every part of his diseased frame. All
this he now brings before Jesus; it is all comprehended
in the petition, "Thou canst make me clean." There are
times when we lead the life of many years in a few
moments; there are also expressions, and sentences,
in which we wrap up a multitude of thoughts; thus is
it here; no doubt the leper concentrated into this interview the energies of many years; no doubt also he concentrated into this petition the story of many miseries;
concentration on his part as the petitioner, and on Christ's
as the granter, are a chief characteristic of this scene.
Let us follow His example in whatever sufferings come
upon us; all classes and forms of suffering were brought
before Jesus in His sojourn on the earth; let them be
brought before Him also, now that He is seated at the

right hand of the throne of GOD in heaven; trouble, sorrow, need, may be brought, as well as gold, frankincense, and myrrh. Oh! poor sorrowful one, do not think that your sorrows will be out of place in the presence of Jesus; do not mark this one bringing Jesus his service; and this other one his money; and yet again this other one the joyous praise of his bounding heart, whilst you have nothing but your sufferings; *bring them;* they also are acceptable when they are brought in faith; they will give Jesus a fresh opportunity of being gracious. He who has any need, has therein something to bring to Christ; it is only he who believes that he has no need in himself, and therefore no need of Jesus, that had better stay away. And mark

The conscious misery of this poor leper. That was another great characteristic of his life. By no possibility could that afflicted man shake off the consciousness of his wretchedness; it was stereotyped upon his flesh; it pervaded the very marrow of his bones; it was ingrained in him, so as to be a very part and parcel of himself; no doubt the one absorbing thought of his whole being was this, 'I am a leper.' Surely, it is exactly with such persons that the Saviour has to do. When He sees a poor creature coming to Him, and saying, "Behold, I am vile:" (Job xi, 4;) "I acknowledge my transgression, and my sin is ever before me:" (Ps. li, 3;) "The crown is fallen from our head, woe unto us, that we have sinned:" (Lam. v, 16;) then He sees one for whom He can do something; He sees a conscious emptiness, which is in point of fact a capacity for receiving what He has to give. So far, then, from being downcast at a consciousness of our misery, and above all, so far from trying to get rid of it by diverting our attention to other things, let us rather be incited by it to come into the presence of Jesus; our consciousness of misery will appeal to His consciousness, to His memory, His sympathy, all, all that can work in our behalf. This was on the leper's part,

A painful display of human infirmity. No doubt he felt it very much himself; he was not accustomed to come near people; the company which he had for a long time been obliged to keep, was that of his fellow lepers; and now he had to make a full display of his disease before the Lord; if he came to Christ at all, he must come with his leprosy; and this he did.

Dear reader, let us bear in mind, that we must ever come *with* our sins or sorrows; and if we do not chose to bring them with us, we must stay away; for we can never get rid of them ourselves. How many mistakes have been made on this point, not only by those who are trying to make themselves a little better, and somewhat acceptable before they come to Christ for the first time, but also by God's own dear people when they have fallen into sin. Their sin is now fresh, and clear, and sharp, and well-defined before their mind's eye; and instead of bringing it at once to God, they wait until they have, as they think, repented enough; or gained some victory in the very point in which they have been overcome. And when this is the case, men are not bringing before the Lord their guilt, but rather the palliations of their guilt; not the deep demerit of their offences, but the merit of their repentance for them, or their efforts against them. All this is a grand mistake; let us do our best with sin in any form, we cannot make it look otherwise than

what it really is, *i.e.*, "exceeding sinful;" we had much
better bring it all as it is; we cannot hide from it, or
diminish it, by any effort that we make. The Lord's
dealings with all these efforts at hiding are very marked.
Hear how sharply He speaks in Isaiah xxviii, 14, &c.,
"Therefore hear the word of the Lord, ye scornful men,
that rule this people which is in Jerusalem. Because ye
have said, we have made a covenant with death, and
with hell are we at agreement; when the overflowing
scourge shall pass through, it shall not come unto us;
for we have made lies our refuge, and under falsehood
have we hid ourselves: therefore thus saith the Lord
God, behold, I lay in Zion for a foundation, a stone, a
tried stone, a precious corner stone, a sure foundation:
he that believeth shall not make haste. Judgment also
will I lay to the line, and righteousness to the plummet:
and the hail shall sweep away the refuge of lies, and the
waters shall overflow the hiding place......for the bed is
shorter than that a man can stretch himself on it, and
the covering narrower than that he can wrap himself in
it." "Mine eyes," says the Lord, in Jeremiah xvi, 17,
"are upon all their ways, they are not hid from my face,
neither is their iniquity hid from Mine eyes." Incalculable evil has been done by our attempting to modify
our guilt, to clothe our nakedness, to make less pitiable
our appearance before God; and this evil is often
suffered by the Lord's people. Insensibly the wicked
One puts repentance and moral efforts in the place of
plain, quick, and unadorned confession, and the consequence is bad; henceforth let our experience be that of
the Psalmist, "I acknowledged my sin unto Thee, and
mine iniquity have I not hid. I said, I will confess my

transgressions unto the Lord; and Thou forgavest the
iniquity of my sin:" (Psalm xxxii, 5.) This is the way
to blessing, to being enabled to say with him, "Thou art
my hiding place, Thou shalt preserve me from trouble,
Thou shalt compass me about with songs of deliverance."
The worst display which we can make of our misery, falls
far short of all that Jesus already knows about it; we
gain nothing, we lose much, by every effort to extenuate
or conceal. Nor may we pass over

*The bringing into immediate conjunction the darkness
of the present distress, and the brightness which would
follow if Jesus only willed to put forth His power and
heal.* Deep dark shadows and bright glorious lights are
brought here into a proximity which no painter would
venture on, whatever might be his skill. "Thou canst
make *me* (and look what I am) clean." (Oh! think what
I might be made!) This contrast the leper brought
before the mind of Jesus, when he presented himself
with his leprosy, and asked for a cure; but the contrast
was no doubt still more powerfully presented before Him
by the omniscience of His own mind. There, before
Him, lay the leprous creature in the dust; let Him but
speak the word, and he would rise from it no longer with
a scaly skin, but with skin like that of a little child; no
longer an outcast from his fellow men, but one whom
everyone might embrace; no longer the bondsman of
disease, but the freedman of health; if the Son did but
set him free, he should be "free indeed." And thus let
each distressed one bring his case before the Saviour,
saying, "See what I am, see what Thou mayest make
me." Oh! Jesus knows the power of contrast well;
He only knows the intense depth of the shadows of

darkness; He only, the exceeding brightness of heavenly light; and if we are constrained to say to Him, "I am in darkness, oh! give me light," He knows the depth of the meaning of those words, far better than we do ourselves; He will act in the power of the contrast as it is presented to His own mind. How wonder-working, how transforming is that power! "Know ye not that the unrighteous shall not inherit the kingdom of God? Be not deceived: neither fornicators, nor idolaters, nor adulterers, nor effeminate, nor abusers of themselves with mankind, nor thieves, nor covetous, nor drunkards, nor revilers, nor extortioners, shall inherit the kingdom of God. And such were some of you: but ye are washed, but ye are sanctified, but ye are justified in the name of the Lord Jesus, and by the Spirit of our God:" (1 Cor. vi, 9—11.) *There* is a contrast; and we have another painted for us by our Lord Himself, in Luke xv, when He shows us the prodigal, who a little while ago was amid the swine, now clothed in the best robe, with a ring on his finger, and shoes on his feet; no longer filling his belly with the husks which the swine did eat; but feasting upon the fatted calf, which had been killed in honour of his return.

Is it not comforting to think that this powerful contrast is presented before the mind of Jesus; that it is brought before His benevolence; that He thinks, 'I know what this man is, I know what I can make him to be?' Oh! it is well for us that Christ knows so much more about us than we know about ourselves; let us bear this in mind, whatever be our plague, when we come before him, and say like the leper of old; "If Thou wilt, Thou canst make me clean."

There is one more thought suggested to our minds by the leper's words, "If Thou wilt," and it is this :—

A kind of obligation was here thrown upon Jesus to be gracious. The method of the leper's appeal might have no weight with us, but it had with Jesus ; and perhaps a little thought will explain the reason why.

The obligation flowed (1.) *out of Christ's very mission.* It was part of the mission of the Lord to heal the sick, not merely as a physician would do, without any ulterior object, but amongst other reasons, as an evidence of His good will to man—as a type, in which was wrapped up the pledge of a higher healing—the healing of that deadly leprosy of sin, of which the disease now in question was pre-eminently the type. Christ must not allow it to be said of Him, that He sent any one away who came to Him in faith and need. He filled the hungry with good things ; it was only those who were rich in their own eyes, that He sent empty away. Shall not we also in all our need make use of the known mission of our Lord ? Shall not we say to Him, " O Thou blessed One, didst Thou not come to seek, and to save that which was lost ? Didst Thou not come to bind up the broken-hearted ? Didst Thou not manifest Thyself to attract all misery to Thyself? Thy mission was to the weak, the weary, and the heavy laden, and such am I. Fulfil, O my Saviour, Thy mission to me!" And Jesus will do this ; He will see in thee, poor afflicted one, a fit object for His work ; when thou challengest Him with a holy faith and boldness, to fulfil His mission in thee, and in thy needs, He will not—He cannot—send thee empty away ; for thee Christ hath an "I will ;"—and His "I will" is this : "Be thou clean."

But we are not limited to the obligation which Christ has graciously caused to hang as a natural consequent upon His mission; we may throw ourselves also (2.) upon *that which proceeds from His very nature.* The Lord of life and glory loves to put many toils close to men's hands, wherewith they may bind Him, and hold Him fast.

We know what is the nature of our Lord; all that He ever said, and did, goes to shew, that He is full of compassion and love; He has revealed that nature to us in order that we may use it; and so, any poor afflicted one may come in his need, and say, "I know Thee, who Thou art," yea, "I know Thee, what Thou art; Thou art kind in Thyself; oh! be kind to me." If you touch a harp-string it will vibrate and give forth its own peculiar tone; if you touch the nature of your Lord, it also will give forth its own peculiar voice; it is from an inner depth there will come forth the sound you want to hear—Christ's great "I will;" the gift of what you need.

Yet once more, (3.) *the Lord by His previous acts has furnished us with grounds both for argument and encouragement.* We make much of precedents in life; we base calculations upon them in mercantile transactions; we raise arguments upon them in courts of law; and many of our own reasonings are insensibly founded upon them; and why should we leave them unused in our spiritual life? Oh! there is great power in the fact, that Jesus did so-and-so; He never acted upon the caprice of the moment; there was a reason for everything He did; the principles out of which His actions flowed in former years, are the same now; like effects will flow out of like causes; let us use what Jesus did, as well as what Jesus said. You may use His acts, somewhat after this fashion in prayer. "O Thou who didst still the wildness of the tempest, and walk upon the troubled sea, walk upon the troubled waters of my soul, and calm the agitation there. O Thou who didst feed the famishing multitude, look upon this my low estate of hunger (either of body or of soul) and feed me, even as Thou didst feed them; and let me have enough and to spare. O Thou who didst restore the withered hand, mark the paralysis that there is over me, infuse fresh life into me; bid this withered part be whole!" Thus might we follow our Lord through all the doings of His life, pleading well-established precedents in all our times of need; and He will never, by denying us, practically repudiate what He has formerly done; He will shew Himself to be the same yesterday, and to-day, and for ever; and perhaps speak to us and say, "Knowest thou so well what I have done? then thou shalt know also what I can do." Then will follow the great "I will;" the herald of the blessed words; the pledge that we shall receive what we require.

"Thou canst."

Whatever measure of ignorance or even unbelief, there might have been in this poor leper with regard to Christ's *will*, there seems to have been none with reference to Christ's *power*. There was a great difference between the "canst" of this leper, and that of the father whose son was afflicted with the fierce and dumb spirit. When he described his need to Jesus, he said, "but if Thou canst do anything have compassion on us, and help us," (Mark ix, 22,) and mark the answer which Jesus gave him: He did by him just as He did by the leper—

took him exactly where He found him; the man said, "if Thou canst do anything;" Jesus answered, "if thou canst believe :"—the poor leper said, "Thou canst;" and Jesus said, "Be thou clean."

There was in this leper *a recognition of the existence of secret springs of power in Jesus;* without that, all would have been of no avail; there was here a strong substratum of faith, whatever shiftings and inequalities there may have been upon the surface.

Is not this precisely the case with many in the present day? They believe in the power of Jesus, though they are uncertain about His will; but perhaps they do not believe in His power in altogether the same way as the leper before us now. He doubtless must have believed in its secret springs; he knew how his blood and very being were interpenetrated with disease; he knew that Jesus could send through them a healing power which would altogether reverse his curse. It is thus that all who come to Christ for healing should believe in His power; you must believe that His power is unlike all others—that it has secret and irresistible methods of operation—that it has ways of doing everything that is to be done. The leper recognised the power that was exactly suited to his case: so, dear reader, let it be with you; see a power, not only which can do many other great things, but, what is far more to the purpose, which can do what *you* require.

And we must not fail to observe that there is deep importance in the repetition of the word "Thou"—if 'Thou' wilt, 'Thou' canst. Leprosy was curable by Divine interposition alone; the skill of the physician, the healing influences of the most precious herbs, could not remove even a single one of its hideous scabs, or purify a single drop of its tainted blood—there lived no physician on earth to whom the leper might have applied and said, 'Thou'—thou canst do something for me. It may have been, that there was a peculiar emphasis in the unhappy man's expression of that word " Thou;" that all his faith, his hope, the terrible energy of his whole being, now moved to its very depths, threw their mighty strength into this single word; and Jesus felt the whole weight of the man's need and hope thrown upon Himself alone. Here was a recognition of His ability to put forth Divine power; the man's need demanded this, and nothing less. And is it not thus, dear reader, that the poor sinner is brought before his Lord? is he not taught the great truth, that none can do anything for him, but Jesus Christ alone? his eye is turned upon an individual, and that individual—Jesus.

Oh! it is a matter of the utmost importance that there should be One to whom the sinner can say, "Thou"—an individual upon whom he can fix his eye, and centre all his hope. Such an one is Christ; and as such, He desires to present Himself to our view. An example of this we find in the raising of Lazarus : (John xi ;) our blessed Lord associates His disciples with Himself in the journey into Judea : " Then, after that, saith He to His disciples, let *us* go into Judea again :" verse 7; they were His companions and friends, and had a common sympathy with Him in the bereavement at Bethany—" a common sympathy !" so far as any, who were mere men, could have community of sympathy with Him. There is much grace dropping from the lips of Jesus in the use of this word " us ;" but when the invitation of sympathy is to be exchanged for the declaration of power, the "us" is changed to "I;" and the Lord of life and glory stands upon the scene supreme, majestic, and alone! It is "*I*," were the words He spake as He moved upon the face of the waters : (Matt. xiv, 27.) "'*I*' go that *I* may awake him out of sleep," are His words as He announces His intention of raising Lazarus from the dead.

It is true there were disciples accompanying Jesus; they were around Him and followed Him, but they were nothing; the eye of faith must fix upon the central figure alone, by whom anything could be done. As it was on this occasion of the raising of Lazarus, so also is it now; the leper fixes all his attention on Jesus. A Divine power was as much needed for healing the leprosy as for raising the dead; and just as Martha said, "But I know that even now, whatsoever *Thou* wilt ask of God, God will give it *Thee:*" verse 22, so the leper says, "If *Thou* wilt, *Thou* canst make me clean."

We cannot overstate the importance of a man's looking at Christ *personally* for all he needs. Jesus says, "Come unto *me*, all ye that labour and are heavy laden, and *I* will give you rest;" His complaint against the Jews was, "And ye will not come unto me, that ye might have life." This 'Thou' of the leper is a distinctive 'Thou;' if it was to be the "Thou" of faith, it must of necessity be so; and in making it thus, the leper found his cure.

May it be given to all who read this book, to look away from every one surrounding Jesus, to Jesus Himself. How apt are men to allow themselves to be diverted, by what one might call, the surroundings of

the Lord Jesus Christ; how much looking is there to
ministers, preaching, and so forth; when one distinctive
glance at Christ would be worth it all.   Oh! never
weary of saying, "Thou"—He has what you want, dear
reader; tell Him, you know He has it; tell Him you
want it from Him; and He will give it.   Press the Lord
Jesus hard with His personality; say not only 'the
thing can be done,' but 'Thou canst do it;' yea, more
than that, 'Thou only canst do it;' and, whatever be thy
plague, thou shalt certainly be made whole.

Let us not leave this part of our subject, without
saying a word or two upon the important little word
"If."   What a volume might be written upon this little
word, in all its various uses in Holy Scripture! but we
do not propose to consider this "If" as we should if we
were giving it its particular place in such a volume,
with all its distinctive teachings; we cannot, however,
altogether pass it by.

Well! to come even to a state of 'If,' is not to be
despised.   There are some divines who would immediately raise a hue and cry after this little word, and hunt
it forthwith to death.   I too would join in the chase if I
were sure of being able always to run it down; but I
know from personal experience, and from the experience
of others, that this little "If" can outlive an entire pack
of the longest-winded sermons; and if it be brought to
bay, can fight as stoutly for its life, as other words of
more pretensions and weight.

I certainly do not mean to defend this word "If;"
for whatever evil there is in it, let it be condemned, but
if there be any good in it, by that good let us be taught.

And in truth, this little word, as used here, is a mixture of good and evil; it has but two letters, and yet it embodies two of the most powerful principles in the divine life, namely, 'belief' and 'unbelief;' and it occupies this strange position, that it may be used powerfully as an exponent of either. Let us leave the bad side for the present, and turn for a moment to the good. Who can tell what processes this man's mind may have gone through before he arrived at this "If?" How he had to struggle with the knowledge of the natural incurability of his disease; and with his consciousness of its power as felt in himself; and with all his past long season of despair, the links of whose iron chain had been riveted into him long long ago, so that now they had become embedded in his soul. To be lifted up out of this despairing state, was no mean attainment in itself; and our Lord does not despise this "If"—Oh no—He who knew what was in man, knew what was in this little word; He knew of what it was the exponent, and so He did not crush it; "The bruised reed did He not break, and the smoking flax did He not quench."

Let us beware of crushing those whom we perceive to be defective in faith; if we will aim a blow with a poker at a fly that perches on the forehead, we run a great risk of knocking out the brains. Coarse dealings with spiritual deficiencies are productive of incalculable ill; they were never adopted by our Lord. Let us bless God that some of our friends can even get as far as an "If;" perhaps the reader will have to bless God if he can get thus far himself; what must now be done is to draw out the moisture of unbelief out of the "If;" to reduce its power; and to kindle up the latent spark of fire, which

undoubtedly is here. Some persons come into the
perfection of faith, not by any sudden and irresistible
impulse of the Spirit, but rather by a gradual process;
the Spirit working out unbelief, and working in faith;
He works upon all men severally as He will.

Be encouraged, O thou of little faith; thy Lord will
not crush thee; He will take what is good in thine
"If" to bless thee, and what is evil in thine "If" to
instruct thee. An "If" may be the lisping of faith—the
stammering effort to make a perfect sound; but God
weighs it; and if in it he finds even a grain of faith, He
will not refuse a blessing to the one in whom it is found.

"I will."

Having considered thus far the leper's condition of
body and mind, we are now prepared to hear the words
of our Lord,—of Him of whom it may be truly said,
"Never man spake like this man." Jesus said, "I will."
Let us observe the majestic brevity of this; He comes
immediately to the point—"If Thou wilt;" "I will."
And blessed be God this is no long complicated matter;
the will of Jesus is not entangled with a number of conditions; it is just the outpouring of Himself, flowing
forth even as the waters of a fountain flow, without let
or hindrance, by the simple impulse of their nature.
Jesus comes to the point at once; to the very point to
which He has been brought by the measure of the leper's
faith; it was His will that the leper challenged, and it is
the will that gives the response.

Is not this subject of 'bringing Christ to the point'
a very important one? Men dare not essay this with
earthly monarchs; they have, as we say, to beat about

the bush for a long time ; perhaps they cannot make the
great man understand; perhaps he is not willing to understand : but mark the condescension of the blessed Lord ;
He is willing to be brought to the point by even weak
faith ; and He does not wander from it—it heralds the
leper's cure.

Have you tried, dear reader, to bring the matter to an
issue in the great affair of the cleansing of the soul—to
get Jesus to say, then and there, "I Will?" If you have
not, oh try it now—Jesus will always come up to the
measure of our prayer. Are not some destitute of present peace, because they really have never sought it? you
sought a cure at some future time ; and perhaps, in seeking that, you received an answer, a good hope of being
saved : but have you brought the Saviour to the point of
saving you now ? If not, try Him—the "I will" that
He spake to the leper, yea, all the "I wills" in this book
have not exhausted Him ; He has been saying "I will"
to poor sinners, ever since He took up His seat at the
right hand of the throne of the Majesty on high : He
has got another "I will" for you.

Observe also the *comprehensiveness* of it. We might
have thought there was no necessity for Christ's using
those words, "I will." Could He not have taken up the
point on which the leper was perfectly clear, viz : His
power, and healed him without any mention of His will ?
Did He not prove His will by working the miracle, and
was not that enough ? This might have been man's plan,
in whose brevity and business-like way of doing things
something is frequently left undone. Brevity may be too
brief; dogmatism may be too dogmatic; it is at times
as dangerous to say too little as too much. We think

we can see good reason for our Lord's repeating the
leper's words, and declaring His will. "I will, be thou
clean." Does He not here take up the very point of the
suppliant's doubt? Does He not apply Himself to
strengthening the weak point? Does He not reveal the
depths of His own loving nature? Does He not shew
how His whole heart, inclination, sympathy, and desire
enter into the subject of the need of those who appeal to
Him? We are thankful that those words have been
spoken; we know now what the mind of Christ is
towards a needy one; we see here an encouragement
which is sufficient for us to go on, even if we had
nothing else; when we are weak and trembling we can
say to ourselves, "He said 'I will.'" This "will," thus
shewn in the curing of the leper, is the same as that
which brought the Saviour from heaven to earth, Psa. xl,
7—the one Will which embraces, in its readiness to cure,
all man's lower as well as higher needs. Where the
leper's weak faith most needed a manifestation of what
was in Christ, there He gave it; and the leper's "If"
departed, doubtless, to be heard no more again for ever.

Think too, dear reader, of the *authoritative power* of
this "I will." It had a deeper meaning than assent—
it implied a will with power. And herein differs the
will of Jesus from our mere human wills, in that He is
always able to link His with power: if He say "I will"
we may rest assured that it will be done. The resources
of the Godhead are all in waiting upon the will of Christ.
And what a prospect does this open out for us; how does
it dispel all emptiness and formality; how does it assure
us that there is a reality in the word of Christ—there are
no mere forms with Him—His words are irresistible:

might we not say of this "I will" even what they did,
who were all amazed, and spake among themselves,
saying, "What a word is this!" (Luke iv, 36.)

"Be thou clean."

Quick following upon the expression of Christ's will
came the declaration of His power. No long interval of
heart-sickening delay intervened between the declaration
of mercy and the performance of it; Christ did not
leave His work half done; He gave the command, "Be
thou clean." The cause of the leper's disease was
operated upon; the poisoned blood heard that word
rolling its mighty sound over its sluggish tides; and
festering sores, and whitened scales, and all the hideous
developments of leprosy shrank before the wonder-
working voice, and vanished before that healing breath.
Then, cannot we imagine how this poor man sprang up
from the dust at his Deliverer's feet; how, at the more
than magic words, he felt the hideous monster, that had
so long enthralled him, loose his foul hold, and depart,
to return upon him no more? Oh! cannot we faintly
picture to ourselves, how, under the influence of reno-
vated life and new health, this poor fellow felt as though
he could have almost flown, instead of walked, as he
went, under the direction of his Saviour, to show himself to the priest? What painter could represent the
gaze with which he looked at Jesus? what poet could
perpetuate, in even the most flowing numbers, the music
of his praise? what orator could imitate the impassioned
utterance of his thanks? he who would succeed in doing
this must not only be poet, orator, and painter, but a
saved leper too! And now he is away to the priest; he

speeds as doubtless he never sped before, but the way seems also doubtless longer than ever it did before. Perhaps the leprous man has a wife to return to ; who knows but that he had been stricken almost at her very side; fond memories of the past come crowding into the heart—the old soft words and sunny looks of healthy days, the sweet communion of love, ere he had to leave his home, bearing the leper's brand upon his brow ; and now he can clasp that wife to his arms once more, and feel her heart beat close to his ; and they twain can be one again ; and it may be that there come trooping into his mind the images of little ones who once clasped his knees, and twined their arms around his neck, sporting with him in that high holiday which children alone can make ; it may be that there were brothers at home ready to grasp him by the hand, and that aged parents would totter forth upon their staves, to fall upon his neck and kiss him, their own long lost one, with flesh come upon him again like the flesh of a little child. The Psalmist said, "When the Lord turned again the captivity of Zion, we were like them that dream :" Psa. cxxvi, 1. And now, in this substantial dream, on speeds this almost breathless man to the priest. And what will he with the priest ? there is no more healing needed; all that now he wants is the declaration that he is made whole. Happy leper, to have said, "If Thou wilt." Happy leper, to have met with one who said, "I will."

"*I* will," "Be *thou*"—mark Christ's "I," giving; mark our "*thou*," receiving; it is an epitome of the gospel; it is the one distinctive grouping of its figures : the giver and receiver brought near together ; the giver—Christ; and the receiver—man !

The "I Will" of Confession.

Matthew x, 32.

MATTHEW X, 32. (LUKE XII, 8.)

"Whosoever therefore shall confess Me before men, him will I confess also before My Father which is in heaven. But whosoever shall deny Me before men, him will I also deny before My Father which is in heaven."

THE heart thrills at the thought of the noble army of martyrs! Far back in the ages of the past, it sees drawn out in long array the warriors of God, who were stoned and sawn asunder, who were tempted, who were slain with the sword. (Heb. xi, 37.) Yet nearer are to be seen the victims of the Pagan and the Jew, banded in unnatural unanimity against the people of the Lord; nearer still, the host murdered by the church of Rome —men, women, and children, bearing upon them the marks of the stake, the halter, and the sword; until almost before our very eyes we see men and women from the missionary field, and from the persecutions of this bloody church of Rome, enlisted for that army in which every one is a true hero, as well as a glorified saint. Heroism's loftiest annals are to be found in the history of the church of God.

But we must not fix our admiring gaze upon the

noble army of martyrs alone; there is a vast body of
confessors upon the earth; yea, and a vast body of them
with Christ in glory, who have deep claims upon our
notice; with the men who have passed through blood,
must be associated in some measure those who are ready
so to do, should there be a cause. These are God's
disciplined troops, who have enlisted under His banner,
sworn allegiance to His cause, and taken up the cross,
they are men who have for the most part tasted more
or less of the cup, which the martyrs drained to the
dregs; they are confessors, and they are ready, when
need be, to empty their veins, and become martyrs.

It is of such confessors that we have now to think
for a little while; it is of them our blessed Lord speaks,
in the passage in which we find this "I will." "Whosoever therefore shall confess Me before men, him will I
confess also before My Father which is in heaven."

And at the outset let us remember, that the ranks of
confessors number amongst them "all sorts and conditions of men." In those ranks may be found the king
on his throne, and the beggar in the streets; and there
may be as great a difference between the places in which
confession is made, as in the confessors themselves; the
true confessor is to be found alike in the blaze of the
most open publicity, and in the shade of deepest
privacy; the confession may be amid "trials of cruel
mockings and scourgings, yea, moreover of bonds and
imprisonment; amid wanderings about in sheep skins
and goat skins; amid destitution, affliction, and torment,
in deserts, and in mountains, and in dens and caves of
the earth;" or it may be only amid the petty persecutions of an ungodly home. Sometimes men prick us

with their swords to see if we will confess Christ; and sometimes they only stick pins into us to try whether we be in the faith; but confession is confession, wherever and however it be made; we are required to be confessors in the circumstances in which God places us, and we must not seek out circumstances for ourselves; we may rest assured, it will always give us quite enough to do, to be equal to *present circumstances;* in them we may make the confession before men, and at last be confessed before the Father which is in heaven.

Let us now look a little closely into this matter, with reference to daily life, and see at once our duty and our reward.

And first of all let us look at this confession with reference to ourselves; what are we, who are, perhaps, only common-place people, likely to have to do with it in our daily life?

It might be said by some, 'Oh, we are confessors; we acknowledge Christ to be the Lord; we would not deny that truth for the world.' No! not the abstract truth; but what about that truth, when it makes demands in daily life?

We must at once clear out of our way the idea that we in this land of professing Christians are confessors, because we call ourselves Christians; it would require far more boldness for us in this country to confess the Devil, and say we were not Christians, than to confess Christ and say we are.

There was a time when even to call oneself a Christian was to make the very highest confession, and to run the risk of martyrdom; what would some of our confessors have done, if they had stood before Nero, and heard the howl of the wild beasts which were ready to break their bones? bare confession was something then; and it is something now in many a heathen land; and just see what it is to a Jew.

"Whatever displeasure" (says a converted Jew) "may arise in the minds of nominal Christians, when their relations are in earnest about the salvation of their souls, and give up all for Christ; it falls far short of what the poor converted Jew has to encounter, when about to publish to the world, and confess in the church, that the Lord Jesus Christ is his Redeemer. No one can adequately describe the sufferings, persecutions, and deprivations of the Jew, when he enlists under the banner of the Lord. Every endearing tie is torn asunder; he is spurned from the parental roof, detested, shunned, and excommunicated by every individual of his nation; his business, too, is quite ruined, in consequence of his former friends abstaining from all intercourse with him, in secular concerns."

Such suffering this poor fellow was soon called upon to endure. His first troubles came upon him at the time of the Passover. "My wife," says he, "went to see my parents on the day preceding the festival. After the usual salutations, my mother said, 'I have been informed of something, which I hope is not true—that your husband has been baptized.' My poor wife being quite unprepared for such an address, could only reply by saying, 'You will see your son, and he will answer any questions you may wish to put to him.' My mother continued, 'Mrs. W. says, that we shall be disappointed in our anticipated enjoyment of the holidays,

for that our son Henry (meaning myself) has been
baptized.' My mother added, 'If my son has been so
mad as to act thus, I am confident that neither you nor
your children will follow his example.' My poor wife
returned home quite cast down; she was hardly able to
utter a sentence, and I confess that I felt sorely grieved,
not because it was discovered that I had openly confessed the Lord, but that it was such a blow to the
feelings of my dear parents and friends, towards whom,
as well as towards all my kinsmen according to the
flesh, I entertained the sincerest affection.

"I understood that my mother intended to visit me.
She, however, gave up her intention, and the elder of
my two sisters came in her stead. After a little common-place conversation, she said, 'Mrs. W. has informed
me that you have been baptized, but I cannot believe it.
Tell me if there is any foundation for such a scandalous
report? I hope it is a false rumour, and I shall be
greatly rejoiced to find it is so.' I was now put to the
test, whether I would deny Christ, and subject myself
to be denied before the Father of our Lord Jesus, or
confess Christ, and be declared before His heavenly
Father, to be one of the sheep of His fold. I was not
a moment in deciding what to do. 'The truth is, dear
sister,' I replied, 'that in the desire of doing all things
to the glory of God, I *have* received the ordinance of
baptism.' I had scarcely uttered the words, when my
poor misguided sister, unable to restrain her indignation,
at first gave vent to her feelings by a flood of tears,
and then, as if reproaching herself for her weakness, she
arose, and changing her countenance, (which before had
been placid,) to an expression of scorn and hatred, she

said, 'then, sir, we must have done with you for ever—
you have made us all wretched—we shall be ashamed
to see any of our friends; you have brought disgrace
and scandal upon us, and will bring the grey hairs of
your parents with sorrow to the grave. If your heart is
not yet so hardened as to be incapable of being moved
at the grief and anguish you have occasioned your aged
parents; if you do not desire to be an outcast from your
family, from your nation; if you will serve the God of
your fathers, instead of being led astray by those Christian idolaters, I entreat you to turn away from them.
You are but little acquainted with them as yet. They
may appear favourably disposed towards you for a short
space of time; but they will soon contemptuously leave
you to deplore your consummate folly in giving your
society to the heathens, in preference to that of God's
chosen people; and the company of strangers, to those
of your father's house.' I endeavoured (by appealing to
her better reason) to soothe her agonized feelings, and
assured her, that I did not look to man, but only to
God. I said, that the Shepherd of Israel was gathering
His sheep into His fold. She would listen to no more,
but turning away, instantly left the house. After her
departure, she gave vent to her outraged feelings in
a flood of tears, and I was afterwards informed, that
she was three several times attacked with violent
fits.

"This was a season of great temptation to me; I
loved my relations very dearly; for in addition to my
having for them a natural affection, I now loved them
for Christ's sake, and for their souls' sake. But even
had it been possible for me to have loved them better

than I did, my love to Jesus was paramount to all, for the love of Christ constrained me to give up all for Him, whom my soul loved. I now prayed earnestly that I might be enabled in this time of sore temptation to stand my ground, and that the word of God sown in my heart might take deep root. My family were determined to leave no means untried to win me back to them. Their mode of attack was cautiously planned; they did not offer any violent opposition to me at first, for they expected that *that* would at once have put an end to their hopes of regaining me. They knew how much I was attached to my youngest sister. We were nearly of the same age, and from our earliest infancy, our mutual affection attracted the attention of all who knew us. In all our little joys and griefs, there was a genuine sympathy of kindly feeling; and this attachment did not only exist in our early days, but continued afterwards unalloyed by any misunderstanding, up to the time when I was called upon to decide between the love of my redeemer and my relations. Therefore this sister was deemed a most proper person to be the bearer of the wishes of my family regarding me: they thought that I could not refuse her any request, and that I should yield to her tears and entreaties. The morning following the day that my eldest sister came, I received a visit from the youngest. She came in and looked at us most piteously, then sinking down on a seat, covered her face with her hands and sobbed convulsively, in a manner that would have been distressing even to a stranger; what must it then have been to a brother who had always shared her sorrows? We sat like so many statues. I now needed as much as ever the strength of

an Almighty arm to lean upon—my natural feelings
were overcome, and had I conferred with flesh and
blood, I should undoubtedly have yielded in this moment of trial, but God was my stay.

" Nearly an hour had elapsed, before my poor sister
could give utterance to a word. Vain would any
attempt of mine be to describe her appeal to me. It
was delivered in broken sentences, now gently reprov-
ing, now affectionately entreating; showers of tears
continually preventing her speech. ' Oh Henry,' she
said, ' If any of that love remains which you have
always shown to all your family, and particularly to me,
you will now prove it by saving us from the disgrace
and shame of *one* of our family abjuring the religion of
his forefathers; you will assuredly break our hearts if
you do not relent.'

"I must here digress for a moment, to observe, that
if a Jew has renounced his religion, and embraced
Christianity or any other religion, if he recant, he may
again be admitted to the privileges of his nation, by
performing some penitential act or acts, imposed on him
by the chief Rabbi, who is commonly, but erroneously,
termed the High Priest. To that personage my dear
sister urged me to have recourse; that, being by him
absolved from the reproach I had brought upon myself,
I might be received with open arms by my friends, and
be more endeared to them than ever. ' Consider,' she
continued, ' that either your wife and children will share
your disgrace, or being restored to us, they will share in
the joy your return will occasion to us all.' She proceeded for a length of time in the same strain; but how
shall I describe the inward-conflict in which I was

now engaged, or the struggle I had with my natural feelings?

"My sister began to have hopes (judging by my silence) that she had gained her point, that her appeal to my affections had not been in vain: she was however greatly mistaken—I was silently praying to my God to give me the spirit of wisdom and of truth, as well as a door of utterance, that I might speak boldly in the name of the Lord Jesus. The Lord was with me, and His grace enabled me to rouse myself from my apparent lethargy, and fearlessly and unshrinkingly to witness a good confession. I assured my dear sister that however great my love might be to her, and to my parents, or to my wife and children, or any creature, the love I bore to my blessed Saviour was infinitely above all other considerations; and that all other love was as nothing, when we are assured of His love to us, His sovereign love, which is unmixed with human passions —in short, I told her that no earthly power or inducement could draw me away from God, my Saviour. Finding that her tears and entreaties had all been spent in vain, she arose to depart. 'Henceforth (said my sister) I shall abhor Christians, their very name will be odious to me.' With an aching heart, and swollen eyes, she returned home to bear the sad tiding of the failure of her mission to the other members of the family, who were waiting her return in deep anxiety.

"My two sisters next paid a visit to the Rev. Mr. ——. They accused him of being the chief instrument in leading me to Christianity. He assured them that he was not instrumental in any way in bringing me to the knowledge of Christ. He said, 'When I first

saw your brother, I found him a Christian already.'
He then took the opportunity of briefly laying before
them the truths of the gospel; and although they were
not able to controvert the proofs he gave them, yet,
being so tenacious of their own preconceived notions,
they expressed strong disapprobation of the step I had
taken.   Mr. —— offered to go to my parents, and
endeavour to soothe their agitated minds, and reconcile
them to the will of Providence; but his kind and
well meant offers were peremptorily refused.   Mr. ——
related to me the substance of his interview with my
sisters, and told me how much pleased he was with
their intelligent conversation; with the energetic manner
with which they entreated him to restore me to them;
and with their respectful behaviour to him, although
they were labouring under excited feelings.

"Their next recourse was to try what my wife's
family could do.   Accordingly we received a visit from
her brothers.   My wife's family were always noted for
the great unanimity existing amongst them.   Her eldest
brother began by asking her if she could reconcile her
mind to live with an apostate.   She assured them, that
from all she observed, she was satisfied that I was seeking to walk in the paths of truth, and holiness, and
added, 'I cannot dissuade him.'   I then thought it right
to address a few words to him, in support of the choice
I had made.   He would not allow me to proceed, but
continued addressing my wife.   'My purpose in coming
to you is this; if you will take your children away, and
leave your husband, I will settle a sufficient annuity
upon you to support you comfortably.'   Now as I have
before stated, they always attacked me where they

thought I was the weakest; and knowing my attachment to my wife and children, they flattered themselves that I would rather yield to anything, than to a separation from them. Here again they were foiled. My wife replied, 'I am ready to share with my husband in all circumstances, whether of reproach, contempt, adversity, sorrow, or sickness, or in any other way in which it may please God to visit us.' 'Then,' said he, 'you are as deep in guilt as he is, and perhaps you are the worst of the two, for had you disapproved of his conduct, he would not, probably, have persevered in opposing your wishes, and rendering you unhappy and miserable.' They went away dejected and sorrowful. We were wonderfully supported in those struggles, for however willing the spirit may be, the flesh is weak; and we must have sunk under the weight of these efforts had not the Lord held us up, proving the truth of His own promise, that His grace was sufficient for us.

"I had now a duty to perform, nor could I rest till it was performed; which was, to go and see my parents. We had not met for some time; and although I knew it would be a most painful interview, yet to have omitted a visit to them, at this particular time, would have amounted to a virtual admission that I acknowledged myself in error.

"'Thou, O Lord, art a shield for me, my glory and the lifter up of mine head.' Never shall I forget the morning I went to my parents; it was the last time I saw them, and in all human probability we shall not meet again in this world. A servant admitted me, and I fancied I could read in her countenance that I was considered an intruder. I felt much agitated as I entered the room where my parents were sitting at breakfast. As I approached them, they averted their faces from me. I bade them good morning, and inquired after their health; a pause ensued, and for two or three minutes I received no reply. My father then raised his head from his hand, on which he had been leaning, and turning to me with a look of contempt and indignation, addressed me nearly as follows: 'How dare you have the temerity, sir, to enter the house of parents you have so grossly offended?' I said, 'In what have I so much grieved you?' He replied, 'By the abominable act you have committed; for ever separating yourself from your family and nation.'

"I attempted to speak about the Messiah, but he would not allow me to proceed. 'You have brought shame and reproach upon your father's house.' I asked if we were not under the curse pronounced upon all who did not keep *all* the Commandments; and endeavoured to shew the difference of being under grace and under the Law. My father said, 'I will not enter into any discussion with you : you were at liberty to maintain your own opinions, if you objected to the forms and services of our religion; but you had no occasion to make it publicly manifest that you disapproved of them. In your own house you could do as you pleased; but in public you might have kept silence concerning anything you deemed objectionable in our institutions.' I replied, that in doing so I should have been a decided hypocrite. My father said, 'You have connected yourself with hypocrites, and deceivers, and worshippers of devils, in preference to the worshippers of the true and only God.' I was about to explain who and what we worshipped, and how completely the Jews were in error in not worshipping the *Triune* God of the Christian, whose existence was as manifest in the Old Testament Scriptures as in the New; but he would not suffer me to reply.

"'Go,' he said, 'and never dare to enter this house again, unless you repent of this wicked deed, and for ever renounce the society of idolaters. If you had committed any crime, however heinous, short of apostasy, I could have forgiven you; but now I shall try to forget you. You are breaking the hearts of your parents, but you will not go unpunished; for a time you will be a slave to these Christians, and do just as they please; they will then despise you, and cast you off, leaving you to the remorse of your own conscience, and to the scorn and derision of Jews and Gentiles.' I said, 'I did not expect that such would ever be the case.' He thereupon mentioned several cases which had come under his own observation, to bear him out in what he asserted. I said, 'I did not fear what man could do to me, for God had promised He would not forsake those who put their trust in Him.'

"He replied, 'The promises are not to you, for you have forsaken God.' My poor dear mother, with uplifted hands, and with her aged cheeks bedewed with tears, besought me to seek a reconciliation with God by taking penance, that is to say,—to go to the chief Rabbi or High Priest, and express my contrition for the abominable sin I had committed in embracing Christianity; and state how desirous I was of returning to Judaism. He would then appoint certain acts of penance for me to perform, and after the expiration of a few days, I should receive absolution, and be restored to the privileges of the Jewish religion, to the joy of all the people, more especially of my kindred, who considered a triumph would be thus obtained over the Gentiles.

"This appeal from my dear mother afflicted me greatly—O could I have been spared this!—this was indeed as a thorn in my flesh—but I felt assured that I was under the guidance of the Lord, and he was my strength and my stay. I therefore addressed my dear parents, and told them, how exceedingly pained I felt at being unintentionally the cause of so much grief and distress of mind to them, in consequence of their erroneous views of the late occurrence. I assured them that so far from my filial love and duty being diminished, it was continually increasing, for that I now felt greater interest than before in their spiritual welfare. I appealed to my former conduct whether I had ever offended them in word or deed. 'However,' said I, 'you may contemn me, and cast me off, my constant petitions shall be offered up for your welfare; and be assured that, through the grace given unto me by the keeper of Israel, I will never do anything that shall bring shame or discredit upon myself, my relations, or my nation.'—'That is false,' said my father, 'for you have done that already, by openly renouncing your God, and the God of your fathers; and now,' he continued, 'I wish for no more arguments with you; you had better leave this house.' I replied, 'As my presence appears to cause you so much uneasiness, I obey, and may the God of Abraham, Isaac, and Jacob, by His holy Spirit comfort you and guide you into all truth.'

"And now by this dispensation of Providence, my Saviour became more precious to me, for no one can sympathize with His people like Jesus. My father and mother had forsaken me, but the Lord hath taken me up. What astonishing mercy! O may I be ever willing to suffer the loss of all things, so that I may win Christ!

"I knew there was nothing now before me but affliction, poverty, distress, and persecution, but I like-wise knew that God was able to supply all my need according to His riches in glory by Christ Jesus. We were considered as *dead* by both our families; and on such occasions the parents, brothers, and sisters of the deceased are compelled, according to the Rabbinical law, to sit for seven days on very low seats, to rend their garments, and to mourn for the departed soul. During that space of time they must not leave their houses, nor transact any business, and I believe their misguided zeal would (if they had possessed the power) have actually realized what was done in semblance, *i.e.*, they would have buried me."

Well, dear reader, for a man to confess under these circumstances is something; and if your heart glows at all within you, and you think, "I wish I had an opportunity of confessing my Lord," you will be glad to see that the thing can be done, and that the opportunity lies almost at your very door.

Where shall we go to look for a confessor's sphere of action? It lies in *society*, in *trade*, in *politics*, in the *social circle*, in *expenditure*, in *pursuits*, and in a word, *everywhere*. Some people think that a profession ought to be made in public, while there is no necessity for it at home : while others say, 'we ought to be religious at home, but we need not be thrusting our religion upon people abroad:' but the truth is, the sphere of confession is so wide, that the sweep of its circle embraces abroad and at home—every place where there is a heart to feel, a head to think, a tongue to speak, or an ear to hear.

I ask you, dear reader, an important question, when I say, are you known as a true Christian in the society in which you move—in *all* the society—not only in the good tea-party branch of it, but in all of it?'

"Not long ago an officer was accosted by a brother-officer thus—' *You're* the right kind of Christian,—— not bothering people about their souls this way!' The speaker himself made no pretensions to serious godliness; and the allusion was to certain officers who had a way of speaking out very intelligibly for Christ. Our friend had himself been converted; but, up to that time, he had been too timid to utter any articulate testimony. As his visitor left him that day, he began to reason with himself—'Well, if that man thinks I am the right kind of Christian, it is time I was looking about me and considering my ways.' It was a somewhat novel point of departure; but, from that hour, our friend has been another man, boldly confessing Christ and labouring to win souls."

Are you the world's right kind of a Christian, or God's right kind? There is much religion to which the teapot is the river Rubicon; to get past it is an almost insuperable task; it may excite a smile, but it is nevertheless a sad and solemn truth, that in the devil's hand even a teapot may be made the means of leading a soul to hell. Look at this person at a religious tea-party, and at an ordinary dinner-party; is it the same person, or does he hold the same principles? Look at this young man as a member of a young men's society, and is he just the same young man as a member of a rifle corps? We hear of all sorts of pocket things, and they are always considered handy—surely we may add to them a pocket religion; and of its exceeding handiness in some respects there can be no doubt. But a pocket religion will not always satisfy the conscience, as we can see from the following fact:—

"A chaplain-general once related an incident of a young soldier who on one occasion had consulted him upon a question of Christian duty. 'Last night,' said the young man, 'in my barrack, before going into bed, I knelt down and prayed in a low voice, when suddenly my comrades began to throw their boots at me, and raised a great laugh.' * 'Well,' replied the chaplain,

---

* Another man, whom for three months we had been teaching to read, was sent by his employer to a job of work in the country; he told me on his return how difficult he had found it to try and keep up his reading, for his fellow workmen would knock the book out of his hand, besides using very coarse language, and when " I knelt to pray they pitched all sorts of things at me, and jeered and swore at me, (there were several men lodging in the same room) but I would not give it up, and after a time they let me alone, and I prayed for them."
—"Life Work," by L. N. R.

On the morning which succeeded the memorable night of Captain Hedley Vicars' conversion, he bought a large Bible, and placed it open on the table in his sitting room, determined that an "open Bible," for the future should be his "colours." "It was to speak for me," he said, "before I was strong enough to speak for myself." His friends came as usual to his rooms, and did not altogether fancy the new colours. One remarked that he had "turned Methodist," and with a shrug, retreated. Another ventured on the bolder measure of warning him not to become a hypocrite: "Bad as you were, I never thought you 'but suppose you defer your prayer till you get into bed; and then *silently* lift up your heart to God?' A week or two afterwards, the young soldier called again. 'Well,' said the chaplain, 'you took my advice, I suppose? how has it answered?' 'Sir,' he answered, 'I did take your advice for one or two nights; but I began to think it looked rather like denying my Saviour; and I once more knelt at my bedside, and prayed in a low whisper as before.' 'And what followed?' 'Not one of them laughs now, sir; the whole fifteen kneel and pray too.' 'I felt ashamed,' added the chaplain-general, in narrating the story, 'of the advice I had given him; that young man was both wiser and bolder than myself.'"

The word *society* seems almost, in the public mind, to preclude the idea of religion; and yet, if a man have true religion at all, where does he leave it when he goes into society? how does he contrive to separate himself from it? on what peg does he hang it? in what drawer does he stow it? in a word, where is it?

There are three great confessors spoken of in the Old Testament, and let us turn our attention to them for a few moments, for in this matter they can teach us much: yes! not only they, but their garments, and we must never be above learning from even the least of the circumstances or things by which God would teach. In

would come to this, old fellow." So, for the most part, for a time, his quarters were deserted by his late companions. During six or seven months he had to encounter no slight opposition at mess, and "had hard work," as he said, "to stand his ground." But the promise did not fail.—"The righteous shall hold on his way, and he that hath clean hands, shall wax stronger and stronger."—"Memorials of Captain Hedley Vicars," p. 33.

revelation and in nature, God teaches us by little things; the sparrows are made the medium of instruction as to God's providence over our life, and the grass-blades are our preachers to invite us to cast all our care on Him who careth for us, and not to wear ourselves out by anxiety about our daily need.

The three great confessors to whom we allude, are Shadrach, Meshach, and Abednego, and the circumstance to which we wish to draw particular attention is the fact, that they were bound in their coats, their hosen, and their hats, and their other garments, and so were cast into the burning fiery furnace.

Let such as think that confession is something special—something that must be prepared for by some special process—observe that these men had to give their testimony without any special preparation. They were probably engaged in their ordinary business when they were suddenly seized; and when sentence was pronounced against them, they were allowed no time for preparation to meet their God—none for prayer: the king's commandment was urgent,—the executioners did not even take time to strip them of their clothes; but threw them into the burning fiery furnace just as they were—with their coats, their hosen, and their hats.

Far be it from us to say anything against special preparation, whether it be for meeting anticipated trial, or for doing anything that is difficult in our Christian course; it is excellent in its place; it is excellent when we can avail ourselves of it. Would to God that we all knew more of special preparation than we do; that we chose our smooth stones from the brook before we hurled them from our sling; that we followed the example of

Him who knelt in Gethsemane before He ascended Calvary; immense blessing and power would flow forth from such preparation; the seed thus steeped would surely sprout; but we must remember that there may be no opportunity for this preparation; there was none, as far as we know, for Shadrach, Meshach, and Abednego; what would have become of them, if they had had to depend upon such preparation as they could have made upon the moment? it may be that life would have been more sweet to them than honour; that the image of Nebuchadnezzar would have received the worship due to the Most High; that they would have bowed the knee to the idol, instead of offering their bodies as a living sacrifice to God; and cornet, and flute, and harp, and sackbut, and psaltery, and dulcimer, and all kinds of music, would have proclaimed, in their unhallowed strains, the disgrace of the cause of God, and the triumph of the image of gold.

Remember, dear reader, you may have no opportunity given you for preparation, in any of the trials which may be coming on you. You may find yourself suddenly in such a position that you must deny Christ, or suffer grievous loss; if you be in such a spiritual condition, so half made up in mind for God, that you absolutely require special preparation to enable you to meet special trial; then, should such special trial come on unawares, you will be undone.

But it must not be supposed, that the three great confessors before us now, were men without preparation and training, albeit there was no *special* preparation for this, their great testimony and confession before Nebuchadnezzar; and for facing those hideous flames, which darted like serpents' tongues from the mouth of the burning fiery furnace, heated seven times more than was its wont. As these men were ready to testify even unto death in the coat, the hosen, and the hat; so in the coat, the hosen, and the hat, the habiliments of daily life, had they been trained.

The account of this training we have in Dan. i, where we read of their refusing the daily provision of the king's meat and the wine which the king drank; for three long years they saw others feasting on that which their own natural palate might have liked, but of which their consciences would not allow them to partake; they had only pulse when others had meat; they had only water, when others had wine. Thus, amid this world's luxuries, they were kept separate for God; they were trained and prepared for their great confession, and for the trial of the furnace, in a long process of daily life; their training was not in the garment of an anchorite, but in the coat, the hosen, and the hat. All God's true people are being educated, and strengthened, and prepared in daily life. David was trained to fight Goliath by the previous conflict with the lion and the bear; and Moses was prepared to lead a host through the wilderness for God, by long solitude with Him in that wilderness itself; and Shadrach, Meshach, and Abednego were trained, by feeding the body upon pulse, to yield those bodies willingly to the fires. Each had a different way in which to glorify God; and each in God's great school was fitted in a different way for his peculiar work. Let us recognise the variety of ways in which God's people are called upon to give testimony for Him; let us also recognise the great variety of ways in which they are prepared for doing so.

Oh! may it not slip from our minds that in common places, and common relationships, and common garments, we are to confess our Lord. Let us give up that ideality in religion, which would dissever it from the commonest of the common occupations of daily life. Let us not be afraid of vulgarizing our faith, because we have to stand up for it, and act it out in our coats, our hosen, and our hats. Some people worship God on Sunday, and profess Him on Sunday, in their Sunday clothes; with their Sunday clothes they put on their religion on Sunday morning, and with their Sunday clothes they put it off at night; but may every reader of this book witness in his week day clothes, in his coat, his hosen, and his hat; for these are what are worn six days out of seven; and these six days form the largest portion of the time for which we shall have to give an account to God. In thread-bare hose and fustian coats some of the noblest testimonies have been given for God; let us go and testify in the garments of daily life, as we are called to witness by our God. Each of us has marked out for him the way in which he is to testify for the Lord; your way, dear reader, may not be mine, and mine may not be yours; to one the sphere of testimony may be like David's battle field; to another like the furnace heated one seven times more than was its wont; to another like the wilderness of Moses; but there lives not one who reads these lines, that is not called to witness in the ordinary garments of common life, even as David did, who, putting off the armour of Saul, met Goliath in the shepherd's coat; and these three men, who, seized upon in the midst of their daily business, dared the vengeance of the king, and were cast into the midst of the burning fiery furnace, bound in their coats, their hosen, and their hats.

And here let me observe, that there is as much diversity in the way in which men are trained, as in the fields in which that training is to come into practical exercise. God prepares and trains His people in common life. I must not say that such an one is not being trained, because his discipline is not the same as mine; nor must he say that I am not being trained, because my discipline is not the same as his. There are many different forms and books in the school of God; there is the training of the lion and the bear; the training of the wilderness; and the training of water and pulse. But however diverse the methods of God's training may be; let us bear in mind that spiritual character must be acquired; and that unless we have a character out of which to act, we shall probably come wofully short when our trial time comes on. God's people are often taken up very quick, just as they are; they must give their testimony in coats, and hosen, and hats; the very suddenness of their trial forms no inconsiderable element in it.

Might we not profitably ask ourselves, how do we stand in this matter this very day? Should we be called upon suddenly, are we prepared? Can we trace any discipline of God upon our souls, which would produce fruit in our trial hour? The question is an important one; for, let us remember that undisciplined souls are not likely to confess Christ on earth, or to be confessed by Christ in heaven. It may be that some are expecting time for preparation, and thinking that they will do very well if they have time given them for this;

but as no time was given to Shadrach, Meshach, and
Abednego, so perhaps none may be given to us; let us
remember that these men were bound in their coats,
their hosen, and their hats.

It is just possible that some reader may think that
sublime truth cannot be witnessed to in ordinary life;
that there must be a stage, with gorgeous scenery and
wide expanse for its development; and that the actors
upon this scene must be suitably attired.

It is a great snare of the devil which, by such a
thought, is spread before our feet; these men, whose
case we are now considering, had in ordinary life to
witness the sublimest truth.   Taken before Nebuchadnezzar just as they were; they had to confront the idol,
and the one by whose order it had been made; and declare, that there was but the one true, and living, and
everlasting God. The idol was made, no doubt, of gold—
"gold"—which is many a man's god, even though it be
in the rough—uncast into any idol form; it glittered in
the eastern sun with dazzling light, and the music
played to its honour, was in itself enough to drug the
soul; but the living God had His shrine in these men's
hearts, and they were ready to confess *their* God, even
amid heathenish music, and in the very presence of the
heathen god.

Let us be assured, dear reader, that we, even as these
men were, are often called upon to witness to the
sublimest truths in the common habiliments of daily
life.   We make a great mistake if we connect the
sublime and the uncommon together; as though anything to be noble and grand must of necessity be out of
the way.   The truly sublime is to be found in even the

commonest walks of life, and upon its flattest plains; there, no doubt, there is an abundance of what is base, but there also, there may be a sublime protest against what is base; it was in the flat plain of Dura that Nebuchadnezzar's image was set up; it was there also that Shadrach, Meshach, and Abednego refused to worship it, and nobly stood up for God.

Let me remind any of my readers, who are inclined to think it dull work, that they have only common truth to illustrate by their life, that it was only a common truth for which Shadrach, Meshach, and Abednego stood up—but for which also they were ready to die. If any think that if they were arrayed in the panoply of a warrior they would fight for God; or if they were vested in the garb of a minister they could testify for God; let them remember that it was in their coats, their hosen, and their hats that Shadrach, Meshach, and Abednego glorified their Lord.

Let us remember, that even the commonest truth of religion is sublime; and that the acting of it out is sublime also. God does not look for the chief confession of His name from beneath the cathedral's fretted roof, but from the commonest paths and homes of life; not from surpliced ministers or chanting choirs, but from men in their coats, their hosen, and their hats. If the consciousness of the sublime will uphold us, let us remember that the commonest truths and acts of real religion are sublime in the eyes of God. Oh! that we could see things in the light in which God sees them; then we should perceive altars of service thick scattered over the earth—altars, to be served by believers, who the apostle tells us are God's priests: the fittest vest-

ments for whose ministering would be the common
vesture of their daily clothes.   Sublimer deeds of heroism have been done in coat, and hosen, and hat, than in
warrior's mail; and the histories of heaven are fuller of
what has been done in the common walks of life, than of
what has been done in the battle field.   Angels arrayed
in brightness ineffable perform their ministry in the
world invisible; but we, as ordinary men, must perform
our ministry amid that which is seen.   Our service by and
bye will be in the shining garment, but now it must be
in the hosen and the coat.   The unideality and unsenti-
mentality of the vesture may drive away from the service
half-hearted men; but it was with three men who were
thrown into the furnace thus arrayed, that there walked
a fourth; and His form was like the Son of God.

And let us just bear this in mind before we turn
from the consideration of these three confessors; thus
bound in their common clothes these men were
cast into the midst of the burning fiery furnace.   Do
we not catch the teaching in a moment; do we not
perceive that as it is as ordinary men we must witness
for God, so as *ordinary* men we must expect to take the
consequences of our testimony, and suffer for God?
There is no special garment for suffering in, any more
than there is for confessing in.   In our coat, our hosen,
and our hat, we are within reach of the world's bonds,
and can be cast into its furnace; it is in our daily
relationships, perhaps in our daily business, that it will
try to do us hurt.   If any of our readers think it hard,
that they should have to suffer for their religion, even in
the commonest little things of life, let them remember
how Shadrach, Meshach, and Abednego suffered; let them

look at how they were arrayed as they confessed before the king; aye, and at how they were arrayed as they walked triumphantly within the fires. No doubt the scene is one in which even angels might have gloried to take a part; but one descriptive touch shows us that these heroes were not angels, but, even as we are—men; "then these men were bound in their coats, their hosen, and their hats, and their other garments; and were cast into the midst of the burning fiery furnace."

We shall be pardoned, we trust, by our readers, for dwelling at such length on this particular case, for the instruction which it affords is so entirely to the point.

Thus the confessors of Christ should be found in *society;* they ought to be found in *trade* also.

There is no doubt but that to confess Christ in trade, becomes daily a harder and harder task. Competition is exercising such a tremendous pressure, and as people say, " cutting things so fine," that in some instances it is cutting altogether too fine the distinction between right and wrong. It is better to make a little on good principles, than much on bad ones; plain fare and a good conscience will do us more good than a dainty morsel with a bad one.

And in speaking of this subject, we must not forget the position into which men are brought in their connection with others, as members of corporations, boards, committees, and so forth. There is an old saying that "Corporations have no conscience;" and how often do we see this verified in practice. Men *pro*fessing Christ, but not *con*fessing Him, will do things as members of boards, which they would utterly shrink from in their individual capacity; they contrive to lose themselves in the crowd; to dilute their responsibility with that of others; "it wasn't *they* who did it—it was the board," "these things are decided by the majority," and so forth. No doubt this latter statement is true; but was this professing Christian well out in the minority? if there were no one else to make a minority, did he make it? even if there were no one to second his resolution, did he propose it? amid *pro*fessors, was he a *con*fessor, known and read of all men? If a man ask what will be the practical good of all this? the answer is, you deliver your own soul; when in the awful day of great account (that day when in strictest measure each man's share of responsibility will be meted out) this matter is inquired into, you will be found to have herein delivered your soul. If this be not a practical good, we do not know what is; but moreover, you may do more good than you think; you may raise thoughts in the hearts and consciences of others, the good result of which it is impossible to foresee. One thing, however, is certain; he who acts thus, confesses Christ before men; in confessing His principles, we confess Himself.

The like may be said of *politics*. How many are there who are afraid to confess Christ on the hustings, or in "the House;" they are willing to make themselves representatives of other people's opinions instead of their own; they have many masters, and the fear of losing the favour of these many masters, makes them forgetful of the favour of that greater Master than them all, even Jesus Christ.

And now let us leave all these wider spheres of confession, and come to the inner and narrower circle

of our own families and homes. It is by no means
always easy to confess Christ in one's own home. Sometimes children of God have to contend with ungodly
relatives always living with them; sometimes the mis-
tress of a house is visited by worldly relatives or friends,
who do not like religious ways; and perhaps there is
the fear of offending some person; perhaps the dread of
being pooh-poohed, sneered, or laughed at; and there
is the temptation to change some of the religious ways
of the house to suit Mr. or Mrs.——, Sir——and Lady
——, or Lord and Lady so and so. Now if all these important folk are gentlefolk, as we must presume them to
be, let us remind our Christian householders that those
who accept their hospitality will conform to the rules of
their house. The writer well remembers a consultation
which was held at an evening social meeting, as to
whether the usual custom of having evening prayer could
be adhered to because Sir——, Bart., was present. This
gentleman, (long since dead) was well known to make
very light of religion; what would he say if prayer were
proposed? At length with some hems and haughs, the
baronet—mighty in his irreligion—was approached, and
asked if he had any objection to evening prayer. 'Oh dear,
no, not he—he had no objection; he should be most happy,'
and he repeated the Lord's prayer as loudly as anyone,
ending up with a sonorous 'Amen.' It is much to be
feared that there was but little sincerity in the prayer;
but one lesson was taught by the baronet, and learned,
it is to be hoped, by some present, viz.: that some
obstacles to confessing one's Lord are imaginary; and
that if men go forward boldly, they will find them melt
away at their approach.

To this let me add a word from "Fuller's Good Thoughts."

"A person of great quality was pleased to lodge a night in my house. I durst not invite him to my family prayer, and, therefore, for that time omitted it; thereby making a breach in a good custom, and giving Satan advantage to assault it: yea the loosening of such a link might have endangered the scattering of the chain.

"Bold bashfulness, which durst offend God, whilst it did fear man! Especially considering that, though my guest was never so high, yet, by the laws of hospitality I was above him, whilst he was under my roof. Hereafter, whosoever cometh within the *doors*, shall be requested to come within the *discipline* of my house; if accepting my homely diet, he will not refuse my homely devotion; and sitting at my table will be entreated to kneel down by it."

Let such as are afraid of great men, be afraid of a still greater God. Thus was Hans Joachim Von Ziethen, one of Frederick the Great's best generals, commonly known as Father Ziethen, or the Huzzar King.

"Ziethen was never ashamed of his faith. On every occasion he openly professed it before high and low. Once he declined an invitation to come to the royal table, because on that day he wished to receive the sacrament. The next time he was at the palace, the king, whose infidel tendencies were well-known, made use of some profane expressions about the Holy Communion, and the other guests laughed.

"Ziethen shook his grey head solemnly, stood up, saluted the king, and said with a firm voice, 'Your Majesty knows well, that in war I have never feared any danger, and everywhere have boldly risked my life for you and my country. I am still animated by the same spirit, and to-day if it were necessary, and your Majesty commanded it, would lay my grey head at your feet. But there is one above us who is greater than you and I, greater than all men. He is the Saviour and Redeemer who has died also for your Majesty, and has dearly bought us all with His blood. This Holy One can I never allow to be mocked or insulted, for on Him repose my faith, my comfort, and my hope, in life and in death. In the power of this faith your brave army has courageously fought and conquered; if your Majesty undermines this faith, you undermine at the same time the welfare of the State. This is undoubtedly true. I salute your Majesty.' This open firm confession of the old general immediately silenced the scoffers, and made a powerful impression on the king. He felt he had been in the wrong, and was not ashamed to acknowledge it; he gave Ziethen his hand, placing his left on the old man's shoulder, and said with emotion, 'Oh, happy Ziethen, how I wish that I could also believe it. I have the greatest respect for your religion, hold it fast. This shall never happen again.' The king rose from the table, dismissed his other guests, but said to Ziethen, 'Come with me into my cabinet.' What passed there no one has ever learnt."

Is Christ confessed when those who habitually attend an evening service on the Lord's day, give it up, because they have some careless or ungodly person dining with them? Is He confessed when masters and mistresses, for their own selfish purposes, give their servants Sunday work which keeps them from the house

of God, even though they themselves are particular not
to be absent? Is He confessed when most of the year's
income is spent on self, and "God's tenth" is left un-
given? On looking over domestic account books, I find
columns for almost every imaginable class of things,
some curious minutiæ even find place there; pepper and
salt, and little condiments, can all be set down in their
proper place, but I have never seen one yet which had a
column ruled for 'charity;' so that even if one had got
so far as to tithe the mint, anise, and cummin, one
would not know where to put it down. Publishers are
always glad of something new; and it is well known that
it is often harder to find a good name for a book, than to
write the book itself; it will be a decided novelty to
produce an account book with a column for "charity;"
and by all means let it be called "The Christian House-
keeper's Account Book." Yes! Christian reader ask
yourself the question, Is Christ confessed in my expenditure? He may be *pro*fessed in your guinea for pew
rent, but is He *con*fessed in the proportion which, what
you give to Him, bears either to your expenditure or
your income? But you say, this is a very private confession; this has nothing to say to confessing Jesus
before men. Ah! it has more than at first sight appears;
the introduction of this one word 'charity,' and its corresponding column into the account book, would make
quite a revolution in all the columns of that book; and
would change the aspect in which many an one now
appears before the world. For, if Christ had His own,
there would not perhaps be so much left for a brave display of dress; or for entertainments, and such like; it
may be that one horse must be kept instead of two; or

perhaps not a horse at all; it may be that a smaller house and establishment generally must be made to do ; and are there not many who could not bear thus, as they think, to come down in the eyes of the world? and so their lack of confession of Christ at home, robs them of the power of confessing Christ abroad.

But we need not dwell longer here; all spheres afford their opportunity for confession; the question hereafter will not be as to the size of our various spheres, but as to the way in which we filled them.

Let us now turn to some of THE CHARACTERISTICS OF THIS CONFESSION.

Are we called upon always to confess in precisely the same way? Certainly not. Just as our Lord acted differently at different times, so must we. We must deal with matters as they arise; we need not go out of our way to make opportunities of confession, they will spring up of their own accord ; to fill worthily the sphere presented to us will always give us as much as we can do. We may expect to find blessing and help in the spheres of God's appointing; we cannot be so sure of this in the spheres which we make for ourselves. And here let us carefully bear in mind, that the kind of confession which we make, must not of necessity be always the same. There are times when we must speak out openly. There are times when we must testify by silence—a silence unmistakable; a silence ominous; a silence with a peculiar voice of its own. Cecil's advice to Mrs. Hawkes was this, " Be careful in your commerce with the world, to act up to the character you profess. Do not put on a Pharisaical manner of 'Stand by, I am holier than thou;' yet let it appear, that while you are under the necessity of hearing their vain conversation, you have no taste for it, no delight or interest in it; a humble kind of silence often utters much."

There is a very interesting instance of this in the "Life of Madame Guyon."

"There was a certain learned lady, who was very fond of talking, and who had read the writings of the Christian Fathers. Madame Guyon was in company with her and another lady; and these two latter had much conversation with each other in relation to God. 'The learned lady,' says Madame Guyon, 'as might be expected, talked very learnedly of Him. I must confess, that this sort of merely intellectual and speculative conversation, in relation to the Supreme Being, was not much to my taste. I scarcely said anything! my mind being drawn inwardly to silent and inward communion with the great and good Being, about whom my friends were speculating. They, at length, left me. The next day, the lady with whom I had previously had some conversation came to see me. The Lord had touched her heart; she came as a penitent, as a seeker after religion; she could hold out in her opposition no longer. But I at once attributed this remarkable and sudden change, as I did not converse with her the day previous, to the conversation of our learned and speculative acquaintance. But she assured me it was otherwise. She said it was not the other's conversation which had affected her, but my *silence;* adding the remark that my silence had something in it which penetrated to the bottom of her soul; and that she could not relish the other's discourse. After that time we spoke to each other with open hearts on the great subject.' "

But a greater than any merely human being meets us

here; our blessed Lord Himself knew the power of silence in testimony, and He used it too. After He had uttered the searching sentence, "He that is without sin among you, let him first cast a stone at her, He stooped down again, and wrote upon the ground:" John viii, 8. And the accusers of the woman could not stand that silence; no sound broke in upon the workings of their consciences; "they went out one by one, beginning at the eldest, even unto the last, and Jesus was left alone, and the woman standing in the midst:" verse 9. What that silence did for the woman also, eternity alone will tell; it may be that then the first seeds of eternal life dropped into her sin-stained soul.

Again we meet with this power of silence before Pilate. "And when He was accused of the chief priests and elders, He answered nothing. Then said Pilate unto Him; hearest Thou not how many things they witness against Thee? And He answered him to never a word, insomuch that the governor marvelled greatly:" Matt. xxvii, 12—14.

Our common proverb says, "Silence gives consent;" and so no doubt it does in many cases; but the silence of the confessor is an unmistakable one; and if it be a right kind of silence, every one present can read it in his face. Yes! the confession of the countenance is no mean confession of the Lord, and it is often one which has no mean effect; many a time it has thrown a damper upon ungodly mirth; many a time has it continued during a dinner party, or for an evening, a protest against what was going on; many a time has it raised thoughts in the hearts of those who felt it—who heard it—for after all, silence has a voice which speaks to the inner

depths of the soul, and leaves an unmistakable impress
there.

Reader, beware of a *sheltering* silence; be prepared
to give a *confessing* silence, when that is the kind of
testimony required from you. Be assured that you will
not lose anything, but on the other hand gain much by
it; you must not give the world the opportunity of
mistaking you. "I have already," says Mrs. Hawkes,
"experienced great advantage from endeavouring to follow my wise counsellor (Mr. Cecil) in avoiding, not only
a too great degree of pliableness of temper, but also a
mean, sneaking, irresolute, shame-faced behaviour among
worldly people. I find by experience that they soon
discover when the mind is made up; and on making
this discovery, cease to persuade you to join with them
in their pursuits, while they secretly respect the con-
sistency of your character, I perceive this *strongly* in
the remarks made by certain persons."

But should we be called upon to speak out, as indeed
in most cases we are, let us be neither ashamed nor
afraid so to do.* Let us remember the conduct of Peter

* The following instance of speaking out, is from a sketch of the
life of Scott, the commentator:—"I had frequent invitations to dinner parties but I seldom returned home without dissatisfaction, and
even remorse of conscience. One Queen's birthday I met at the house
of an opulent tradesman a large party, among whom were several
other ministers. The dinner was exceedingly splendid and luxurious,
including every delicacy in season. In the evening a question was
proposed on the principal dangers to which evangelical religion was
exposed; and being called on to speak, I ventured to say that conformity to the world was the grand danger of all. One thing led to
another, and the luxurious dinner did not pass unnoticed. Perhaps I
was too pointed, and strong expressions of disapprobation were used at

and John before the high priest and his kindred in Jerusalem, who, when they were called and commanded not to speak at all nor teach in the name of Jesus, gave this answer, "Whether it be right in the sight of God to hearken unto you more than unto God, judge ye; for we cannot but speak the things which we have seen and heard:" Acts iv, 19, 20.

There are times when it is quite impossible for us to keep silence, and yet retain our distinctive character of confessors of our Lord. On such occasions let us make our confession with meekness but with boldness; with gentleness but with decision; with no accompaniment calculated to irritate the man, though with precision enough to rebuke his sin. And we shall be more successful than we at first, perhaps, suppose; and not only so, but we shall escape with, perhaps, less personal insult than we had reason to expect.

It is related by Dr. Scudder, that, on his return from his mission in India, after a long absence, he was standing on the deck of a steamer with his son, a youth, when he heard a gentleman using loud and profane language. "See, friend," said the doctor, accosting the swearer, "this boy, my son, was born and brought up in a heathen country, and a land of pagan idolatry; but in all his life he never heard a man blaspheme his Maker until now." The man coloured, blurted out an apology, and looked not a little ashamed of himself.

the time; but I went home rejoicing in the testimony of my conscience. The gentleman never invited me again but once, and then our dinner was a piece of boiled beef. He was, I believe, a truly pious man, but misled by bad examples. He continued to act towards me in a friendly manner, and left me a small legacy at his death."

And now let us change the scene, and we have a poor man, both faithful and prosperous in his confession.

A merchant and shipowner stood at the entrance of his store, conversing with a gentleman on business. A good old sailor belonging to one of his vessels approached the store with the intention of entering it; but observing that the door was occupied, modestly stepped aside, not willing to interrupt the conversation. As he stood waiting patiently an opportunity to pass, he overheard some allusions made to Christ; and turning to look, he perceived that it was his employer who was speaking. Instantly he changed his position, and stood in front of the gentleman with his head uncovered, and his hat under his arm, and addressed his employer in the following language: "Sir, will you forgive me if I speak a word to you?" The gentleman, recognising in the sailor one of the crew of the vessel recently arrived; and supposing he might have something to communicate affecting his interest, kindly encouraged him to speak. Without further hesitation the sailor proceeded,—" You won't be offended, then, sir, with a poor ignorant sailor if he tells you his feelings?" The gentleman again assured him that he had nothing to fear. "Well, then, sir," said the honest-hearted sailor with emotion, "will you be so kind as not to take the name of my blessed Jesus in vain? He is a good Saviour; He took my feet from the horrible pit, and the miry clay, and established my goings. Oh, sir, don't, if you please, take the name of my Jesus in vain! He never did anyone harm, and is always doing poor sinners good." The rebuke was not lost upon him for whom it was intended; a tear suffused his eye, and he replied to his urgent request,

"My good fellow, God helping me, I will never again take the name of our Saviour in vain." "Thank you, sir," said the faithful witness for Christ, and putting on his hat, he hastened off to his work.

Sometimes weak women have to be confessors; and they are matched against those who in mere argument are able to overcome them; but God can give them suitable words, if only they be faithful to Him. He who can give His people words before magistrates and rulers, can give them words also before their fellow men in society; or in whatever position they are called upon to confess.

A lady once thus completely shut up a pretended freethinker, who had been repeating a number of absurdities to prove that men had no souls. The company seem contented with staring at him, instead of replying. He addressed this lady, and asked her with an air of triumph, what she thought of his philosophy. "It appears to me, sir," she replied, "that you have been employing a good deal of talent to prove yourself a beast."

And for the encouragement of female confessors, we may add another instance of successful interference for Christ.

A few years ago, a young naval officer who was passing in the cars from Newark to York, constantly introduced the most profane oaths into his conversation. His shocking profanity greatly annoyed a young lady who sat near him. At last, turning to him, she said, "Sir, can you converse in Hebrew?" "Yes," was his reply, in a slightly sneering tone. "Then," said she, "if you wish to swear any more, you would greatly oblige me, and probably the rest of the passengers, if you would do it in Hebrew." The young officer's colour came and went. He looked at the young lady, then at his boots, then at the ceiling of the cars; but he did not swear any more, either in Hebrew or English.

God often chooses the foolish things of the world to confound the wise; and He chooses the weak things of the world to confound the things which are mighty; and things which are not to bring to nought things which are, (1 Cor. i, 27.)

But we must be prepared for suffering in some form, if we take up a position in the ranks of the noble army of confessors. Ours may not be the martyrdom of the body; but we may have to undergo the martyrdom of the mind. There are writhing feelings as well as writhing limbs,—quivering nerves of the mind as well as of the body,—emptying and desolations of the heart within, as well as of the home without. St. Paul suffered the loss of all things, yet did he count them but dung so that he might win Christ. We marshal in the rank of the noble army of martyrs, only those who have actually shed their life-blood for the Lord; we associate their name with deeds of violence, with the halter, the faggot, and the sword; but it may be, that God will number in that glorious host many whom we think of as only confessors, but who, if the truth were known, lost their lives for Christ. Yes! unkind words and looks, long protracted, cut into their soul; petty persecutions at length wore them out; their blood was not spilled upon the earth, but it curdled in their veins, until at last its crimson tide ceased to flow; the heart stood still; the victim was worn out,

and died.   Just as they who have been worn out in the
privations of a campaign die as truly a soldier's death,
as they who fall by the bullet or the sword; so these
who are worn out by so long continued endurance of
despitefulness for Christ, are as truly martyrs, as if they
bled upon the block, or burned at the stake; they
burned with a slow fire at a stake which no man saw;
they bled beneath an axe with which no headsman
struck; they surely have come out of great tribulation;
and their proper place shall be assigned them by the
One they so nobly served.

Let me give two instances of stout confession of the
Lord Jesus Christ, one from private life, where the
confession involved the secret martyrdom; and the other
from more public life, for its scene was the great Indian
mutiny, and so far as the religious history of that great
catastrophe is concerned, there are few names more
memorable than those of which we are about to speak.
Let us first retire into the privacy of home.

"Now, girls, I *have* got news for you!"

The speaker was a showy girl, dressed in the height of
fashion. She was just entering the room where sat several young
ladies, her cousins, pursuing various household employments.

"What is it, Ada?" cried one and another.

"You'll never believe it; Lizzy Ashbrook has professed
religion!" was the half serious, half laughing reply.

"Lizzy Ashbrook!"   The girls repeated the name, more
or less in surprise.

"Lizzy Ashbrook," said the elder cousin, Julia, seriously;
"why! she was for ever making sport of the subject."

"And such a fashionable girl; why, she would hardly
look at a person who was ill dressed;" remarked another.

"Her father, an infidel of the rankest sort, too, what will he say?"

"I heard that he had turned her out of the house," said Ada.

There was a long silence.

"Well,"—it was abruptly broken by the youngest of the family,—"we shall see now if there is the reality in religion that Christians talk about. I don't believe there is a single person in any branch of her family who is religious. She will have unusual trials to undergo; I wouldn't be in her place."

"Trials! phsaw! there's no such thing as persecution in these days; it would be a rare thing to see a martyr!" This was lighly spoken by Ada, who had been Lizzy's nearest friend, and who felt an unusual bitterness springing up in her heart towards the young girl, who she knew could no longer enjoy her companionship as of yore.

The cousins made an early call on Lizzy, who received them with her accustomed grace, and a sweeter smile than usual. Yet she was pale, and though there was a purer, a holier expression on her beautiful face, yet she appeared like one wearied a little from some external struggle, in which she was the sufferer. Although she did not speak directly of the new vows she had taken upon her, the new peace she had found, her visitors could see clearly and distinctly the wondrous change in dress, in manner, and even in countenance.

Lizzy was engaged in marriage to a thorough-bred man of the world. George Philips loved his wine, his parties, the race course, the theatre, the convivial and free and easy club. The Sabbath was his day of pleasure, and many a time had Lizzy graced his elegant equipage, radiant in beauty, on the holy day, as they swept off to the haunts of the gay—to some hotel—or some meeting of kindred spirits. He bore a dashing exterior, was intellectual—a sparkling wit, courted, caressed, admired everywhere.

His brow darkened as he heard the news. What! the girl of his choice, the woman he would place at the head of his brilliant household become a canting Christian! Nonsense! he didn't believe it; he would see for himself. He didn't furnish his parlours for prayer-meetings. He wanted no long-faced ministers to visit his wife, not he. It was a ridiculous hoax. It must have originated in the club-room. What! the daughter of Harlan Ashbrook, the freest of free-thinkers? "Ha! ha! a capital joke—a very clever joke—nothing more."

He called upon her not long after the visit before mentioned. His cold eye scanned her from head to foot; but how sweetly, how gently, she met him! Surely the voice that was melting music before, was heavenly in its tones now. All the winning grace was there; all the high-bred ease; the merry smile dimpled her lips; but there was a something that thrilled him from head to foot with apprehension, because it was unlike her usual self. What could it be?

At length, lightly laughing, he referred to the report he had heard. For one moment the frame trembled, the lips refused to speak; but this passed; and something like a flush crossed her beautiful face, it lighted her eyes anew, it touched the cheek with a richer crimson, as she said,

"George, please don't treat it as a jest, for truly, thank God! I have become a Christian! O George!"—her clasped hands were laid upon one of his—"I have only just began to live! If you knew——"

The proud man sprang to his feet, almost throwing her hands from him in his impatient movement; and not daring to trust his voice, for an oath was uppermost, he walked back and forth for a moment. Then he came and stood before her. His forehead was purpled with the veins that passion swelled, his face was white, and his voice unsteady, as he exclaimed :—

"Do you mean to say that you will really cast your lot among these people, that for them you will give up all—*all?*"

"I *will* give up all for Christ!" The words were very soft and low, and not spoken without reflection.

For one moment he locked his lips together, till they looked like steel in their rigidity: then he said, in a full passionate voice :—

"Lizzy—Miss Ashbrook—if these are your sentiments, these your intentions, we *must* go different ways."

This was very cruel—this was a terrible test; for that young girl had, as it were, placed her soul in his keeping. Before a higher, a purer love was born in her heart, she had made up her human love—an absolute idolatry; and the thought of losing him, even now, caused her cheek to grow ashen and her eyes dim.

As he saw this, his manner changed to entreaty. He placed before her the position he would give her; lured her by every argument that might appeal to the womanly heart. And he knew how to win by entreaty, by the subtlest casuistry. His was a masterly eloquence. He could adapt his voice, his language, his very looks, with the most adroit cunning, to the subject and object of his discussion. More than once the gentle spirit of the young Christian felt that she must give way—that only help direct from the fountain of life could sustain her with firmness to resist him to the end of the interview.

At last it was a final—"All this will I give you, if you will fall down and worship me !" It came to this—"Christ or me !" There could be no compromise, it was—"Christ or me." And standing there, clothed with the mantle of a new and heavenly faith, with its light shining in her heart, and playing over her pale features, she said, with a firmness worthy the martyrs of old,—"Christ!"

Though his soul was filled with rage so that he could have gnashed his teeth, the slight figure standing there in its pure white robes against the background of crimson hangings, —the eye that cast an earnest, upward glance,—the brow that seemed to have grown white with spirit-light,—the attitude, so self-possessed yet so modest, so quiet yet so eloquent, filled him with a strange admiring awe. But the hostility towards religion was so strong in his heart, that it bore down all his tenderness, almost crushed his love, and he parted from her for the last time coldly, and like a stranger.

The engagement was broken off; but who can tell the struggles it cost?

This was but the first trial: there came another, while yet the blow lay heavy on her heart.

Her father had never been very loving towards her. He was proud of her; she was the brightest gem of his splendid home. She was beautiful, and gratified his vanity; she was intellectual, and he heard praise lavished upon her mind, her person, with a miser's greedy ear, for she was his—a part of himself; she belonged to him.

He called her into his study, and required a minute account of the whole matter. He had heard rumours, he said; had seen a surprising and not agreeable change in her; she had grown mopish, quiet. What was the cause? It was a great trial, with that stern, unbelieving face, full of hard lines, opposite, to stand and testify for Christ! But He who has promised, was with her, and she told the story calmly, resolutely.

"And do you intend to join the church?"

"Yes, sir." A gleam of hope entered her heart; she did not expect his approval, but she could not think he might refuse to sanction this important step.

"You know your Aunt Eunice has long wanted you to become an inmate of her home."

"Yes, sir," the gentle voice faltered.

"Well, you can go now. Unless you give up this absurd idea, and trample it under your feet, I do not wish you to remain with me. Be as you were before, and you shall want for no luxury, no affection; follow this miserable notion, and henceforth I am only your father in name."

She did forsake all for Him; but her step became slow, her form wasted, her eye hollow, her cheek sunken. The struggle had been too much for a frame unable to cope with any overwhelming sorrow. Her pastor, as he marked the brilliant hectic and the trembling frame, thought of the graveyard and the mould,—she thought only of the glorious immortality *beyond*. Swiftly she went down into the valley, but it was not dark to her. Too late the man who had so sorely tempted her, knelt by the side of her bed and implored her forgiveness. Too late? No, not too late for his own salvation, for in that hour his eyes were opened to the sinfulness of his life, and by her dying pillow he promised solemnly to give his heart to God. Her father, too, proud infidel though he was, looked on his wasted child, triumphing over death, with wonder and with awe. Such a dying scene it is the privilege of but few to witness; she had given up *all*, absolutely *all* for Christ, and in the last hour she, like Stephen, saw heaven open. Her face was angelic, her language rapture, her chamber the gate of heaven. And like one who, but the other day, untied the sandals of life and moved calmly and trustingly down the one step between earth and heaven, so she said, with a smile inexpressibly sweet,—"Sing!"

And they sang,—

> Rock of ages, cleft from me,
> Let me hide myself in Thee,
> &c., &c.

At its close they heard one word—the last. It was—
CHRIST."

And now let us change the scene and behold a confessor, yes, many confessors, witnessing for Christ and
confessing Him at the peril of immediate death.

"The Rev. Gopenath Nundy, a native missionary of
the American Presbyterian Board, was stationed at
Futtehpur, where he had been a faithful labourer for
several years. When the insurrection broke out, he
and his family escaped without much difficulty to
Allahabad. Finding the fort much crowded with European families, and thinking that, as a native, he could
make his way in comparative safety; he set out, with
his wife and two children, for Mirzapur. They had not
gone far before they fell into the hands of robbers, who
stripped off their clothing, and otherwise cruelly treated
them With difficulty they returned to Allahabad. Of
their subsequent sufferings he has drawn up the following narrative, which we have taken from the pages of
the 'Foreign Missionary,' for November, 1857.

"We inquired from our host about the fort, and the
fate of the Europeans who were in it. The poor man,
as far as his knowledge extended, said the fort was
taken by the mutineers, and its inmates murdered.
This sad news, at this critical time, grieved us greatly,
and brought us to utter despair. Our host, seeing us in
such a state, said that a moulwí had come from Kurria
with some men, to shelter and help the distressed and
afflicted, without any distinction of creed or colour.
This was rather cheering news, and we made up our
minds to go to him. About sunset we directed our

course towards that side, and when we came near the
police station-house, we found out that he was hostile to
the English; and all the Christians, whether European
or native, brought before him were massacred. This
greatly alarmed us, but to turn our course in any other
direction then was utterly impossible, as we were surrounded by thousands of infuriated Mussulmans; so we
made up our minds to go to the moulwí, and throw
ourselves on his mercy, to do with us as it pleased him,
either to kill or spare our lives. Accordingly we went
to him; but, before reaching his place our lives were
often in jeopardy by those who surrounded us, for they
wanted to kill us; but we besought them not to do so
until we had an interview with their head, the moulwí.
They accordingly brought us to him. We found him
seated on a chair, attended by a number of men with
drawn swords, and he put the following questions to us,
viz:—'Who are you?' 'A Christian.' 'What place do
you come from?' 'Futtehpur.' What was your occu-
pation?' 'Preaching and teaching the Christian religion.' 'Are you a Padré?' 'Yes, sir.' 'Was it not
you who used to go about reading, and distributing
tracts in the streets and villages?' 'Yes, sir, it was I
and my catechists?' 'How many Christians have you
made?' 'I did not make any Christians, for no human
being can change the heart of another; but God
through my instrumentality, brought to the belief of
His true religion about a couple of dozen.' To this the
man exclaimed in a great rage, and said, 'Tobah!
tobah! (fy! fy!) such a downright blasphemy! God
never makes a person a Christian, but you Kafirs—
Infidels—pervert the people. He always makes Mo-

hammedans, for the religion which they follow is the only true one. How many Mohammedans have you perverted to your religion?' 'I have not perverted any one; but, by the grace of God, ten were turned from darkness into the glorious light of the gospel.' Hearing this, the man's countenance became as red as hot iron, and he said, 'You are a great haramzuda (a wicked rogue.) You renounced your forefathers' faith and became a child of Shoytan (Satan,) and now use every effort to bring others in the same road to destruction. You deserve a cruel death: your nose, ears, and hands should be cut off at different times, so as to make your sufferings continue for some time, and your children be kept in slavery.' To this, Mrs. Nundy said to the moulwí, 'You will confer a very great favour by ordering to kill us all at once, and not torture us.' After having kept silent for a while, he exclaimed, 'Soovan Allah! (Praise be to God!) You appear to be a repectable man: I pity you and your family. I, as a friend, advise you to be Mohammedans: by doing so you will not only save your lives, but will be raised to a high rank.' My answer to this was, that we perferred death to any inducement he could hold out. Then the man made an appeal to my wife, and asked her what she meant to do. Thank God her answer was as firm as mine. She said she was ready to sacrifice her life in preference to any inducement he held out as to the renouncement of the true religion of Jesus. The moulwí then asked if I had read the Korán. My answer was 'Yes.' He then said I could not have read it with a view to be profited by it, but simply picked passages to argue with Mohammedans. However, he

said he would allow us three days' time to think over
the matter, and then he would send for us, and read a
portion of the Korán: if we believed, and became
Mohammedans, all right and good, but if otherwise, our
noses were to be cut off. We further said there was no
occasion to wait till that time: as long as God con-
tinues His grace we will not renounce our faith; so he
had better at once order our heads to be taken off. He
then pointed to his people to take us to prison. It
was a part of the Sarie, where travellers put up, guarded
by his men, with drawn swords, not very far from
him.

"While on the way to the prison, I raised my heart
in praise and adoration to the Lord Jesus for giving us
grace to stand firm, and to overcome all the temptations
which the moulwí held forth; and while repeating the
11th and 12th verses of the 5th chapter of St. Matthew, I
thanked Him for counting us worthy to suffer for His
name's sake. When we reached the place of our imprisonment, we found two other Christian families, one
native and the other European; the former from Mr.
Hay's printing establishment, and the latter, Mr. Con-
ductor Colman, his wife, and five children. We felt
extremely sorry, seeing them thrown in the same difficulty as ourselves. After conversing and relating each
other's distress, I asked them to join with us in prayer,
to which they all of them readily agreed; and when we
knelt down, one of the guards came and gave a kick on
my back, ordering me to keep quiet, or pray according
to Mohammedan form. Our lips were truly closed, but
our hearts were in communion with Him who required
the emotions of our hearts more than the utterances of

our lips. Next day Ensign Cheek, an officer of the late 6th Native Infantry, was brought in: he made his escape when his regiment rebelled, and his bearer took him on the other side of the river Ganges. There he was attacked by a Jemadar, and some other people, who wounded him most cruelly. He made his escape from their wicked hands, and hid himself for three days. At nights he used to hide himself in a tree, and, during the day, he kept himself under water, with his face above the water. At last when he was exhausted, and could not keep himself hidden any longer, he was brought, with severe and putrified sores, to the moulwí as a prisoner, who sent him where we were.

"His sufferings were excessively great and severe: he was unable to sit up or lie down on the bare ground, which we all had to do; but I, a prisoner, and hated the most, yet felt it my duty to do what I could to relieve the agonies of poor Cheek. I went up to the Daroga (jailer,) and begged him hard to allow him a *charpoy* (coarse bedstead.) The hard-hearted jailer condescended to grant my petition with the greatest reluctance, and though he gave a charpoy, yet it was a broken one, for their object was to see how much we could suffer. He was in a state of fainting, and evidently sinking, as he had had no food for three days and nights. We had a little cherttoo and gúr, which we brought with us before coming to the prison, and which I turned with a little water into a kind of gruel, and gave it to him. Taking this, and drinking a full mud-pot of water, he felt greatly refreshed, and opened his eyes. Finding me a fellow prisoner, and a missionary, he opened his heart at once to me, and told the history of his sufferings: he also requested me to write to his mother in England, and aunt; which I intend to do as soon as I can spare time. The wicked Daroga, finding that I was attentive and kind to poor Cheek, ordered my feet to be fastened to the stocks; after which they removed me to a different place, thus causing a separation, not only from Ensign Cheek, but from my poor family. To this I made a great resistance, and a body of the rebels fell upon us with weapons, and forced my feet into the stocks, at the same time holding out the offer of pardon if I became a Mohammedan. They dragged my poor wife by the hair, and she received a severe wound on the forehead. While they were maltreating us so cruelly, poor Cheek cheered our spirits by saying, 'Padré, Padré, be firm, be firm, do not give way.' His meaning was, do not become Mohammedans.

"At this time the danger of our lives was most imminent, and the temptation was strongest, but the Lord delivered us from their wretched designs, and rescued us from the snares of Satan. To aggravate my sufferings, they put me out with the stocks in the hot burning sun. But notwithstanding all the exposure to the sun, and hot winds, and privations, our gracious heavenly Father did not permit the disease in my head to be increased, but it remained as it was before.

" We were in the prison from Wednesday the 10th to Tuesday the 16th. All this time our sufferings were great indeed; for, for our food we received only a handful of parched grain in the middle of the day, and at night a single *chapaty* (a cake made of coarse flour, about three ounces in weight.) Water was supplied only twice daily, and that sparingly. Every five minutes the

Mohammedans used to come and threaten to take our lives if we did not become Mussulmans. Once an ill-educated moulwí came with a portion of the Korán, and read a part from it. When I asked the meaning thereof he could not give it, as he himself was ignorant of it. To this I answered, 'How can you expect to make proselytes of others, when you yourself do not understand what you read?'

"Instead of the moulwí sending for us on the third day, as he arranged at first, he came himself on the sixth day, and drawing near to us, he inquired of the Darago where the Padré prisoner was; and when I was pointed out, he asked me if I were comfortable. My answer was, 'How can I be comfortable when my feet are in the stocks? but I take it patiently, as it is the will of our heavenly Father.' I then begged of him to order a little milk to be given to our baby, which was in a state of starvation. He reluctantly gave the order, which was never executed.

"The moulwí left nothing untried to make us converts to his faith. He made our sufferings of the worst kind, threatening to take our lives every moment; and yet why he spared us I cannot tell. It was, I believe, that he thought it would promote his glory, and that of his religion, by making us converts and preachers of the same, more than by killing us, who are but natives like himself. Whatever it was, this much I know, that the finger of God directed the whole course. He sent these dangers and difficulties no doubt to try our faith, and gave us grace sufficient to make a full confession of it before the world. The saving of our lives was a miracle, for they were no less exposed than that of

Daniel of old. Thanks be to the all-protecting hand of
God!

"On the sixth day of our imprisonment, that is, on
the 15th June, Captain Brazier came out with some
European and Sikh soldiers to meet the enemy: he had
a regular fight not very far from the place where we
were confined, and totally defeated them.

"The next morning, about three A.M., the enemy
retreated, and forsook Allahabad, leaving us prisoners.
When we saw that they were all gone, we broke the
stocks, and came into the fort, where our Missionary
brethren, Messrs. Owen and Munis, rejoiced and welcomed us in their quarters. They all heard that we had
been killed by the mutineers." *

---

* To the above we may add the instance of the stout squire, Peter
Paasch, although we cannot of course approve of his striking the
Turk.

In the year 1717, there was a great war between the Germans
and the Turks. The good and brave Marshal, Prince Eugene, won
many glorious victories over the infidels; and so great was the patriotic
spirit excited all over Germany, that nearly every village sent a con-
tingent to aid the Emperor's army against the unbelieving foe. From
the village of Hermannsburg rode forth the brave knight, Staffhorst,
with his two squires, Peter Paasch and Hans Puffel. In the great
battle near Belgrade, in which the Germans were victorious, Puffel
was killed, as he was rescuing his hardly pressed master from the
hands of the Turks. Staffhorst fell at the subsequent storming of
Belgrade, after he had forced his way into the city. Peter Paasch,
full of grief at the death of his beloved master, pursued the flying
Turks so rashly, that he was surrounded by the fugitives outside the
walls and taken prisoner. They tied him to his horse's tail, a Turk
mounted the horse; and Paasch was obliged to run by the side, naked
and barefoot, for the Turks had robbed him of everything. Late in
the evening they halted in the wood, where they thought they were
safe from the Christians; and now they determined to take their long
desired revenge on the Christian prisoner, for they had remarked how

Who can tell? perhaps the confessors in the home circle, and these of the Indian mutiny, may not find themselves far apart in the position assigned them for eternity.

We hope that our readers will not think that we have been too long in coming to the "I will" of Christ,—

many Turks Paasch had slain in the battle. So first they placed two sticks in the form of a cross, one over the other; they spat on this cross, and endeavoured, by blows and tortures, to force Paasch to do the same. But Paasch, who was now unbound from the horse, and from whom no resistance was expected, struck the Turk who had spitten on the cross, so violently about the ears, that they again bound his hands and feet together. Then they cut him with knives and daggers to force him to spit on the cross; and as all this was of no avail, they nailed both his hands over his head to the trunk of a tree, and tried, by horsewhippings, and the wounds caused thereby, to make him pronounce the name of Mohammed. But as often as they repeated this name, he said, "Jesus Christ." Then the enemies of the Lord determined to kindle a fire at his feet, and thus to make him deny Christ, or to kill him by the tortures of a fiery death. When Paasch saw that his end was so near at hand, he prayed, with earnest and devout voice, the Lord's Prayer, and repeated the Creed; and the Lord gave the brave warrior such peace in his heart, that he even prayed for his murderers, as our Saviour did, and the holy Stephen. And he was now filled with such lofty, celestial joy, that he could not refrain from singing, with strong, deep voice, the grand old Passion chant, "Oh, innocent Lamb of God, slain on the cross for us," &c. When he had sung to the end of the third verse, and ended with the words, "Grant us thy peace, O Jesus, Amen," the clang of trumpets was heard from without the forest. German horsemen rode in, the Turks fled, and the horsemen beheld, with astonishment, Paasch nailed to the tree, and the fire at his feet. They at once unbound him, and he fell fainting in their arms. After they had bound up his many wounds, washed him, and provided him with clothes, he came to himself again, and his first question was, how God had sent them to him just at the right moment? They replied, "We were sent out in pursuit of the Turks, when we heard from the forest, the song, 'Oh, innocent Lamb of God.' That is a Christian, said we, and that blessed "I will" which follows on all this confession, and it may be suffering; which sweetens its darkest trials to the Christian, and enables him, by grace, to go forward through its most rugged passes.

The promise, then, of our blessed Lord is, that whosoever confesses Him before men, him will He confess before the Father and before the angels which are in heaven.

"Verily I say unto you, he shall in no wise lose his reward," is the language of Scripture; not only with regard to those who give a cup of cold water in the name of Christ, but also with regard to everyone who does anything for Jesus, be it great or small. There are great rewards like jewelled crowns; there are little rewards like diamond dust; the great deed of love shall receive its great reward, and the little deed shall receive its measure too; and so it shall be found hereafter that nothing was forgotten.

We have already considered the history of some who confessed their God even at the peril of their lives; and these three men have doubtless in no wise lost their reward. They found in those furnace fires jewels of immeasurable price; and they won in that short sharp trial, glory which they shall wear in peace for ever and for ever. They had respect to the recompense of the reward; and now let us see whether there be not

rode into the wood: the Lamb of God, whom thou trustedst, has saved thee." Then they brought Paasch to Belgrade. The story came to the ears of the good Prince Eugene, who ordered him to be well cared for, visited him himself, and rejoiced in his simple child-like faith, and, as he was no longer fit for service, sent him back to his country. He lived ten years afterwards, and died, in 1728, in faith, after he had sung for the last time, "Oh, innocent Lamb of God."

something to encourage us also, so that we, like they, may confess our Lord.

Our great encouragement is 'The confession which Christ will make of those by whom He is confessed.' " *Whosoever, therefore, shall confess me before men, him will I confess also, before my Father which is in heaven.*"

Now the first point to which we are to direct our attention is

The *personality* of this confession. Individuals are to be acknowledged or confessed by an individual— 'men,' by 'the man Christ Jesus.'

There shall be an individual owning of the confessor, —"'him' *will I confess.*" No doubt there shall hereafter be a great glorifying of holy principles: these principles are at present vilified and trampled under foot by the world; they are not the principles which are in fashion; or which attract favourable attention; or which secure the admiration of the world: but hereafter they shall be glorified and admired, when God comes to set all principles of action in their proper light.

All this is very comforting; it will be a great triumph to the believer to see the principles on which he acted, acknowledged as the true ones by God; but we have before us a still brighter prospect than this. Principles and *persons* are here linked together; and Christ will acknowledge His people *man by man.* 'Him' will I confess; the personal element at once invests this confession of our Lord with a vividness and distinctness, which gives us the highest interest in it. The triumph of holy principles will be embodied in individuals; Jesus will confess as His, every one who confessed Him. The man who has made a great discovery, knows what it is to be received with acclamation by his fellow men; the man who has fought and won great battles, bears, in the stars and medals on his breast, the history of his achievements, and has a patent of nobility conferred on *him:* both these men may have only pushed to their legitimate conclusions principles previously well-known, but *they themselves* are honoured; so will it be with the saints; they, the confessors, shall receive in their own persons the reward of the confession they have made.

The personal interest is the strongest that can be appealed to in man; and it is here used by Christ. He says to you, dear reader, "If you confess me, I will confess *you*—not only will I put you amongst a class who shall be blessed, but I will acknowledge you as an individual; you shall not be lost or merged in a crowd; you shall occupy your own distinct place in my estimation; you shall have your own distinct position amongst the millions of the redeemed; you shall have your own personal feelings of happiness and triumph.

It is not selfishness to enjoy the thought of this, or to allow it to have some place in energizing us for Christ. God gave us our own individual beings, that we may be responsible in them, and that we may feel in them; and He meant our personal hopes and fears to be instruments in influencing us to what is right, and keeping us from what is wrong; and we *may* be cheered and energized by the thought, that we shall *individually* be confessed of Christ; if *I* suffer in my confession upon earth, or am put to shame because of it, I may encourage myself by the thought that *I* also am to be blest by Christ's con-fesssion of *me* in heaven. Oh! think of this, and the vividness with which the future will thus be clothed, will give a vividness to the present also; you will say, "It is not enough that Christ should *be* confessed, *I* must confess Him;" and you will ask yourselves more particularly, "Wherein do I confess Him now?"

Oh! it is a wonderful thought that each confessor shall come out with personal distinctness hereafter,—that Christ will think each one worth confessing,—that He will say, "I own such an one, and such an one, for mine." Here is a poor creature who now stands alone in the family, witnessing for Christ in all meekness, amid the indifference of some, and the taunts and sneers of others. Christ will hereafter say before the angels of His Father, "I acknowledge *thee;*" and here is a Sabbath School teacher, and here is a servant, and here is a little child, all nobodies in the estimation of the world; but Christ recognises them above, and remembers how they filled up their little circles of daily service, and stoutly confessed Him before their fellows; and now He calls them—his own sheep by name, and says, "I confess thee, and thee, and thee."

And following upon that—Christ's individuality of confession—will be Christ's individuality of reward; then He will say, "Well done, good and faithful servant, enter *thou* into the joy of thy Lord." There will no doubt be a general word for all,—"Come *ye* blessed of my Father;" but there will also be a particular word for each,—"Enter *thou* into the joy of thy Lord."

And it will be for you, dear reader, to ask yourself, whether you be now so personally and individually in confession for Christ, that you have reason to believe that you will personally be confessed by Him. After having been nothing particular on earth, it is not reasonable to expect to be some one particular in heaven; and unless you be accounted worthy by Christ of individual notice, you will not be accounted worthy of anything at all. In that day, when men shall be known by what they were, and by what they did, what shall be known of *you?* Oh! this is a solemn thought for many who read these lines; when it comes down to the *particulars* of confession of Christ—when no mere vague generalities will be admitted,—where will you be found? "Him *will I confess*,"—"him ;"—are there not, alas! too many, of whom the question might be asked—what can be said of "him," and "him?" May all readers of these lines lay hold of this subject, and solemnly question themselves, "wherein am *I* individually a confessor?" When Jesus speaks, and grounds what he says upon definite acts in the past—what! oh what will He say to me? And as this offers a subject for very solemn enquiry to some, so does it also offer very solid encouragement and comfort to others.

Encourage yourselves to personal confession, by the soul-inspiring thought of being personally confessed. Do not, with a mistaken humility, cast away from you that which God intends to be a great encouragement— the certainty of your being personally acknowledged by Christ. To us it may seem too much to be confessed by Christ, before such men as Paul, that beaten, and imprisoned, and stoned, and shipwrecked man; or before those three, who fell down bound in the midst of the burning fiery furnace; or before that solitary man, who spent an awful night within the lions' den. We might say "Who are we that we should hold up our heads amongst those who had trials of cruel mockings and scourgings, yea, moreover, of bonds and imprisonments? Who are we that we should be mentioned before such as were stoned and sawn asunder, tempted, and slain with the sword; before men who had to wander about in sheep-skins and goat-skins, being destitute, and afflicted, and tormented, of whom the world was not worthy? Shall we who dwell, even in the worst cases, comparatively at ease, be mentioned in the presence of those who once had to wander in deserts, and in mountains, and in dens and caves of the earth?" Yes! who and what are we, that we should expect all this? We are, in our own sphere, confessors for Jesus before men,—we are men, as marked in our testimony in the workshop, or the drawing-room, or the counting-house, as these were in the den, the prison, and the cave; we are men who openly and unmistakably confess Christ; and who humbly, yet faithfully, lay our hand upon His own promise, " *Whosoever, therefore, shall confess me before men, him will I confess also, before my Father which is in heaven.*"

We see then, that there shall be individual owning of a person, even the confessor; let us now turn our consideration for a few moments to the fact that the individual confessor shall be acknowledged by *an individual Christ*. If there be much important teaching for us in the fact that it is as "persons," that believers shall be acknowledged, there is much teaching in the fact that it is "a person," an individual, who is to acknowledge them—even Jesus Christ Himself; " him will I confess."

There will be personal confession for personal service. As Jesus *Himself* was served, so Jesus *Himself* will acknowledge the service. He will say, " Come ye blessed of my Father, inherit the kingdom prepared for you from the foundation of the world; for I was an hungered and ye gave me meat; I was thirsty and ye gave me drink; I was a stranger and ye took me in; naked and ye clothed me; I was sick and ye visited me; I was in prison and ye came unto me. Verily I say unto you: Inasmuch as ye have done it unto one of the least of these my brethren, ye have done it unto *me*."

And if we think for a moment, we can see, how here also the introduction of the personal element increases the greatness of the reward. If we look no further than human sovereignties, we see that it is considered a great enhancement of a reward, if it be given by the sovereign in person. He who wears the cross which men receive for deeds of special valour, thinks all the more of his distinction, if the sovereign have with her own hands pinned it on his breast; and personal receptions, and autograph letters, and all into which the living individual sovereign enters, are far more highly prized than what is official and nothing more.

Now, He who will hereafter confess and reward His people, will doubtless do so in the character of a mighty king. "Then shall *the King* say unto them at His right hand." But it is not in His official capacity alone that He will speak, but in His personal also. The living being and energy of Christ will enter into His words, and give them depth and life; all who hear them will know that His heart goes out to those to whom they are spoken; there will be intense reality in what he says.

And, even from ordinary life, we can gather what a great increase the happiness of the saints will receive from the fact, that Jesus Himself will, with His own

lips, tell them that He owns them.   Do not we ourselves
realize a power in the *spoken* word which we do not feel
in a message or a letter, even though the substance be
in each instance the same?   When a person tells us he
loves, or hates, face to face, do not his tones of voice tell
it? do not his eyes tell it? do not the very muscles of
his face tell it? assuming that he be earnest in his love
or hate—no letter, no messenger could tell us what that
living, breathing man does, whose very being is thrown
into the feelings he would express.   And if it be thus
with these sluggish natures of ours, poor and unim-
passioned, compared with a spiritual nature like our
Lord's, oh! can we not see what a great enhancement it
will be of the joy of the acknowledged saints, that it is
by Christ *in person* that they are confessed.

No doubt, even without this, it would be well worth
our while to confess our Lord; even if Jesus never
spake, yet would it not have been well worth our while
to have confessed Him, if at His command some high
archangel proclaimed aloud, with trumpet voice, our
names and our acceptance by our Lord; if listening
myriads with rapt attention, were gathered round, and
the silence were to be broken by your name or by mine.
Who would not buy at the cost of all he has (if it could
be purchased by gold,) the weighty honour of being thus
proclaimed—of having it said of him by the high angelic
herald; the King of kings and Lord of lords confesses
him as His—owns him from His heart's core before
martyrs and apostles and prophets, before all the hosts
of heaven?' But that which is in store for every man
who confesses Jesus Christ in truth, is more than this.
Jesus will not delegate to any of the heavenly hosts, the

privilege of proclaiming the name of the man that He will confess before the Father; that He reserves for Himself— *" him will ' I ' confess before my Father which is in heaven."*

Oh! if we think coldly of Christ's thus personally confessing us, is it not because we are, alas! only too cold in our own dull hearts? Hearts palpitate and bosoms heave and pant, and thrillings undefinable vibrate through all the mysterious chords of our being at the sound of the voice of one we intensely love; and shall it be a matter of indifference to us, that we shall hear the voice of Jesus calling us—His sheep—by name, and confessing us before His Father that is in heaven. May it not be so; may our dull and laggard natures wake up; may our appreciation of true honour become more vivid; may our love to Jesus become more personal, and more intense; and then we shall feel the power of that wondrous promise, *" Whosoever, therefore, shall confess me before men, him will I confess also, before my Father which is in heaven !"*

There is yet one more aspect of this personal confession of Christ, at which we must glance, *i.e.* :—

The great value that is to be attached to it from our Lord's omniscience, and from His authority to judge.

A confession of our being His, will be indeed of solid worth, when made by Christ. With that confession will go forth all the authority and weight which must attach, in heaven, to every word that is uttered by Him.

And how entirely will that confession of Christ stamp the genuineness of every one whose name He will confess! Be it so, that in his earthly career there were many short-comings and imperfections—that, even in the judgment, the evil one could bring many things against him; Jesus, who knows the heart, has pronounced His confession of the poor believer as His own; henceforth, conscience, and devils, and evil men, and all who would accuse must hold their tongue.

Dear readers, Jesus knows who is confessing Him and who is not; and none who are thus confessing can be hid. If you be hidden to Jesus now, you must be unknown to him in that day when He will confess those and those only who have confessed Him.

Question yourselves, then, "what does Jesus know of me now?"—what grounds will He have for confessing me by and bye? Oh, think of your honour, should He, who knows all hearts and lives, acknowledge you as His—how *genuine* you will then know yourself to be, and others shall know you to be; and how *safe;* for, when within the very shadow of the judgment-seat your Lord has confessed you as His own, who can impeach you in the position which that confession gives?

Away, then, shall flee all fears as to whether you be Christ's or no—away shall flee all depressions and doubts, and that for ever; Christ Himself will have proclaimed you as His; acknowledged you! named you! glorified you! and there can be no more room for fear!

Come then, and let all readers who know the Lord, confess Him henceforth with more courage and distinctness than ever, remembering what is in store for them— even confession of them by Jesus in His glory.* Men

---

* "Life is sweet," said Sir Anthony Kingston to Bishop Hooper at the stake, trying to persuade him to recant, "and death bitter." "True, friend," he replied, "but consider that death to come is more bitter, and the life to come is more sweet."

who, perhaps, are civil enough to their poor relations
when no one particular is near, often slight them when
grand people are at hand; but Jesus will not act thus;
great indeed is the disproportion between *our* confessing
Him, and *His* confessing *us;* but He will confess us
before the angels of heaven; before sainted martyrs and
prophets and apostles—yea! why speak we at all of
these? before the mighty Lord of all—the Father—the
Most High Himself—"*Whosoever therefore shall confess
me before men, him will I confess also,* BEFORE MY FATHER
which is in heaven!"

The "I Will" of Service.

———

MATTHEW iv, 19.

MATTHEW iv, 19.

"Follow Me, and I will make you fishers of men."

———◆———

AS God clothed the immortal soul in a body of clay, so Christ clothed immortal truths in homely images and words; condescending to use for His high purpose even the commonest circumstances of daily life. The bread which men handled and ate, was made the medium of teaching deep truth about the bread of life; the little children who formed part of their earthly households were made to shadow forth the mind and character of those who should be of the household of God; the hairs upon the head, the fowls in the air, the lilies of the field, all formed simple texts from which He, the great teacher, drew forth most wondrous truths.

And here, in commissioning two of His disciples, we find our Lord making use of one of the commonest avocations of daily life. He tells them what He will make them, even by reminding them of what they are—they, fishers of fish, shall become fishers of men.

We need have no hesitation in giving this subject a place in the present volume; for the words of our Lord speak not only to Simon and Andrew, but to all who hear and obey (even as they did) the solemn words "Follow Me." Every one who follows Christ is to become a fisher of men; and no man can be a true fisher of men, unless he be a follower of Him.

It is the earnest desire of the writer to win, by the Spirit's influence, some of the readers of this chapter to become fishers of men. "Why stand ye here, all the day idle?" are the words of the blessed Jesus, Himself a toilsome worker; yes, why are not believers working for their Lord? "Why call ye Me Lord, Lord, and do not the things that I say?" Why are souls perishing and Christians idling? May this chapter be a net, the meshes of which will catch some at least of its readers; happy indeed will the author of it be, if his Lord should say of it, "I will make it a fisher of men."

Let us classify what we would say upon this subject under these three heads:—

 I. THE APPOINTMENT ⎫
 II. THE WORK   ⎬ of the Fishers.
 III. THE REWARD   ⎭

And now, I. WHO IS IT THAT APPOINTS THE FISHERS? It is the blessed Lord Jesus Christ; the One of whom it is said, in Psalm viii, "Thou madest Him to have dominion over the works of Thy hands, Thou hast put all things under His feet; all sheep and oxen, yea, and the beasts of the field, the fowl of the air, and the fish of the sea, and whatsoever passeth through the paths of the seas."

The One who appoints, is the One into whose hands all things are committed of the Father, and it is in His power and wisdom that this fishing is to be carried on.

The Lord's people are sent to fish by One who knows where each fish is to be found. When the piece of money was wanted, and it was to be supplied through the instrumentality of a fish, that particular fish was brought to the apostle's hook; this should afford great comfort to the people of God; their master does not send them forth on hap-hazard; He knows and appoints with the finest minuteness every item connected with their success. There is no pursuit so uncertain as fishing for fish, none more certain than fishing for men. The word wherewith we fish has this said of it; "My word shall not return to me void."

He who brought the solitary fish to the apostle's hook, was also the One who brought the miraculous draught to the net; at His word the net was let down, and the draught was great. We are commanded to go forth by the very One who has the power of giving us good speed. Special direction will, no doubt, be given in the providence of God, as to where and when we are to fish; but the very fact of our following Christ compels us to become fishers on His behalf. How many spheres are open to us for this fishing, we shall presently see.

Let us now turn our attention for a while to the work of the fishers of men.

What is this work? It is the attempt to influence souls for Christ, and to draw them out of the world to Him; the watching all opportunities of winning the attention of careless men to divine things, and bringing them, in knowledge of their need, to the cross of Christ. What Cecil says of a minister, is in its measure true of all Christians, " He is a fisherman, and the fisherman must fit himself to his employment.   If some fish will bite only by day, he must fish by day; if others will bite only by moonlight, he must fish for them by moonlight."

Now, it has been well remarked,* that there is here *a relation of the conscious agent to the unconscious subject ;* the fisherman, with all his human intelligence and skill, is represented as coming into contact with the fish, in which there is no knowledge; and in divine things, the fisherman for Christ, himself possessed of a knowledge of eternal life, and conscious of it, is represented as using this intelligence and consciousness, in his dealings with poor ignorant souls—alas ! how unconscious of everything really spiritual or divine.

This was precisely what our blessed Lord Himself did; He, the conscious One, knowing God's love, and holiness, and justice, and mercy, applied Himself to men, all unconscious of them in any real practical sense, and drew them to Himself.   This was what the apostle did, "Knowing therefore the terrors of the Lord, we persuade men ;" this is what every believer is to do; he is to bring his knowledge of the Lord to bear upon the ignorant and deluded world; he must say, "We speak that we do know." "We also believe, and therefore speak :" (2 Cor. iv, 13.)

Have you, dear reader, the conscious element in you; do you know the Lord vitally yourself ?   If so, that very consciousness is a talent; it must not be allowed to lie

* "Olshausen on the Gospels," Vol. I, p. 262.

idle; even if you have no actual gifts, that one of spiritual intelligence is enough; with no more than this, many a believer has won souls to Christ.

But what is to be the scene of our operations for Christ? The fishers are to fish in the sea; they are to launch out into the deep. The ever shifting world, troubled and restless, is to supply the fish for the gospel net. Now there is much in the world to daunt timid disciples of Christ; they shrink from its turmoil, from the storms which they must encounter, and from such a complete going out of self as is involved in a launching out into the deep. Many an one will not venture much for Christ; the very timid Christian will throw in a hook and line from the shore, or even venture out into some little bay or creek, which washes almost his own door, but he will not venture out into the deep. Well! we would just observe in passing, that some of the best fish are caught in deep water; however, far be it from us to think lightly of every one that skirts the shore. No doubt there are shore fish as well as deep water fish; and happy is he who fishes at all, and catches anything; we are glad if any of our readers have thus commenced, even as it were just at their own door; we pray that in God's good time they may be encouraged to go forth into the deep. For the encouragement of such, let us give the experience of a city missionary in one of the worst parts of London.

"My experience in mission work is, that its discouragements gradually lessen, while on the other hand its encouragements continually increase. At first a missionary enters on his work with fear—fear, lest the important truths which he wishes to make known should be mocked at, and their value lost upon persons engrossed in the every-day duties of life. Probably this is the feeling which induces so many private Christians to seek any outlet for their zeal, rather than that of speaking to neighbours about their souls. Those fears, however, soon wear away; especially if a genuine sympathy for others in their wants and woes is possessed. During the past year my access to the people has greatly increased. I will mention a few of its causes. I have before me a row of sixteen cottages, to only one of which I could gain an entrance on my first round. At my last round, I could make known the gospel at the fireside of each. I believe this has arisen simply from the frequency with which I have passed these houses, in going to other parts of the district. Certain it is, that this kind of familiarity, instead of breeding contempt, as the copy has it, rather tends to slacken the cords of enmity with which the hearts of the unconverted are bound. A second source of access, is a gradual good opinion of the missionary among the people, as his labours are known, which are told from one to another. I have sometimes been refused admittance at one visit, when on a second visit, some one else being present of those I visit, that person has said such a word in my favour, as to prevent my being again sent away. And then on a third visit, affliction often softens down the people. 'Lot of beggars going about!' said one woman of us; but when the frost set in, and she was in the greatest of distress, she was altogether on another key. But, above all, the report throughout a district of real good effected in some of the people, has a wonderful influence in helping the missionary with others whom he visits."

They who venture little for Jesus, generally get little; "Be it unto thee according to thy faith," is said many a time now, even as it was in the days of Christ.

The history of the church of God is full of instances of the courage of His servants in launching out into the deep—depths of ignorance, of persecution, of resistance, of vice, and such like; and of their having met with great success in doing so. Let us consider a few examples of this launching forth, and perhaps they will have the blessed effect, of at least encouraging our timid ones, to venture a little farther than they do. Our first example shall be rather a formidable one, but all the more encouraging on that account.

"During the revolutionary troubles of the year 1848, a band of robbers had established themselves in the great manufacturing town of Lyons in the south of France. They were rough fellows, with faces that looked fit only for the gallows, and hearts hard as the street paving of the town. To judge from their appearance, they would think no more of taking away a man's life than of blowing out a rushlight. But nothing prospers in this world without some sort of government, and these robbers knew it; so they chose one of their number for a captain, and in this case it was the one most accomplished in all kinds of robbery and murder. And then they raised their hands to heaven and swore, that none of them would ever leave or betray the band, and if any should nevertheless break the oath, the rest would pursue and kill him. And now they went forth to plunder and murder, and all the people of the neighbourhood, who besides their heads had temporal goods to lose, were full of terror and dismay.

"At this time there was assembled in Lyons another band, which, like these robbers in the forest, sent out their messengers in every direction, and so hunted after all sorts of people. And where these messengers appeared, many an one has trembled. It is true they were not armed like the robbers with pistols, and such murderous weapons, but out of their wallets peeped large and small books; and when the messengers read out of them, it was to many a listener as if a two-edged sword pierced through his soul. For in the books was much written about the holy God, who brings sinners before His tribunal, and about the Saviour Jesus Christ, who so mercifully takes upon Himself the sins of those who heartily repent and seek forgiveness from Him.

"One of the missionaries of this society resolved one day to go into the forest to the robbers; not, indeed, that he might become one of them, but, with the help of God, to put an end to their unrighteous profession. It was truly a dangerous thing to do, and I really begin to tremble when I think how the lawless fellows in the forest yonder will handle the poor man. He might well think about it too; but God had given him a brave heart, so that he didn't trouble himself about it, further than to say to himself that at most they could only destroy his body, but were not able to kill his soul. 'If I fall,' he thought, 'I shall go straight to heaven, and there it is far better than in this poor world, especially in France. And would not my life be amply repaid if, by the word of God, the soul of one of these robbers should be saved?' So he filled his wallet with Bibles, and stepped away bravely into the wood. Soon he was lost in the thicket, and, after a few miles, he came upon the outposts of the camp.

"'Who goes there?' cried a rough voice, which seemed to pierce our Bible distributor through bone and marrow. Soon several horrible-looking forms came out of the thicket, surrounded the adventurous intruder, and scrutinized him with curious looks. He had, meanwhile, recovered courage to meet their wild scornful faces.

"'What brings you here, fellow?' cried the robbers.

"'I come,' replied he, with a firm voice, 'to bring you the word of God, and to warn you from the path of ruin, before the judgment of God breaks over you.'

"A wild, fiendish laugh interrupted the address. 'Ha! ha! ha!' cried the comrades, 'this is a capital fellow, and a good roast for our captain! There you can finish your sermon. It's just what he likes, and he'll reward you for it. Pack up your books: over yonder you'll do more business! March! On with you!'

"With these words they thrust him forward, and brought him to their captain. At the sight of such a body of ruffians, playing with their muskets as if they were toy guns, the stoutest heart might have quailed; but our man of God stood calm.

"'What do you want, fellow?' asked the captain, haughtily.

"'I come to bring you the word of God,' replied the missionary, firmly.

"'Do you know who we are? Do you know us?' he asked again.

"'Certainly, I know you,' was the answer. 'You are the wickedest of the wicked, the most daring of sinners. You are the terror of the neighbourhood; but the anger of God will burst over you, and destroy you before you think it. He is a righteous God, and will not leave the wicked unpunished.'

"As before, the fearless speaker was now interrupted by a burst of laughter. A flood of sneers and curses was poured on him, but he did not allow himself to be disturbed, and only raised his voice the louder.

"'Repent!' he cried, 'even for you there is mercy and forgiveness: even for you is the Saviour, the Son of God, come, if you repent, and be converted. Now is the time. His love has sent me here; the arms of His love are opened to you.' The wild laughter was stilled, but instead of it a low murmur was heard The wild eyes glared with rage; involuntarily they pointed their muskets at the daring missionary; but a glance from the captain, and he would have paid for his boldness with his life. But the eye of God watched over him, and his courage was undisturbed.

"'Do you know,' shouted the captain, 'that your life is in our hands?'

"'Without God's permision you cannot touch a hair of my head,' replied the missionary, raising his warning and exhorting voice still louder, and distributing his Bibles right and left. By degrees the murmur was hushed. The robbers began even to show respect to the courageous man. Many a heart might have trembled at that moment, but the devil had bound their chains too firmly. They had taken that fearful oath, never to leave the band. It could be broken only by death. Presently the captain exclaimed, 'take the man away, but do him no harm!' He was obeyed, and, with oaths and curses.

they led him out of the wood; and he, praising God in his heart, made the best of his way back to Lyons.

"Now many may think the Bible distributor might have spared himself his troublesome journey, for that robbers will be robbers still. Have patience. The word of God never returns empty, but will accomplish whatever He pleases. But to proceed.

"The captain had himself received a New Testament, and, as he was one day strolling through the wood, he took the book out of his pocket and read it, to pass away the time. He was astonished at what he saw there, and he read on and on. He had never heard such things before. His conscience was awakened, and the life he had led appeared darker and darker to his mind. He became uneasy. Every day he separated from his comrades, and wandered about the wood. To them such conduct appeared somewhat suspicious, and they began to whisper among themselves. But he became every day more alive to the misery of his sins; the judgment of God was to him fearful, and the love of Christ burned in his hard heart: he could no longer belong to the band. But how could he leave it? Should he run away? Now we should not think it wrong, but our captain would not break his oath, even with robbers. For a long time he struggled thus with himself; but at last he assembled the band. They hastened together, in the hope that he was going to lead them out again on some profitable expedition. But they were not a little astonished when the captain addressed them as follows:—

"'Comrades!' he cried, 'hitherto I have been your leader: henceforth I am so no more. This book here

has shown me that we are on the way to ruin. A
fearful oath bound me to you; but my resolution is
taken. I am in your hands. If you wish to kill me,
you can do it; but never again can I bring myself to
lead the cursed life of a robber!'

"In mute astonishment the comrades listened to
their leader. A murmur of rage ran through the company, but soon anger gave place to sympathy. After
long consultation, they came to the determination of
letting the captain go quietly away. Once more he
raised his warning voice to his old companions, reminding them of the wrath of God, whose commandments
they had broken, and of the great love of the Redeemer,
if they repented, and urged them earnestly to quit with
him their life of sin. Soon afterwards the band broke
up. Many of its members followed their captain, and
were converted; and the society which first sent their
missionary into the wood has received several of them
into its office, as companions of its labours." *

* " From the Berlin " Neueste Nachrichten aus dem Riche Gottes,"
December, 1850.

The following tradition of the early church will also, doubtless,
interest the reader; in some respects, it bears a remarkable similarity
to the circumstances mentioned in the text :—

" Clemens Alexandrinus in his book, entitled, " What rich man can
be saved ?" narrates the following :—

" Listen to a story, or rather to a genuine tradition of the apostle
John, which has been faithfully treasured in memory. On his return
from Patmos to Ephesus, he visited the neighbouring regions, to
ordain bishops and organize churches. While he was engaged in exhorting and comforting the brethren in a city near Ephesus, whose
name is given by some, he noticed a handsome spirited young man,
toward whom he felt himself drawn so powerfully, that he turned to
the bishop of the congregation with the words, 'I commit him to you,
before Christ and the congregation, who are witnesses of my heartfelt

But we can find examples amongst ourselves. "Of the courage and tact necessary for the missionary's work, as well as of its influence under the most unlikely circum-

earnestness.' The bishop received the young man, promised to do all in his power, and John, at parting, repeated the same charge. The elder took the youth home, educated and watched over him, and finally baptized him. After he had given him this seal of the Lord, however, he abated in his solicitude and watchfulness. The young man, too early freed from restraint, fell into bad company. He was first led into lavish habits, and finally drawn on to rob travellers by night. Like a spirited steed that springs from the path, and rushes madly over a precipice, so did his vehement nature hurry him to the abyss of destruction. He renounced all hope in the grace of God; and, as he considered himself involved in the same destiny with his companions, was ready to commit some startling crime. He associated them with himself, organized a band of robbers, put himself at their head, and surpassed them all in cruelty and violence. Sometime after, John's duties again called him to that city; when he had attended to all the other matters, he said to the bishop: ' Well, bishop, restore the pledge which the Saviour and I entrusted to thee, in the presence of the congregation!' The bishop at first was alarmed, supposing that John was speaking of money; and charging him with embezzlement. But when John continued, 'I demand again that young man, and the soul of my brother,' the old man sighed heavily, and with tears replied ' He is dead!' 'Dead?' said the disciple of the Lord, 'in what way did he die?' 'He is dead to God,' responded the old man; 'he became godless, and finally a robber. He is no longer in the church, but, with his fellows, holds the fastnesses of the mountain.' The apostle, when he heard this, with a loud cry, rent his clothing and smote his head, and exclaimed, 'To what keeper have I committed my brother's soul!' He takes a horse and a guide, and hastens to the spot where the band of robbers was to be found. He is seized by their out-guard; he makes no attempt to escape, but cries out 'I have come for this very purpose; take me to your captain.' Their captain, completely armed, is waiting for them to bring him; but recognising John as he approached, flees, from a sense of shame. John, nevertheless, forgetting his age, hastens after him with all speed; crying, 'Why my child do you flee from me—from me—your father, an unarmed old man? have compassion on me, my child; do not be afraid. You yet

stances, the night preceding the execution of Mullins
may be taken as an example. The public-houses were
then thronged till the hour of closing, when the inmates
were off in a body to await all night in the open air the
solemn scene of the morning. Into a public-house that
evening a missionary entered. As he crossed the bar to
enter an inner room, the landlord cautioned him not to
go in, as it was unsafe. But, in language characteristic
of a city missionary, the missionary writes :—'On hearing this, in I went.' In the room he found about sixty
men and youths, all their hair dressed in the favourite
style with that class, known as 'the Newgate cut,' and
a number of them smoking short pipes. His entering
among them caused great excitement, and the only
words which he could hear for some time were such as
these, 'Bonnet him,' 'Kick him out,' and the like, until
one man, gifted with a louder voice than the others,
shouted to the potman, 'Here, bring a quartern of Old
Tom, and two outs for me and this chap, to drink

have a hope of life. I will yet give account to Christ for you. If
needs be, I will gladly die for you, as Christ died for us ; I will lay
down my life for you. Stop! Believe Christ has sent me !' Hearing
these words, he first stands still, and casts his eyes upon the ground.
He next throws away his arms ; and begins to tremble and weep
bitterly. When the old man approaches, he clasps his knees, and with
the most vehement agony, pleads for forgiveness ; baptizing himself
anew, as it were, with his own tears ; all this time, however, he con-
ceals his right hand, but the apostle pledging himself, with an appeal
to God for the truth, that he had obtained forgiveness from the
Saviour for him, implores him, even on his knees, and the hand he had
held back, he kisses, as if it were cleansed again by his penitence. He
finally led him back to the church ; here, he pleaded with him
earnestly, strove with him in fasting, urged him with monitions, until
he was able to restore him to the church, an example of sincere
repentance and genuine regeneration.

Mullins's health with.' These words were no sooner
spoken than the rest rushed to the door to cut off the
missionary's retreat. The missionary, seeing his position, and that they desired to frighten him, advanced
quickly to the middle of the room, and, raising his hand
to heaven, exclaimed, 'If a thousand savages were here,
I'd have my say out, and do you think I'm to be cowed
by fifty or sixty Englishmen? Why, I have come to
tell you of the last dying speech of a friend who was
executed.' This last observation was so appropriate to
the state of their minds, that it caused silence, which
was generally called for by them in words of their own
vocabulary, such as 'Shut up,' 'Muzzle,' 'Hold your
mug,' Then the missionary began to tell of the two
condemned to death, and of the thousands who poured
out of the city to see the well known thieves and murderers die. Then he proceeded to tell of One greater
than these, who was suspended between them, while
increasing throngs 'came together to that sight.'
He was permitted to describe the whole scene, and
while he told them of the darkened heavens, and the
trembling earth, their silence became intense. On his
repeating to them the last words of the sufferer, ' It is
finished,' their pipes all went on the table, and they
gazed in wonder at the tale of the Saviour's finished
work, which was described by the missionary with much
fulness. He then called on them, in His name, to repent. No resistance was made, when at length he
proceeded to leave; but several of them rose in
respect to him as he did so, and two followed him out.
One of these was a ticket-of-leave man, and both he
and his companion promised the missionary, in the

strength of prayer, to separate entirely from their old companions."

Another missionary in humble life, (Roger Miller,) writes:—

"In —— Court there were three men who were the terror of the place. Having repeatedly heard of their determined violence against me, and of their saying that they would kick me out of their house if I should go there when they were at home—a threat which all the neighbours believed they would accomplish—I at once resolved to call upon them; and as they were only at home on Sundays, I arranged to visit their families on one of these days. I accordingly did so. The neighbours, on seeing me enter the first house, were alarmed, and held themselves in readiness to interfere, in the event of violence. The family was at breakfast; I apologised. The man bid me make no apologies, as he had heard of me, and knew that my intention was good. I had a long talk with him, and the result was that he assured me that he should be glad to see me at any time, and he thought he should begin to go to some place of worship."

"Mr. and Mrs. B., of —— Place, were extremely poor and ignorant, and were in their persons, house, and children, uncommonly filthy. When I first called upon them, and told them the business and purpose of my visit, Mr. B., vociferating a stunning oath, bid me begone and never again trouble him with any of that 'ere non-sense.' I left a tract, and said, 'I will call again at some future day.' 'Yes, you do,' replied he, 'and I will soon kick you out—that's all!' I however called. He was not at home himself, but I met with his wife, and found her but little better than he. Her children, I saw, were in her way, and occasioned her much vexation; so I invited her to send them to the infant school, representing to her the advantage that would arise out of this, as she would herself get rid of them during the day, and they would learn to read. I offered, if she would wash their hands and faces, to take them with me immediately. I accordingly did take them. This care for her children pleased her much. I continued to visit them, and after some months again met with Mr. B. at home. In the meantime, his children had received considerable instruction, and amongst other things, had learned to sing a number of pretty little hymns, and he himself had been called to task but a few days before, for commencing dinner without saying grace; so instead of '*kicking out*' his friend, as he had *threatened*, he received him most respectfully. 'I don't know how it is,' said he, ' but the children seem to learn a great deal at your school; I should like to come and see them.' The man was quite subdued and won. He began to attend a place of worship himself, became increasingly regular in doing so, and ended, an anxious inquirer for the best of things."

"Mr. and Mrs. ——, of 25, —— Street, were a somewhat aged couple. They had long lived together, strangers to themselves and to God; rarely if ever attending a place of worship, and entertaining the most perfect contempt for religion. At first when I called, they would not hear anything I had to say, but I continued my visits. They gradually became more and more free and friendly, and at length I was permitted to read and pray with them. Their minds were open to receive my instructions and counsels, and they became hopefully converted to God. The case of this poor man and his wife, at my last visit, appeared truly affecting. Both wept like children, and said with great feeling, 'Oh, sir, if you had not come to us as you did, we should still have been living in our sins, and we have often wondered that you should have troubled yourself to come a second time to see us, as we used you so bad when you first called on us. We never go to bed now, nor get up, without praying for you ; as we know that others serve you as we did when you came to us at first.' 'But, oh! what mercy,' exclaimed the old man, 'has the Lord bestowed on us ; to think that he should send His Son to die for a poor old sinner such as I am.' The poor old man was soon after visited with an attack of paralysis, which occasioned his confinement to his room. His wife became a member of the Wesleyan Society in Broadwell."

We are afraid often to launch out into what might be called *the depths of hopelessness;* but God has His own ways of bringing even the most unlikely fish to our gospel net.

"I will now," says a city missionary, "give a few illustrations from the district, and the first instance will show that effects may be produced, even among the most hopeless kind of persons. Among the most uncouth persons I ever met with was a man named————, and his wife. Years passed away before any perceptible progress was made, even in the way of access. It required more than ordinary means to subdue this man. It pleased God, therefore, to afflict him very much. Four times did he meet with accidents by the breaking of his limbs ; till at length he was disqualified for labour altogether. This gave me more opportunities of meeting with him, and, in the change of circumstances that

followed, I had occasion to use my influence on his behalf
in temporal things. These combined influences operated
on him; he began to show more interest in spiritual
things, and in the reading of the tracts. He was much
influenced with 'the Bar of Iron,' and he would not rest
satisfied till I had procured him the second part, which
he also read with much interest. Ultimately he was
induced to attend church, and has done so for some time,
although his crippled state renders it very difficult for
him to walk; and he said one day, while I was visiting
him, 'The more I goes the more I likes it.' No persons
manifested more sympathy on my leaving the district
than these persons. He missed me from calling, and one
day I met him in the street, and he asked the cause. I
told him it was through illness, and I saw the tears in
his eyes; but when I added it was probable I should
leave, his countenance quite changed, and for a few
minutes he could not speak. At length, with quivering
lips, he said, 'I am so sorry, I am so sorry!' It moved
my heart to see this, for it was what I never expected
to see. They both pressed me to give them a parting
visit, which I did. They expressed much sympathy and
regret, and showed it by many wishes for my future
welfare. I do not say this man is converted, but I give
the facts of the change in him as indicating hope, and as
a source of encouragement to faithful perseverance."

It may be that we shall not succeed in getting out of
such depths a sufficiently large draught to break our nets;
but even if we get one for Christ—one out of such an
unlikely place—one from the midst of such sin, how
great the triumph. And we may get one; though it be
but one,—yet is it one SOUL.

When the missionary Weitbrecht was at the court of
the Rajah of Burdwan, the Rev. Krishna Mohun Bener-
jea visited that place, and, at the earnest request of the
Rajah, Mr. W. took him to call on him. He could not
believe, without ocular demonstration, that one of the
highest class of Brahmins had adopted another religion;
and it led to a great deal of interesting discussion on
the subject with him and his family, which reminded
the missionary of a remark made by the sainted
Martyn, that, "If ever he lived to see a native Bengali
Brahmin converted to God, he would see the nearest
approach he had yet witnessed to the resurrection of
the dead." "Thanks be to God," says Weitbrecht, "the
day has arrived when such conversions are no longer
rare."

Thus from most unpromising depths have some fish
been drawn; our own waters, unpromising though they
also be, yield their increase.

But let us see such success at home:—

"A city missionary, meeting with a man, a Roman
Catholic, the following conversation took place:—
'Good morning; I hope you are well!' 'I am very well
in body, but not very happy in mind.' 'What is the
matter with you?' 'I have an old friend of mine who,
has been after going to mass with me for many a long
year, both in Ireland and in this country; and, sure
enough, I would never be thinking as how he would be
after becoming a child of the devil.' 'What has he been
doing? Committing murder or theft?' 'No, but something worse than all that; for, sure, mercy would then
be in store for him. But sometime since I missed him
(God help me), and went to his house, and opened the

door before he was after hearing me, and he put a book under his bed. I asked him what it was, and, bad luck to him, without fearing the priest at all, he was after saying to me, 'Oh, indeed, and it is the book of books, and fool that I have been not to read it before.' And what do you think?—he had the impudence to recommend it to me,—and, sure, I don't want the curses of the church.' I asked him if he intended to tell the priest? 'Indeed I do,' was his reply; 'for I am bound to do so when I go to confession.' 'Then it is true that you are not allowed to read the Bible?' 'Indeed it is, for the Bible is not true; and if it is, it is not for the like of us to be after reading what the priest alone can understand. The Lord have mercy upon me for not saying his Holiness the Pope first;' and here the poor creature crossed himself, and left me.

"An Irishwoman, who opposed me most strenuously, said, 'I am quite certain we should and ought to be as readily forgiven for the worst of crimes as for harbouring heretics. We are cautioned against receiving your tracts on pain of excommunication; and, sure, if I knew any one Roman Catholic who receives those tracts (cursing them), I would go direct to the priest and lay information. The Lord be merciful to us, you fellows are the plague of our lives. You are worse than the parsons, for the like of you get into the people's houses and into their good graces. Bad luck to you, you make the people uncomfortable and uneasy. Get along with you; I have no common patience with you. Your day will soon come. I heard Father —— say so the other night.' Here the old woman left me, having worked herself up into a perfect frenzy.

" 'So you think we are not right, and that the blessed Virgin has nothing to do with our salvation? I think a precious sight more of the Mother than of the Son, for, sure, He would never have been born but for her. In heaven she asks Him for us, and no prayer can reach Him but through her; and when we go to purgatory it will be a consolation to know that we have so many good priests begging the Mother to beg the Son soon to purify us.' I now attempted to refer them to the Word of God, but was assailed by the other as follows:— 'Sure, is it the Bible you refer to—that awful book of yours? I went into St. Saviour's Church the other day (that church which you (with an oath) Protestants rob- bed us of), on purpose to see Bishop Bonner's chair and his judgment-seat, and I sent up some Paternosters and Ava Marias, that another Bishop Bonner might be raised up to get rid of that ˏbook of yours, and get rid of every heretic out of the land. We are told by Father ———— to pray, and we do—yes, all of us pray that it may soon come to pass.'

" 'Well, what have you there? I suppose "The Irish Schoolmaster" (alluding to the tract bearing that title). Murphy read it the other evening, and, sure, we are all mad against him. Ought not the stone thrown at him and the other at his wife to have settled their business? but the devil favours them that's wrong, and then makes them prosper.' 'But what did he wrong?' 'Sure, and he read the Scriptures, contrary to the rules of the Church and orders of the priest.' 'But we are com- manded by Christ to search the Scriptures.' 'Away with you, you lying heretic; it is not for the like of us, but the priests only.' And here he left me; his passion had overcome him. A person to whom I had given the tract had lent it to him."

But even from such apparently unproductive depths as these, something was to be had.

"This is a most remarkable instance of the power of truth when accompanied by the Spirit of God. Mr.——, an Irishman, living in No.——, —— Place. I found him deplorably ignorant, and I had difficulty in making him understand the most simple language. All he could do was to repeat a few Ave Marias. He had never had a copy of the Word of God, but after a few visits he consented to accept one; and he had it read to him, and the Spirit of the Lord applied its truths to his heart, and the most pleasing of all inquiries was heard, 'What must I do to be saved?' He became a Christian, left the Romish Church, and attended where he could hear Christ and Him crucified preached. Affliction overtook him, and, being in adverse circumstances, he was obliged to go to the workhouse. He recovered, but kept in the house. He was permitted to have a holiday. I called to see him, and was rejoiced to find him in such a happy frame of mind. He said, 'I am happy. Oh, what a treasure Christ is. Strange that I should have been ignorant of Him for so many years, and what wonderful love His must be, to have mercy upon one who, for seventy years, had no love for Him!' 'Are you happy in the house?' 'Yes, with one exception. There are so many wicked characters, and their bad language grieves my very soul; however, I do what I can to show them their error, but they say I am too quiet a man; but, poor things! they don't understand why I am different.' 'God's grace has done it.' 'Well, sir, I can't do much by argument, but I hope what few days I have to remain on earth, to live to Christ. And do seek out those poor creatures who are deluded like I was. I know the difficulties you have to contend with; and the emnity there is in the hearts of all Catholics against the Bible, and the simple truths of the Gospel. They are taught it. I know I was. Well, here am I, a sinner plucked out of their clutches, and out of the clutches of the devil, thanks be to God and to you.' A few weeks elapsed, the old man was taken suddenly ill, and soon expired. His last words were, ' Unto Him that loved me and washed me, &c., &c., be glory for ever and ever.'"

Oh ! that we all had that holy venturesomeness for Christ—a spirit within us ever thrusting us forth into the deeps ; thence should we draw some souls at least for Christ ; thence should we win great honour and profit for ourselves ; for that which we catch for Christ, we catch also for ourselves; Christ's glory is His people's gain.

Be encouraged, dear reader, by what you have already perused of the work of the Lord in the depths ; perhaps some once hardened creature's eyes, albeit long unused to tears, are destined to fill and overflow with affection to *you ;* perhaps some now tightly compressed lips are destined to quiver, when you announce that your work is done, and that you are coming to visit the garret, or the cottage, no more again. Oh ! these are but little things compared with pleasing Jesus, and winning fresh glory for Him, and rescuing souls from eternal woe ; but still they touch the sensibilities of the heart, and surely the vibrating chords sound forth, " Launch out into the deep" —fear not the storms—the height above is greater than the depths beneath ; Jesus Himself has been out upon those very waters long before any of us; there rises not a billow over which He has not ridden; there sinks not a hollow into which He has not descended, "Follow me, and I will make you fishers of men!"

Now let us consider *some of the characteristics of this fishing work,* and this consideration will embrace in it some of the requirements of the fishermen. One great requirement is faith—expectation—yea, even belief that we shall assuredly catch fish. Whatever may have been our miscarriages and failures in ourselves, we also must be ready with our "Nevertheless;" "Nevertheless at thy word I will let down the net." The full belief that we shall catch fish will often energize us to go forth; when if we had not this inducement we might be inclined to stay at home. If it be well known that the fish are going, the fisherman will always turn out; the fish of the fishers of men are always going; they might be almost said to be swimming even around our very doors. Hope cheers the fisherman almost more than the man of any other calling in life; he is always hoping to get a haul of fish; if he be fishing with a net, he does not know the moment when he will meet with a shoal of fish; if with a hook, he cannot tell how soon he will feel the jerking of his line. There may be, there no doubt is uncertainty; but that very uncertainty keeps the fisherman's heart from despair. But the *hope* of the fishers of fish, must turn into *faith* in the fishers of men; we must make sure that we shall catch. And we must not allow ourselves to doubt of success, because we can see nothing; we may die in the very act of hauling the net; we may never see its living freight brought to the surface of the water; but other hands will bring in the fish,

and God will not forget that we hauled the net. If they
who tarried by the stuff, [1 Sam. xxx, 24,] had their
share of the spoil as well as they who went forth to the
battle; and if, while one soweth and another reapeth,
both sower and reaper rejoice together; surely he who
hauled at the net shall not be forgotten, because others
bring in the fish. It may be our part only to let down
the net; or to give a long, strong pull, and die at the
rope, seeing nothing; but when the fish are brought to
land, our share of the profit shall not be held back; the
great master of this superhuman craft will apportion to
every man his reward, and accurately mark out the
part which he has had in bringing about the great result.

There is no doubt that discouragements will meet us
in our work; these discouragements are in themselves
very provoking, and often arise from sources whence we
should never have looked for them; but we must
remember that the Great Fisher of men took experience
of them, and wrought through them; and He shall see
of the travail of His soul, and be satisfied; and so
shall we.

The history of the Lord's servants is full of discouragements; and thanks be to God, of their triumphs
also over them. Let us look at a few instances; when we
see how others have been tried, we shall be the less down-
hearted and discouraged, if we be tried ourselves.

In one of his summer excursions, Romaine was invited
to preach at Bootle, in Cumberland. On ascending the
pulpit stair, he found the door would not open. The
churchwarden observing him pull hard, but in vain,
immediately suspected that a blacksmith in the parish,
who was a great enemy to the gospel, had played them a

trick; and quietly asking the clerk to sing a long psalm, ran away to get pincers and hammer to open the pulpit door. This was done, and Mr. Romaine preached to the great edification of the people.

At Saint Dunstan's, the rector refused the pulpit to Mr. Romaine, though appointed lecturer, and seized it while the prayers were being read, in order to prevent his occupying it. When the rector was compelled to give him the pulpit, he appointed the lecture at an inconveniently late hour; and the church doors were shut against the congregation till the last moment. The consequence was, that hundreds, perhaps thousands, crowded around the walls, and rushed in like a torrent the moment the doors were opened. The Bishop of London (Dr. Terrick), who had known Romaine at Oxford, and honoured his learning and abilities, happened to be passing by Saint Dunstan's church before the service began, and observing the immense crowds, and the church doors shut, inquired the cause of such an assembly. On being informed, he required the church-wardens to see that the church doors should be opened at a proper time, and the lecture be permitted to commence at an earlier hour.

Hannah More experienced like trouble; and on one occasion, the assaults of the enemy were met in rather a ridiculous way.

Of a certain place at which they were endeavouring to establish a school, Hannah More writes:—"Last Sunday, Drewitt preached an hour; after he had finished, the clerk got up and said, 'The parish are desired to meet next Friday, to consult on the best means of opposing the ladies, who are coming to set up a school.'

Bold Drewitt, nothing dismayed, stood up instantly in the pulpit, and said, 'And on Sunday next, the parish are desired to meet the ladies who intend opening the school, at nine o'clock!'"

Scott, the commentator, was driven almost to despair : "I had," said he, "at this time many instructors as to my style of preaching; and some of the directors assumed rather a high tone of authority, while others were disposed to counsel me as the messengers of Ahab did Micaiah. But I disposed of the dictating instruction very shortly, saying, 'Gentlemen, you possess authority sufficient to change me *for* another preacher, whenever you please; but you have no power to change me *into* another preacher. If you do not convince my understanding that I am in error, you cannot induce me to alter my style of preaching.' The vexations, however, which I continually experienced, often overcame for a period my patience and fortitude. On one occasion they led me to say to my wife, 'Whatever be the consequence, I will quit this situation, for I shall never have any peace in it.' But she promptly answered, 'Take heed what you do; for if you leave your station in this spirit, you will, perhaps, soon be with Jonah in the whale's belly.' The check was seasonable, and procured my acquiescence."

None ever met with such discouragements as our blessed Lord Himself; but He toiled on; remembering that He came to do His Father's will, whatever aspect human affairs might wear. "It is enough for the disciple that he be as his Master;" and it will sweeten our lot, if we think that we are sharers of it with Him.

Another characteristic of this fishing work is *labour*. It is laborious work. And this idea of labour is very strongly brought before us in Matt. ix, 37, 38, where our Lord says to His disciples; "The harvest truly is plenteous, but the labourers are few; pray ye therefore the Lord of the harvest, that He will send forth labourers into His harvest." The idea here, as also that in the similitude of the fisherman, is one of toil.

Now this labour embraces going to look for the fish, as well as hauling the net; and, in truth, very little is done without going to look for souls; they seldom swim into our net; rather do God's toiling servants draw the net round them; and perhaps, after a long and laborious haul, bring them to the shore. It is needful to go out into the highways and hedges and compel them to come in. And God seems to bless all the aggressions of His church upon the world; aggression is often the best defence; if the gospel were more used for purposes of assault upon the powers of evil in the world, it would be assaulted far less than it is. Its supineness invites attack. The Christian should be found with the sword of the Spirit, as well as with the shield of faith.

And very wonderfully does God seem to bless the labours of fishers in the present day, who launch out into the deep, and let down their nets for a draught. There is many an one who was never bred to the sea, but who can yet lend a hand to haul a net; and a vast blessing seems to rest upon the labours of many such in the great spiritual fishing of the present day. There is scarce a single new agency upon which the blessing of God has not manifestly rested; and every one of these agencies are aggressive. The "Irish Church Mission" is aggressive, and draws its broad net through the teeming multitudes of our Romish neighbours; the "Midnight Mission" is aggressive, and warily pilots its craft through shoals and quicksands; the "Bible Women" are aggressors, and navigate the intricate windings and turnings of St. Giles', and other localities less known, but equally in need; and so we might catalogue the names of aggressors of this kind, until we showed how great a fleet had put to sea. All these are out after the fish, and verily they have met with goodly shoals.

Let us take one instance of the success of this launching out into the deep, we are indebted to the "London City Mission Magazine" for it; to no better source could we go for instances of success in this class of work:—

"The opening of the Standard Theatre for a second series of special religious services, has been a great blessing to this neighbourhood, doing much towards turning this fountain of evil into a positive good; and being situate in the very centre of the district, I felt that when the committee asked me again to undertake the management of this important effort, it was my duty to accept the invitation, although doing so involved a considerable amount of mental and physical labour.

"How God smiled upon that effort is well known. The people were glad to find a place of worship where rags might find admission; where all seats are free, and the poorest made to feel he was heartily welcome. An average attendance of 2,000 persons has been obtained, of the very class who usually shun the house of prayer, and pass the Sabbath hours in vain attempts to find pleasure in worldly occupations. This large number of persons always maintain the most perfect order and decorum. The police in attendance have never been required to interfere in any single instance; the entire work of keeping order, distributing copies of the hymns, etc., being carried out by a body of twenty working men, selected from the congregation itself, under the superintendence of myself and a brother missionary.

"In the course of my daily visitations many of these persons were met with, and many proofs given that they had not heard in vain.

"One man said, 'I see'd you at the Standard on Sunday. I say, didn't that parson walk into me pretty tidy about swearing, eh?' I replied, 'Well, I hope you have left off that sinful habit.' 'Ah!' said he, 'that ain't so easy to do, guv'ner; but I tell yer what, I don't say one bad word now where I used to say ten.'

"A poor woman said, 'Oh! sir, my home has been a happy place on Sunday; for my husband goes to hear the preaching, and always comes home sober. I go as often as I can, and we send our children to Sunday school.'

"The man now acts as one of the stewards at the Theatre, and attends my meeting as often as his work will permit. His wife has recently passed through a severe illness, during which I visited her constantly, and am encouraged to hope that both will ultimately be led to decision.

"Another person remarked, 'I am so glad you have got my son to come to the Theatre. He was brought up in a Sunday school, and led to a place of worship; but he 'went wild,' and made me very unhappy; but now he is quite steady again, and I hope he will be a comfort in my old age.'

"Observing among the congregation two young women, who came regularly every Sunday, I had some conversation with them, and invited them to my meeting. After coming a few times, they brought father, mother, and a friend with them, who for many weeks were attentive listeners to my instruction. They now attend a regular place of worship on a Sunday, and manifest an earnest, inquiring spirit. The father has since been severely afflicted, and appears to be drawing near to death. I find his mind directed to the true source of consolation, and am led to believe that he is truly converted to God.

"Another interesting case is that of a lame beggarman, who attended the special services, and also my weekly meeting for a considerable time. He wore no hat, coat, or waistcoat, but was always very clean, and remarkably attentive to the service. He told me, that he had often longed to enter places of worship, but was not able to do so on account of his wretched appearance; that he feared to come into the Theatre, until one of the stewards invited him; but he was so pleased with what he heard, that he stayed in London all the summer in order to attend the services. At his earnest request I supplied him with a Bible, which he kept carefully covered, and brought under his arm every Sunday; and some friends who have met him in the street, tell me that the Bible and tracts which I have given him are always found in the bottom of the box which contains his matches, laces, etc., for sale. The result of their conversation with him confirms my own opinion, that he has been brought to believe in the Lord Jesus. Having no settled home, he was compelled to endure much persecution in the lodging-houses where he slept. I suppose he has now gone 'on tramp,' as I have not seen him for some time.

"These are a few of the most prominent cases; but, in many other instances, it was found that persons who neglected public worship for many years have acquired the habit of going regularly to the Theatre services every Sunday evening.

"Recently a prayer meeting has been held after the sermon, to which from 600 to 800 persons have usually remained, greatly interested in such an unusual and solemn service.

"A man, more than fifty years of age, came to me at the close of the prayer meeting, a week or two since, saying that he had never been at a prayer meeting before in all his life; and that what he had heard had so impressed his mind, that he felt most anxious to become a Christian. While he spoke the tears ran down his cheeks as he said, in a tremulous voice, 'I want to know how I can find Jesus.' He is now an attendant at the district church where he resides, and also comes to my weekly meeting. I trust that, in the prayerful use of these means of grace, the way of life and peace will be made plain to him."

A goodly sight we deem it, to see the houses of God which are sown broadcast over the land; we love to see the church's stalwart tower with buttress and battlement, as though garrison were kept for God in an enemy's land; we love to see the church's tapering spire, shooting upwards to the skies, vanishing in airy lightness to a glittering point, as though it would show to man, how all of earth grows less and less the nearer we approach

to heaven; but we have a sentiment above that sentimentality; the deep sentiment of the pricelessness of an
immortal soul; and we believe that he who offers the
water of life to perishing men in a wooden bowl, or even
as it were only in the hollow of his hand, does better
than he who says, 'if thou wilt not drink from a consecrated chalice, then perish in thy drought, thou shalt not
drink at all!'

In this fishing for men, we must expect to have
tossings to and fro, and it may be, even to soil our hands.
There are entries which are full narrow for fashionable
skirts! But is it reasonable that this, which is labour,
should be made an exception to all other labour? and is
it reasonable that what men and women so cheerfully
accord to the toil of pleasure, they should be loth to
accord to the toil of earnest work?

"Excuse me, madam, but what is all that mess?"

"I have taken to photography."

"Dear me! you have quite stained your fingers."

"Oh! one can't help that in photography."

"And dear me! what a disagreeable smell."

"Oh! 'tis nothing when you are use to it."

"And what a troublesome process it seems to be."

"Oh! we can't do anything in this world without
trouble."

"No, dear madam, no—and with not a whit more
trouble, mess, or smell, we could show you how to make
photographs (sun pictures)—the picture of the blessed
Jesus, taken and printed in light upon many a soul that
is now perishing for lack of knowledge."

And thus we might go on, through all the toil of
life's amusements and pursuits, and ask, alas! only too

many, 'Does not what you undergo in earth's toil and
pleasure, (if you be doing nothing for your Lord,) shame
you in the excuses which you make for declining all toil
for heaven?' When Louis Marie, the Montreal colpor-
teur, was subjected to very ignominious treatment, he
never complained. One evening when he returned
home, he was asked what kind of day he had had? He
replied, with a face full of quiet Christian joy, that 'he
had had a very good day, having only been kicked
twice.' Alas! how many are there who would not consider it a good day, if they had to pass an unswept
crossing, or to whiff an unsavoury smell. Many of our
fears are imaginary; they are merely bug-bears raised
up by the enchantments of the devil; they vanish on a
near approach; we may have a very little to endure after
all; but at any rate, we do not know what we can endure
until we try. Take courage, dear reader; in a tossing boat
you may catch much fish; and all the while you yourself
be safe.

Do not be afraid of venturing upon a few visits for
the Lord. There was in a certain minister's district a
public house, in which neither the landlord nor his wife
were professors of religion. It was quite a resort for the
thoughtless and profane, and he dreaded visiting the
place; but conceiving it to be his duty, he nerved himself
up to the task. He was respectfully received and invited
into the sitting room, where he found the tavern keeper
and his wife alone. He conversed with, or rather talked
to them about the interests of their immortal souls; endeavoured to shew them the responsibility of their
station; and urged them to give immediate attention to
the things which belonged to their peace; but could get

no other answer than a promise from the landlord that
he would think of it. He left the house with a heavy
heart, feeling that he had done them no good.

They soon left the place, and the minister knew
nothing of them until ten years after his visit, when he
received a very kind note from the man, informing him
that the conversation which seemed to be so little regarded,
had resulted in the conversion of both himself and wife.

But in this work we must make up our minds to
exercise *patience* and *perseverance.* These are qualities
pre-eminently required in natural fishing, and in spiritual
fishing too. We shall accomplish very little by mere
dabbling as it were with our hands over the sides of the
boat.* The fish may be near at hand, swimming all
about, and looking on with amazement at this strange
phenomenon; but they will not be so captivated by it as
to come near and be caught. He who would fish successfully, must fish in earnest. Now see how patient
and persevering a fisher of souls was with one poor
creature, and how successful in the end; and may this
account cheer us on, when like fish come to our net.

"It was on the 18th of May, 1848, that I commenced
my labours in the district, and on that day I called at
No. —, —— row, which was occupied by a family of the
name of ——, and was informed by a little girl that her

---

* We read that the Rev. Charles Simeon kept the picture of Henry
Martyn in his study. Move where he would through the apartment, it
seemed to keep its eyes upon him, and ever to say to him, *Be earnest,
be earnest; don't trifle, don't trifle;* and the good Simeon would
gently bow to the speaking picture, and with a smile reply, "*Yes, I
will be in earnest; I will, I will be in earnest; I will not trifle,* for
souls are perishing, and Jesus is to be glorified."

mother was not at home. But I soon became well
acquainted with this family. The husband held a situation under the Custom House, and the wife, who was a
stay and corset maker, I found was an inveterate
drunkard, and the dread of the neighbourhood. The
babe at her breast (with the rest of the children) was
deserted night and day by her, while she would be out
getting drunk, and sometimes she would strip herself of
all but two articles of dress for drink. Then the husband
would shut her out, would not allow her to enter his
house, and would declare that she should never darken
his door any more. At these seasons she went about
without stockings or shoes; and being tall, she had rather
a masculine appearance, with a loud, sonorous voice.
She would be seen going through the streets, followed by
scores and sometimes hundreds of children; and, making
a stand here and there, she would make an oration.
Then the rude boys would be calling out 'Polly Long
Stockings,' and behave in the most indecent manner.
In the neighbourhood of Spitalfields, Whitechapel, Hox-
ton, and Kingsland, she was well known by the lowest
of characters, as well as where she lived; and with the
respectable, she was the dread of the neighbourhood.
She would thieve, commit adultery, or do anything for
strong drink. The police stood aloof from her, and
dreaded to have anything to do with her; but sometimes
they were compelled to lock her up and imprison her.
I often visited, warned, exhorted, and counselled her, and
she would express a desire to amend. Sometimes, when
her husband had turned her out, she came to me and
promised fairly; and I have gone and reasoned with him,
and asked him to try her once more. He was a boister-

ous man, and sometimes I had been fearful that he would knock me down, when I have called on him respecting his receiving her home again, and he has said; 'Ah, the rascal! don't mention her to me any more; she's a disgrace to me. If I leave a penny, to buy a little milk for the baby, she'll spend it in the cursed drink. I'll have no more of her!' Early in the morning of the last day of 1848, having been shut out for a long time, she called on me, and begged that I would go and see her husband, and ask him to allow her to come home; promising never any more to have anything to do with intoxicating liquors. I told her that it was useless, for he had said to me that while he had an arm to his body, she should never live with him again. Three times that day she called on me, making the same request. At last, taking the delicate condition in which she was into consideration, I said, 'I will call on him once more, but I expect that he will knock me down.' I went, telling her to be close to the house, so that if I did succeed, I might introduce her. I got him to consent to her request, and stepped out and called her in. I said, 'Mrs. ———, this is your husband. Sit down and tell him what you have said to me.' She did so. I read Ephesians v. The husband and wife kneeled with me in prayer, and the scene was most affecting. Rising from his knees, he wiped the tears from his face, and said, 'May God grant it!' But six weeks had not quite elapsed, when three days after her confinement, she broke out again, and became, if possible, worse than she had been before. But, passing over nearly seven years of her life, (with the exception of thirteen months, during which she kept sober, and got a good business together in the stay and corset making,) she went on in this dissipated career, in and out of prison and the union, a walking pest to society, and a corrupter of morals. In November, 1855, she came to my house in a fearful plight, and asked me to try her once more. I said, 'Well, Mrs. ——, my Master received the outcast, and I must do the same.' I read and prayed with her, and promised to see what I could do for her. The next day she called again, and signed the pledge of total abstinence from all intoxicants. I asked a poor man, eminent for piety, to take her in, as he had a room to spare; both he and his wife consented, and I arranged to pay them 1s. 6d. per week rent. Friends to whom her case was known supplied her with work, and I got her husband to pay her rent, unknown to her. She now went on well. Sometimes she received a friendly visit from her husband, and on the 24th of December that year she was welcomed home again by him. All proceeded well till May, 1856, when she broke out once more. She had tasted the insidious drink, and, in a few days, all her clothes, and everything she could lay hand on, was sacrificed at the shrine of Bacchus. Her husband had now become a witness to her unfaithfulness to him, and she was not allowed to enter under his roof. A gentleman who lived near them, and was continually being annoyed by her brawling, being a guardian of Hackney Union, got her admitted into that institution. As she had forfeited all claim on her husband, she was passed to her native parish, at Doncaster. She remained in that 'union' but a short period, and, at leaving it, she went to Liverpool to reside with a relative. While there she sent me a letter, and entreated me to watch over her children, and to tell them

that she still had a mother's love. They had removed off
my district to Cambridge Heath; and I went, in com-
pliance with her request, and saw her children, but not
one of them seemed to have the least regard for her. I
heard no more of her till the autumn of 1858, when she
had managed to walk from Manchester to Homerton,
dressed in a short dark skirt, a man's jacket, a bonnet,
and a pair of Yorkshire wooden clogs. When she started
from Manchester she was penniless, and she commenced
to beg. Six different persons gave her a halfpenny each,
and she bought three pennyworth of matches and began
trading. She sold them, and bought some bread, and a
fresh stock in trade. Thus she managed to get to the
metropolis once more; and having done so, she took to
selling stay laces, and, in the course of her daily rounds,
Hackney claimed her attention. Many who knew her,
pitied her, and out of compassion bought of her. At
night she lodged in some of the low lodging houses, pay-
ing 3*d.* per night for shelter. When sober she was highly
gifted, clean, and industrious, and none of her companions
in vice would dare to visit her. She was a good manager,
and understood the science of domestic economy; and
now, having kept sober a few weeks, she gained a little
more sympathy from those who had long known her in
Homerton, and she felt that she was not entirely forsaken.
A Christian woman offered to lend her a bed, and she
took a room for herself, went out charing occasionally;
and, by this means, she managed to get a few things to
make a decent appearance once more; she came to me
and signed the pledge, and attended my meetings, and,
subsequently, public worship. After a few months she
made herself look quite respectable, and there were

grounds to hope well of her. She attended the ministry
of the Rev. J. Davies, and manifested a growing interest
in the things of God. About this time, she felt that she
had gained a little standing in society; she had worked
hard, and fared harder still, till she had got a room nicely
furnished by her own industry. The gospel so faithfully
preached by her minister had reached her heart with
power; and she felt an increasing desire to do something
for the good of her fellow creatures. She came to my
temperance meeting one evening, asked permission to
address the meeting, and we arranged for her to do so the
next Monday evening. It having been announced that
'Mrs. —— was going to speak next Monday evening,'
when the time came the room was crowded; and while
she portrayed the evils of drunkenness, and what she had
undergone herself, many a hard heart was touched, and
their eyes melted to tears. A second address was
delivered with the same effect, on which occasion she
brought a large coloured engraving of our Lord and the
Twelve Disciples at the 'Last Supper,' and showed it to
the audience: telling them that such pictures were pre-
ferable to her than any of 'the publican's stuff which they
sold to ruin men's souls and bodies.' The desire she had
now to do good, was as great as it was before to do evil.
Humbled under a sense of her crimes and guilt, she now
was enabled to look unto the Lord for strength to support
her. Her struggles for a subsistence were great; sometimes her fare was a little bread, weak coffee, and a red
herring, which she sometimes cut in two, three, or four
pieces, each to serve a day, according as the case might
be with her finances, till she had got her things around
her comfortable. She kept away from her husband and

family, but felt desirous to do them good; and, having obtained some tracts, she went to the docks, where her husband was on duty. She distributed them, and gave one to an officer, saying, 'Will you be kind enough to give this tract to Mr. ——,' mentioning her husband's name. She then put her veil up over her bonnet, and passed by her husband without speaking. Shortly after this, she met him at Victoria Park, and walked out of it side by side with him, silent. At another time she met him as she was leaving the street in which she lived; they both smiled at each other, and he asked her where she lived. After this he visited her frequently.

"I called on her one morning, and found her ill in bed, when she showed me two new hymn-books which she had received as a present from her minister. She said, 'I very much prize them.' She spoke of her past life; of the great change which she by the grace of God had experienced; and of her hope in Christ alone for salvation. Subsequently her children were reconciled to her, and at the request of my dear wife they visited her. The eldest son, who, after the example of his father, had often bruised her flesh by his blows, and had enlisted in the army, was glad to receive shelter from her for himself and his child; and found he had a friend and a faithful adviser in his once degraded and maltreated mother. It was early one morning in March, 1860, that she called to inform me that her husband was taken very ill, and she was anxious for me to visit him, as he would not allow anyone else to visit him. I went and saw him, and read a portion of the Word of God to him, warned and exhorted him to repent of his sins, and seek the Lord Jesus Christ as his Saviour. He was glad of my visit, and sent for his wife to come to nurse him during his affliction. She complied with the request; and now a scene, which angels must have beheld with delight, was transacted in that abode. The wife of his early fondness had returned,—humble, penitent, and a new creature. The husband, still impenitent, allowed her to take the precious Word of God in her hands to read to him; and was glad to see and hear her at his bedside, on her knees, pouring forth ardent petitions to Almighty God in his behalf. His eyes being opened, he saw the fact that his wife, after all her faults, was a changed woman; and had, by the grace of God, been preserved to him to comfort him in his last days. He told his children to take her advice now, for it would do them good. He recovered from his illness, and occasionally went with her to the house of God. She gave proof of the stability of her character, and saw the minister respecting her being admitted into communion with the people of God. But that step was not hastened. It was thought advisable that she should be long tested, ere that privilege should be afforded her. Her walk was steady and consistent; many highly respectable ladies who knew her, took a very lively interest in her; and with wonder they beheld the power of Divine grace in her soul. She warned and exhorted others of the evils of sin; and made reference to herself as an instance of what the grace of God could do, saying, 'God has done it.' But as with the lovely flower, which is easily nipt by the wind's untimely blast, so was it with her spiritual career on this earth. I heard of her being taken ill, and called to see her. I found that she had been ill a fortnight, and that her husband, who, a week after she had been taken ill, was fondling over her, had been taken ill of the virulent fever and erysipelas, and had died on the evening before I got there, and was in his coffin. She had been unconscious during the whole of the time; did not know even of his having been ill; and was still insensible. Two days after, she died, and on Sunday, October 21, they were both buried together at Victoria-park Cemetery. So that, instead of her joining in holy fellowship with the Church militant on earth, she speedily was taken to join the Church triumphant in heaven; and the plant of the Lord's own planting was removed to bloom in the paradise of God. On the day of their burial I made known in the district that I was going to speak on their solemn deaths, and the meeting-room was crowded. There were some of the most hardened sinners in the district present, who appeared to be impressed by what I said to them from the word of God. May the Lord in mercy grant that many souls like hers may be saved in like manner, who may be our crown of rejoicing at the great day of account."

Or take the case of the old woman who kept a stall in Shoreditch; in one little alley she had lived for fourteen years, and she was a well known character in that neighbourhood for levity and irreligion. In writing of her, the missionary who visited her, says:—

"The heathenish state of her mind was most painful to witness. A Christian lady observed to me some time ago:—'I was asking myself the other day, can it be possible that such a creature really has a soul?' Yes, it was true! within a casket so begrimed, so repulsive and uncouth, there was a precious gem, which the Holy

Spirit could bring to light,—a heart which the love of
Jesus could warm and expand? Many a time, when
invited to the meeting, she has said, ' Oh yes, I mean to
give yer a turn some day;' and, when hope was almost
extinguished, she came at last to redeem her promise.
She was pleased with what she heard; for, when
leaving, she said, as she dropped a curtsey, 'I shall
come agin, 'cause I understands what you say.' Accordingly, she has continued to come; frequently bringing a
companion with her. I do not think she has been once
absent since her first coming; and the same lady remarked
to me the great alteration in her behaviour, saying, 'I'm
very glad —— comes to the meeting; she tells me about
what you say; and I really think that the Word has taken
root, and light is breaking in upon her dark mind.' She
now goes regularly to church on Sunday, and has induced three other poor persons to accompany her, both
to the church and to the meeting-room."

There are some souls which are to be eventually won
only by patience, labour, and perseverance; they are
slow in listening, and then slow in acting; and it may
be, that even when they do act, it is with indecision and
irregularity, and many slips and backslidings, before
they come fairly out for Christ; but just as the fisherman does not cease to haul at the net, because the
fish plunge in its toils; so the one who fishes for men
must not cease to work, because he has to deal with
some one who gives him trouble; it is often found that
the heaviest fish to secure are the most valuable when
they are brought to land.

Let us but attach real value to the fish; let us but
have design and unity of purpose as regards catching

them, and we may all of us do great things for God. If
we esteem souls as of great price, we shall be earnest in
our efforts to catch them; and God will supply us with
opportunities enough. We need not go out of our way
to seek them; they will ever keep presenting themselves
to us day by day; he will be found to have lived a
glorious life indeed, who has availed himself of every
opportunity which presented itself of winning souls.

Dr. Spencer, in his "Pastoral Sketches," gives us an
instance of success in fishing; the result, with God's
blessing, of *perseverance*.

The young man of whom he tells, "belonged to a
pious family; his parents and several of his brothers
were members of the church; he was a moral, staid,
industrious, intelligent young man, always attending
church, and was a teacher in the sabbath school. I had
not supposed that his feelings of opposition to religion
had ever assumed the strong character which he described to me now; and I had never known the means
of their alteration. I happened to ask him:—

" 'Mr. H——, what was it that first called your
attention definitely to religion, when you began to make
it a matter of your personal concern?'

" 'I found there was no escape, I could not get away
from it.'

" 'What do you mean, when you say, there was no
escape?'

" 'Why, the subject met me everywhere. Wherever
I went, there was something to make me think of it.'

" 'Yes,' said I, 'there are things to bring it to mind,
all around us and always, if we could heed them. God
has filled His world with things suggestive of Himself.'

" 'Oh, sir,' said he, 'I don't mean *that* at all. It is true that *now* almost everything makes me think of God and my duty: but I mean things that were done *on purpose* to catch me. It seemed to me that I was pursued everywhere. There was no getting away. If I went to church on Sunday, you never let us off with a descriptive or literary sermon, like a college professor; you always had something about faith, or repentance, or depravity, or the duty of sinners to fly to Christ. If I went to my store on a week day, thinking I should escape there, because I had something else to attend to; my partner would have something to say to me about religion, or something to say in my presence which I knew was meant *for me*. If I met you in the street, you were sure not to let me pass without bringing up that subject in some way or other. If I went home to dinner or tea, religion would be talked of at the table. If I was spending any part of the evening in the family after I left the store, it was the same thing again: religion, religion would come up; every one had something to say which made me think of religion. If I went off to bed, (as I did many a time to get out of the hearing of it,) my sister had put a tract under my pillow. I could not bear all this. I often avoided everybody, and went to my room, where I could be alone, and think of what I pleased; and *there* the first thing to meet me would be some religious book, which my mother or some one else had put in the place most likely to attract my attention; and perhaps left it open at some passage marked on purpose for me. After several of my young associates had become Christians, and began to talk about religion, I avoided them, and sought other company, and pretty soon *they* began to talk religion too! I was provoked at it!'

" 'Did these people, who endeavoured to influence you, treat you rudely or impolitely?'

" 'Oh, no! that was the worst of it; I hoped they would. If they had been meddlesome and impudent, I should have had something to find fault with; and should have told them to mind their own business, and keep their religion to themselves. I should have said, that religion makes men ungentlemanly, and unfit for society; and so should have excused myself. But there was none of that. There was little said to me. All that was done, was only calculated to make me think *for* myself, and *of* myself; and so I could not complain. But religion came up before me on all sides; whichever way I turned, morning, noon, and night, it was there. I could not escape it.'

" 'Did you have a strong *desire* to escape it?'

" 'Yes, I had. I turned every way. I avoided Christians. One Sunday I stayed away from church; but that contrivance *worked the other way*, for I could think of nothing but religion all the morning, and so in the afternoon I went to church, to see if I couldn't forget it there. When I came home I went into an· unoccupied room, because they began to talk about the sermon in the parlour; and the first thing that met me was the Bible, laid open at the 2nd chapter of Proverbs, and a pencil-mark drawn round the first six verses. 'This is some of mother's work,' said I. Finally I resolved to sell out my store, and get away into some place where I should not be *tormented about religion* any longer. I began to make arrangements for selling out.'

" 'Well, sir, what altered your mind?'

" 'Why, just as I was in this trouble to get away from religion, resolving not to live any longer in such a place as this; I began to think what I was after, why I desired to get away. And then, I soon found out it was because I desired to get away from the truth, and away from God. That alarmed me, and shamed me. I thought, then, that if there was no escape from men here, there could be no escape from God anywhere. And though it cost my pride a hard struggle, I made up my mind that I was all wrong, and I would attend to my salvation. Then I began; but I don't think I ever should have begun, if I had not been hunted in every place where I tried to escape.'

" 'Did you have any more temptation to neglect religion after that?'

" 'No, I immediately took my stand. I went among the inquirers openly. Then I was disappointed to find how little I cared any longer for the world, for what people would say, and all such things, as I used to think would be great trials to me. And I believe *now* there is very much gained by getting a sinner to *commit himself* on this matter. Then he will not wish to get off.'

" 'What way do you think is most likely to succeed for inducing any one to commit himself, to attend to his religion?'

" 'Oh, I cannot answer *that*. Any way is good, I suppose, which will lead people to *think*. Judging from my own experience, I should suppose that no irreligious person in the world could put off religion any longer, if his way was hedged up as mine was, so that he could not avoid *thinking* of the subject.'

" Such was a part of my conversation with him.   He
united with the church; and I have some reason to
suppose, that since that time he has aimed to 'lead
people to think,' in such a manner that there could be
'no escape.' "

And now, we turn to *the appliances of the work*—the
nets and hooks wherewith we must go forth as fishers of
men.   These appliances lie ready to the hand of every
one who is willing to go forth and fish for men; none
need stand idle for the want of means wherewith to
work.   Tracts, sermons, conversations, giving and lending good books, rightly spending money for the Lord;
these are some out of the many appliances which are at
hand for whosoever will fish for men.

Many a soul has been won for God in ordinary
conversation; how many in deliberate conversation upon
divine things?   Whoever has a tongue, has a net either
for good or for evil; for winning souls for heaven, or for
seducing them into hell.   The human tongue has in all
probability swept more souls into perdition, than any
other implement of the devil.   "Death and life are in
the power of the tongue:" Prov. xviii, 21.

Experience shows us that there is much need of skill
in the use of this net; but this skill will be always
vouchsafed of God.   The fish are wary; and| it is only
by keeping our one point in view, and steadily turning
always to it, no matter how often we have been foiled,
that we are at all likely to succeed.   Many a time has
the writer been kept half an hour, before he could
succeed in getting the conversation with some sick
person to be decidedly upon the concerns of the soul.

Now and again we seemed on the very verge of what we desired, and then some trivial remark sent us as far away again as ever. Our course was like that of the Israelites in the desert, continually towards the promised land—and almost touching it—and then going back as far as ever again. No more curious book could be written than the conversations of a minister with such persons, *up to* the point where he succeeded in making it bear upon spiritual things.

We must not be discouraged because no immediate result seems to follow upon our conversations for God. We cannot tell when they will turn up, nor when they will open the way for further progress in divine things.

'A missionary called many times upon a certain woman with tracts, and although she received them, it was generally with reluctance. He had almost despaired of ever being any real benefit to her, for though she did not persecute, there was an awful aversion to the truth; and he could never get beyond the street until the hand of God was laid upon her. He was then requested to call and see her; and, to his great surprise, found her in concern about her soul. Her affliction was severe, but it was not that that caused her anxiety, but her everlasting welfare. *What had been said to her at the door had made on impression on her mind not easily to be got rid of*, and her grief was, that she had not yielded to the convictions under which she had been labouring, and that she had not admitted him when she ought to have done so. Her anxiety increased, and with it her affection for God's people. The following are some of her remarks:—Her daughter, who is averse to what she calls 'nonsense,' reproved her for admitting the missionary, and she replied, 'Ah, my child! I know one thing, and I would give the world to know another: I am a sinner—I feel it, I know it; oh, that I could feel that mercy is in store for me!' At another time, in speaking to a relative, she said, 'Never, no never, despise the servants of the Lord; listen to them, they are your best friends; I have found it so.' Indeed, she preaches Christ to all who come to see her."

Perhaps it may be only one word, or one sentence that will hook the fish, as was the case in the following instance:—

" 'How glad I am to see you, Mr. T.!' said a sick woman to a city missionary; 'I'm always glad to see you now; but you know that I didn't used to be so. I didn't like to see you come. I used to think I know'd everything when you came to talk to me, but now I'm different; I see I know nothing at all. Years ago, when I went to your meeting one Sunday night, you spoke on the flood, and you spoke about Noah's carpenters being lost, who had helped to build the ark. I was led to tremble then; but you know, though I promised then to lead a new life, I soon forgot all about it, and went on in sin like a poor, blind old sinner. But that often com'd into my mind *about Noah's carpenters being lost.* I couldn't shake that off. I've thought on it hundreds of times. And though I went on in sin, you know I wasn't happy; I was miserable at times. But ever since you read that chapter about the Pharisee and the Publican, I've been led to see what a poor, vile, and ignorant old sinner I am. 'Twas that chapter that opened my eyes. I thank God that you ever com'd. Now I feel that I want more faith.

I want to feel like as the poor Samaritan leper you spoke of on Sunday evening; and I want to cast myself at the feet of Jesus, with gratitude for what He have done for me.' Her love for the means of grace and for visitation is very great, and she often says, 'Do come and see me as often as you can. It refreshes my soul so to see you, and if I can get out at all now, and can only as it were crawl, I feel that I must and do come to hear you.' She has recently been very dangerously ill, but her faith and hope in the Lord Jesus have been manifest to all around her. She is able with St. Paul to say, 'I know in whom I have believed, and am persuaded that He is able to keep what I have committed to Him against that day.' She is well known to several, who take a pleasure in visiting her, and listening to some of her pithy sayings about what the Lord has graciously done for her soul. His grace is triumphant in her, and makes her glad in God her Saviour."

Conversations will often remain in people's minds, even though they wish to get rid of them; and who can tell the moment when they will turn up?

And bear in mind, dear reader, that the whole thing may be done by a solitary observation or remark.* You

* Here is a good example of following up well an original remark. "Travelling once on the outside of a stage coach, I said to a man, who for a few miles happened to be my only companion, 'Do you care anything about your soul?' 'What is that to you!' he replied, in a tone and manner which he evidently thought would silence me. I at once remarked that certainly it must be of far greater importance to himself than it could possibly be to me; but that if I, a perfect stranger, felt any interest in the question, how much more ought he to feel, since it mainly concerned himself! 'Upon my word,' said the man, 'there is something like good sense in that.' He then listened attentively to

need not be a logician; you may perhaps have no power
of sustaining conversation; you may perhaps be wholly
destitute of brilliancy; one sentence,* even one word,
may do the work. It was to a single sentence that
Merle D'Aubigné owed his conversion. The following
gives us this part of his history:—

"When M. Monod and I," says he, "attended the
university at Geneva, there was a professor of divinity
who confined himself to lecturing on the immortality of
the soul, the existence of God, and similar topics. As to
the Trinity, he did not believe it. Instead of the Bible,
he gave us quotations from Seneca and Plato; Saint
Seneca and Saint Plato were the two saints whose
writings he held up to admiration." And thoroughly did
the disciples enter into the opinions and spirit of their
master. About the time of Mr. Haldane's arrival in
Geneva, there appeared a pamphlet, entitled, "Considerations on the Divinity of Jesus Christ," by Henry
Empeytaz. This pamphlet produced great excitement
among the students in theology, to whom it was
addressed. They assembled in the grand hall, chose

all I had to say. In the course of my address, I saw him try to conceal an unbidden tear; and when he left the coach, which he did at
the next market town, he said, 'Good morning to you, sir, and many
thanks for your faithfulness.'"

* "A number of intimate friends being at dinner on the Lord's day,
one of the company, in order to prevent improper discourse, said, 'It
is a question whether we shall all go to heaven or not.' This plain
expression occasioned a general seriousness and self examination. One
thought, 'If any of this company go to hell, it must be myself;' and
so thought another and another. In short, it was afterwards found,
that this sentence proved, by the special blessing of God upon it, instrumental to the conversion of many."

for their president, one of their own number, and
addressed to the "Venerable Company" a letter, in
which they solemnly protested against what they termed
"the odious aggression." The foremost man on this
occasion, the chosen president of the assembled students,
was no other than Merle D'Aubigné. "But the Lord
sent one of His servants to Geneva," he says, "and I
well remember the visit of Robert Haldane. I heard of
him first as an English or Scotch gentleman, who spoke
much about the Bible, which seemed a very strange
thing to me and the other students, to whom it was a
shut book. I afterwards met Mr. Haldane at a private
house, along with some other friends, and heard him
read from an English Bible a chapter from Romans
about the natural corruption of man—a doctrine of
which I had never before heard. In fact, I was quite
astonished to hear of men being corrupt by nature. I
remember saying to Mr. Haldane, 'Now I see that
doctrine in the Bible.' 'Yes,' he replied, 'BUT DO YOU
SEE IT IN YOUR HEART?' *That was a simple question,
but it came home to my conscience.* It was the sword of
the Spirit; and from that time I saw that my heart was
corrupted, and knew from the Word of God, that I can
be saved by grace alone."

There are often little helps in the way of circumstances which we may avail ourselves of, as in the
following instance, and they will prove very helpful.
The fisher for men should turn everything to account:

A young man who had graduated at one of the first
colleges in America, and was celebrated for his literary
attainments, particularly his knowledge of mathematics,
settled in a village where a faithful minister of the

220 THE "I WILL" OF SERVICE.

gospel was stationed. It was not long before the clergyman met with him in one of his evening walks; and
after some conversation, as they were about to part,
addressed him as follows:—"I have heard that you are
celebrated for your mathematical skill, I have a problem
which I wish you to solve." "What is it," eagerly
enquired the young man? The clergyman answered,
with a solemn tone of voice, "What shall it profit a man,
if he shall gain the whole world and lose his own soul?"
The youth returned home, and endeavoured to shake off
the impression fastened on him by the problem proposed
to him, but in vain. In the giddy round of pleasure, in
his business, and in his studies, the question still forcibly
returned to him, "What shall it profit a man, if he shall
gain the whole world and lose his own soul?" It finally
resulted in his conversion, and he became an able
advocate and preacher of that gospel which he once
rejected.

Many a time has a word turned and shaped the
whole course of a man's career on earth; a word has
made, and a word has unmade him; cast in as your
hook, even a single word; you know not, perhaps you
never will know until eternity, what it will bring
forth.

In Madame Guyon's life, we meet with a very interesting case of the value of a conversation, and especially of
seizing an opportunity. Such opportunities are often
very short, as in the present case. In June or July,
1671, a letter was brought to Madame Guyon from her
half brother, Father La Mothe. The bearer was La
Combe, who was then young, but came highly recom-
mended from La Mothe, who wished his sister to see

him, and to regard and treat him as one of his most
intimate friends. Madame Guyon says that she was
unwilling at this time to form new acquaintances; but
desirous of corresponding to the request of her brother,
she admitted him. The conversation turned chiefly
upon religious subjects. With the clear insight of
character which she posessed, she could not fail to
become deeply interested in La Combe, as one on whom
many religious interests might depend. But still she
could not at that time fully decide whether she should
regard him as truly a possessor of religion, or as merely
a seeker after it. "I thought," she said, "that he either
loved God, or was disposed to love Him; a state of things
which could not fail to interest me, as it was the great
desire of my heart, that everybody should experience
this Divine love." As God had already made use of her
as an instrument in the conversion of three persons,
members of the religious order to which he belonged,
she indulged the hope that she might be made a benefit
to him. And although she says she felt a reluctance
to begin the aquaintance, she now felt a desire to
continue it.

La Combe left her, but he was not satisfied. Providence had brought him in contact with a mind to which
either grace or nature, or both in combination, had given
power over other minds. He desired, therefore, to see
more, and to hear more. And, accordingly, on the basis
of the acquaintance which had thus begun, he repeated
the visit after a short time. Madame Guyon remarks
that La Combe, who seems to have been a man not only
of intelligence, but also of vivacity and generosity of
feeling, was very acceptable to her husband. On this

second visit, he conversed with her husband freely. During the interview, he was taken somewhat unwell, and with the view of recovering and refreshing himself in the open air, he went out and walked in the garden. Soon after, Madame Guyon, at the particular request of her husband, went out for the purpose of seeing him, and of rendering any assistance which might be needed. She availed herself of the opportunity which was thus afforded, to explain to him what she denominates the interior or inward way, *la voie de l'intérieur;* a way which is inward, because it rests upon God, in distinction from the way which is outward, and which rests upon man. He was prepared to receive her remarks, because he inwardly felt the need of that form of experience which was involved in them, and because he perceived from her countenance, her conversation, and her life, that she possessed that of which he felt himself to be destitute. *La Combe always admitted that this conversation formed a crisis in his life.* Her words, attended by Divine power, sank deep into his soul. It was then and there, that he formed the purpose, with the Divine assistance, to be wholly the Lord's. "God was pleased," says Madame Guyon, "to make use of such an unworthy instrument as myself, in the communication of His grace. He has since owned to me, that he went away at that time changed into quite another man."

To these we may be permitted to add the following illustrations :—

"When on a journey for my health in 1812," writes a Christian minister, "on a hot sultry day, I called at a farm house in one of the beautiful towns in Berkshire county to procure a drink of water. There happened to be no one in the house but a young lady, apparently about sixteen years of age, to whom I was introduced by my travelling companion, and from whom I received a glass of that refreshing and healthy beverage which flows in such rich abundance from the hills of New England.

"As I arose to depart I took her hand, and said; 'Permit me, my dear girl, before I leave you, to enquire whether you have yet given your heart to your precious Saviour?'

"She replied in the negative, while the tear that stole down her cheek showed that she was not without feeling.

"I then said to her, 'My child, I am a minister of Jesus Christ; and as such it is not only my duty, but my privilege, to offer you eternal life, upon the condition of your repenting of your sins, and putting your trust in Him; will you accept of this offer?'

"She answered with deep emotion, 'I cannot decide that question now.'

"I said, 'You will have to decide it now. Jesus Christ is beseeching you by me, to be reconciled to God; and if you do not choose to tell me what your decision is, He will take the answer from your heart; and it will be recorded in heaven, that you have either accepted the offer of eternal life, made to you by your Redeemer to-day, or that you have rejected Him again.'

"She seemed to take a new view of her fearful responsibility, and wept convulsively; but could not be prevailed on to tell me what her decision was.

"After repeating some appropriate passages of Scripture, to show her her duty and her danger, I left her, expecting to see and hear of her no more, until we should meet at the judgment seat of Christ.

"Years afterwards, on stepping upon a steam boat in New York to go to Philadelphia, my name being called by some of my friends on board, a gentleman came up to me, and asked if my name was Wisner. On being answered in the affirmative, he inquired if I had ever been in the town of ——, Berkshire county. I told him I had passed through it in 1812. He then informed me, that when he was coming from home, a lady requested him, if he should meet me on his journey, to say, that she was the individual who gave me the glass of water; and what I had said on that occasion sunk so deeply into her heart, that she could find no rest until she hoped she had closed in with the offer of her blessed Lord; and that she wished me to accept her thanks for what was to her, truly 'a word spoken in season.'"

*   *   *   *   *   *

"In 1815, while spending a Sabbath in a place where they had no stated preaching, I put up with a deacon in the church, whose sister-in-law had come from a neighbouring town to spend the Sabbath with him. She was a gay thoughtless girl of about eighteen years of age. Knowing that her widowed mother was a pious woman, and felt anxious about her daughter, I wished to have some personal conversation with her before she went home. She seemed to be aware of my intention, and so entirely avoided me, that I had no opportunity of speaking to her, until she was ready on Monday morning to return home. When she started, I accompanied her to the door, and as I assisted her to get on her horse, I told her that I was deeply concerned for her soul; I felt that she was in imminent danger, and entreated her to remember her Creator now in the days of her youth. She made me no answer, but rode off; and I felt that I had lost an opportunity of doing her good.

"About a year afterwards, I was sent for to administer the sacrament to that church; and after the preparatory lecture, the deacons told me there was a candidate to be examined, whom I found to be the young woman who had so skilfully avoided me on a former occasion.

"On inquiring what it was that first called her attention to her lost condition, she informed me that it was the few words I said to her, when helping her on her horse; that they rang in her ears all the way home, and deprived her of rest until she found it in Christ. Her successful evasion of a more deliberate conversation, was doubtless employed to bring a brief word home the more forcibly to her unguarded heart."

"A number of acquaintances and friends had assembled to spend a social evening together. In the course of the evening they resolved to have a dance, and prevailed on Michael Onions (the man at whose house they were) to go out a distance of two miles to procure a fiddler for them. On his way he met a stranger, who, having missed his road, requested Michael to direct him to Madeley. Michael readily consented to do this, and walked about half a mile with him for this purpose. The stranger ascertained the errand on which Onions was going, and began to talk to him about his soul, showing him the unsuitableness of such follies to a dying man, his need of salvation and a personal interest in

Christ, and his awful danger as an unsaved sinner.
When the stranger left Michael, the conversation had so
impressed him that he dared not proceed on his errand,
but returned to his home. When he opened the door,
his friends inquired,

"'Have you brought the fiddler?'

"He answered, 'No.'

"'Is he not at home? Have you been to Brosely?'

"'No,'

"'Why, what is the matter? you look ill, and are all
of a tremble.'

"Michael then told them that he had met somebody,
but whether a man or angel he could not tell; he never
before heard such a man. He repeated what had been
said to him on spiritual subjects, and added, 'I dare not
go to Brosely; I would not for the world.'

"The party was broken up. The next Sabbath
Michael and some of his friends attended Madeley
church; and there, in Rev. John Fletcher, the new vicar,
he recognised the stranger who had conversed with him.
The impression wrought on Michael was lasting in its
character, and, under the influence of the Holy Spirit,
led to his conversion. He became a zealous, devoted, and
useful Christian. 'A word spoken in due season how
good it is.'"

The late Bishop Wilson, of Calcutta, tells us that an
observation was the means of his conversion.

"One evening I was as usual engaged in wicked
discourse with the other servants in the warehouse, and
religion happening (humanly speaking I mean) to be
started, I was engaged very warmly in denying the
responsibility of mankind, on the supposition of absolute

election, and the folly of all human exertions, where grace was held to be irresistible. (I can scarcely proceed for wonder that God should have upheld me in life, at the moment I was cavilling and blaspheming at His sovereignty and grace). We have a young man in the warehouse whose amusement for many years has been entirely in conversing on the subject of religion. He was saying that God had appointed the end; He had also appointed the means. I then happened to say that I had none of those feelings toward God which He required and approved. 'Well, then,' said he, '*pray for the feelings.*' I carried it off with a joke, but the words at the first made some impression on my mind; and thinking that I would still say that I had done all I could; when I retired at night I began to pray for the feelings. It was not long before the Lord in some measure answered my prayers, and I grew very uneasy about my state."

He who is inclined to fish for souls may also *make use of good books*, and that with great success. Many souls owe their salvation to good books.*

* A poor pedlar, a humble but zealous Christian, stopped at the house of a rich man, and tremblingly knocked at the door. The master himself came and purchased a tract, called the "Bruised Reed," by Dr. Sibbs. He threw it carelessly aside, and thought no more of it; but the Lord had destined it to an important end. That small despised tract the rich man's son saw and read, and, by the Holy Spirit's power it became to him the means of saving grace; that son was the celebrated Richard Baxter, who wrote the "Saints' Rest." But the conversion of one soul does not end there; that soul is much concerned for the souls of others, and seeks to know what the Lord would have him to do, and in a variety of ways his influence spreads.

"Years of despondency passed over John Bunyan before he came to the enjoyment of the peace of the gospel. The light which first stole in upon his soul, and in which his darkness finally melted away, was a clear discovery of the gospel of Christ; more especially a distinct perception of the dispositions which He manifested while He was here on earth. And one thing greatly helped him; he alighted on a congenial mind, and an experience in many respects like his own. Providence threw in his way an old copy of Luther's 'Commentary on Galatians,' 'so old,' he says, 'that it was ready to fall piece from piece, if I did but turn it over. When I had but a little way perused the book, I found my condition in his experience so largely and profoundly handled, as if his book had been written out of my heart.'"

It was while reading a book that Colonel Gardiner saw the celebrated vision which issued in his conversion. "Towards the middle of July, 1719, he spent an evening of folly with some of his gay associates. The company broke up about eleven, and at twelve he had made a criminal appointment. The intervening hour must be bridged over by some employment. A pious mother had, without his knowledge, slipped into his portmanteau

Baxter is dead; but he has left us his "Saints' Rest," which was the means of converting Dr. Doddridge. That holy man died; but the mantle fell on others, the influence did not fail, for he left us his "Rise and Progress of Religion in the Soul," and that conveyed the flame to that holy politician and zealous Christian, Wilberforce. He also died; but his influence was not extinguished, for his "Practical View of Christianity" communicated Divine light to Legh Richmond, who now lives in his "Dairyman's Daughter," and other works, to convey comfort, and perhaps conviction, to many hearts. All this had its rise in one "small tract."

Watson's 'Christian Soldier, or Heaven taken by Storm.'
The title attracted him, and he expected some amusement from its military phraseology. He took it and
read, but it produced no seriousness nor reflection.
While the book was yet in his hand, however, impressions were made on his mind, the fruit of which
must be regarded as the best index to whence they came.
Whether he was asleep or awake at the time, he felt
it afterwards difficult to determine. But if asleep, so
vividly was what he saw and heard impressed on his
mind, that it seemed to be a waking reality. He thought
he saw an unusual blaze of light fall on the book while
he was reading; which he at first imagined might happen
by some accident in the candle. But lifting up his eyes,
he apprehended, to his extreme amazement, that there
was before him, as it were, suspended in the air, a visible
representation of the Lord Jesus Christ upon the cross,
surrounded on all sides with a glory; and was impressed
as if a voice, or something equivalent to a voice, had
come to him to this effect:—'O sinner! did I suffer
this for thee? and are these thy returns?'"

The issue of this vision was, that Colonel Gardiner
became a converted man; and lived to the glory of God
for many years.

Sometimes an isolated passage in a book will do the
work either of convicting or comforting; one sentence
may be fruit bearing, when many pages seem dead.
"Miranda N.," says a Christian minister, "was about
eighteen years of age, much distinguished for personal
beauty, but more for uncommon sweetness of disposition, and great amiability of deportment. There was not,
perhaps, amongst all the people of my charge, one whose

case would have been more promptly cited and perhaps none so effectively, to disprove the doctrine of the entire sinfulness of the unregenerate heart. She was deservedly a general favorite. She seemed to entertain the kindest affection toward all; and every one who knew her loved her. One evening, at an inquiry meeting held at my house, I noticed in a full room, a female in great apparent distress; her loud sobs were a frequent and painful interruption of the silence of the room. On coming to her seat, I was not a little surprised to find myself by the side of Miranda. The first inquiry I put to her was this: 'What has brought you here, Miranda?' With emphasis, she replied, 'My sins, sir.' With a view to test the reality and depth of her convictions, I then said, 'But what have *you* done which makes either your heart or life appear so heinously sinful?' At this second question, she broke out into a voice that reached the extreme part of the room, and thrilled through every heart, for she was known and loved by every one present, 'I hate God, and I know it. I hate Christians, and I know it. I hate my own being. Oh! that I had never been born.' As she uttered this acknowledgment, she rose and left the room in irrepressible agony. A few minutes after this, while walking the adjoining room in great distress, her eye lighted upon a copy of village hymns, which lay upon the sideboard. She eagerly caught it up, and read at the first page, to which she opened, these words—

> 'There is a fountain filled with blood,
>   Drawn from Immanuel's veins,
> And sinners plunged beneath that flood,
>   Lose all their guilty stains.'

"As she finished this verse, she dropped the book and exclaimed, 'I have found my Saviour! This is the Saviour I need; O precious Saviour!' and many other expressions of the same kind. Her enmity to God was gone; her burden was removed."

A hymn-book has often been made the means of blessing. The case we have just referred to is by no means solitary. To it we may add that of a poor wretched female, religiously educated, but afterwards abandoned to sin, misery, and want. This poor creature was horrified at hearing her own child repeat, as soon as she could well speak, some of the profane language which she had learned of herself. She trembled at the thought that she was not only going to hell herself, but that she was also leading her child thither. She instantly resolved that with the first six-pence she could procure, she would purchase "Dr. Watts's Divine Songs," of which she had some recollection, to teach her infant daughter. She did so; and on opening the book, her eye caught the following striking verse:—

> "Just as the tree, cut down, that fell
> To north or southward; there it lies;
> So man departs to heaven or hell,
> Fixed in the state wherein he dies."

She read on; the event was blessed to her conversion, and she lived and died a consistent professor of religion.

The Rev. Mr. Lord, seaman's chaplain, at Boston, mentions a very interesting case of a man's conversion by a book; and of the conversion of a second man, through the instrumentality of the first; a book in this case also, being the means employed.

"The first of these men was converted by reading 'Little Henry and his Bearer;' he went home, but on reflection, made up his mind to go on board a man-of-war, for the purpose of doing good. He shipped at Charlestown, furnishing himself with tracts, Bibles, and the Society's volumes. The crew were so wicked, that at the end of nine months the chaplain was compelled to leave the ship; but this man, and one or two other pious men remained. At last God blessed him. One of the men was sent up to a foretop-sail as a punishment. He asked this man to lend him a book, which he did. He was a wicked man, and had been accustomed to read 'Tom Paine,' and similar works. But now he came down serious, and enquired what he should 'do to be saved.' God opened the windows of heaven; and in three weeks there were between twenty and thirty inquirers, and fifteen or twenty entertaining hope. There was great and continued opposition from the officers. But at the end of three years-and-a-half the vessel arrived; and eleven men, who had endured this fiery persecution all this time, sat down to commemorate the dying love of Jesus."

"When Flavel was in London, in 1673, his old bookseller, Mr. Boulter, told him that some time before, there came into his shop a 'sparkish gentleman,' to inquire for some play books. Mr. Boulter told him he had none, but shewed him Mr. Flavel's treatise of 'Keeping the Heart,' entreating him to read it; and assuring him it would do him more good than play books. The gentleman read the title, and glancing upon several pages here and there, broke out into these and such other expressions, 'What a fanatic was he who

made this book!' Mr. B. begged of him to buy and
read it, and told him he would have no cause to cen-
sure it so bitterly. At last he bought it; but told him
he would not read it. 'What will you do with it,
then?' said Mr. Boulter; 'I will tear and burn it,' said
he, 'and send it to the devil.' Mr. B. told him, then
he should not have it! Upon this the gentleman
promised to read it, and Mr. B. told him if he disliked
it upon reading, he would return him his money. About
a month after, the gentleman came to the shop again in
a very modest habit, and with a serious countenance,
addressed Mr. Boulter thus: 'Sir, I most heartily thank
you for having put this book into my hands,—I bless
God that moved you to do it; it hath saved my soul.
Blessed be God that ever I came into your shop!' And
then he bought a hundred more of those books of him,
and told him he would give them to the poor, who
could not buy them."

A printed sermon of Whitfield's was the means of
a man's conversion, the circumstances of which we
give a place to here, because they show us what people
thought of real spiritual earnestness in those days; not
but that there are many who think Bedlam a very
suitable place for God's people, even in the present day.

"Joseph Periam, a young man in London, who had
read Whitfield's sermon on 'Regeneration,' became deeply
impressed by it; he sold all he possessed, and prayed
so loud and fasted so long, that his family supposed
him deranged, and sent him to the Bedlam madhouse,
where he was treated as 'Methodistically mad,' and as
one of Whitfield's gang. The keepers threw him down,
and forced a key into his mouth, while they drenched

him with medicine. He was then placed in a cold
room without windows, and with a damp cellar under
it. Periam, however, found some means of conveying
a letter to Whitfield, requesting both advice and a visit.
These were promptly given. The preacher soon discovered that Periam was not mad; and taking a Mr.
Seward and some other friends with him, he went
before the committee of the hospital to explain the
case. Seward so astounded the committee by quoting
Scripture, that they pronounced him to be as mad as
Periam. The doctors frankly told the deputation, that
in their opinion, Whitfield and his followers were really
beside themselves. It was, however, agreed that if
Whitfield would take Periam out to Georgia, his release
would be granted. Thus the conference ended, and
the young man went out as a schoolmaster at the
Orphan-Home, where he was exemplary and useful."

And in the present day there is (in this respect at
least) assuredly no lack of fishing gear. Of making many
books there is no end; the press is truly a mighty engine,
either for the ruin or the good of souls. There are nets
and hooks thus supplied to suit the calibre of every
fisherman, and the capacity of every fish; and we may
do much by lending or giving them away. And the book
will sometimes succeed where the tract fails; many a
cne will be pleased with a book that would be offended
with a tract. Sometimes more good is done by lending
a book than by giving it; when you get it back, it is
something like pulling in your line, you have an opportunity of seeing if there be anything at the end of it;
when your friend returns the book you will of course
ask him what he thinks of it; you will get into

conversation with him on it; you will possibly be ready
with some opinions of your own upon it; you will also
have at hand a second volume; and thus, a soul, perhaps otherwise inaccessible, may be won to everlasting
life.

A very cheap, easy, and successful way of fishing for
men, is by means of tract distribution. This mean of
usefulness is within the reach of every one who desires
to do something for the Lord; the daily walk or drive
will afford a ready fishing ground,* with this advantage,
that it is sure to swarm with fish. The author knew a
man who fished a good deal in this way, and, it is to be
hoped, not without success. On one occasion our dili-
gent friend saw a pair of breeches hanging up to dry,
and quick as thought, he popped a tract into the pocket,
let us hope with future edification to the owner; when
the wind was favourable he flew tracts over the walls of
the gardens of persons who would not be likely to take
them by hand; sometimes he twisted them into the
shape of a penny bag of sugar, or an ounce of tea, giving
them a good twist at the bottom, and a neat turn in at
the top; then again by doubling and redoubling them
until they were no larger than a child's marble, and
tying them compactly together, he used to shoot them
through the shop doors as he walked by, and behind the
counters, when a favourable opportunity offered; we

* In the Memoir of Francis Lewis Mackenzie, a young man of
great promise, we are told that "a number of tracts selected and
arranged for different ages, from adults down to the infant were in his
coat pocket, as left by him, when he undressed for the last time."
What a sweet evidence of readiness to be about the Master's business
in daily life; laying down the garments of daily life and the Master's
work *together*, to put on bright raiment and enter into rest.

have known him when waiting at a railway station insert them between the paper and the sugar loaf lying there to be sent to a neighbouring grocer; a rent in the paper affording a favourable opportunity; and many a poor gate-keeper upon the railways has received in the white shower which flew towards him out of the window of the train as it sped by, gospel messengers able to save the immortal soul. It is astonishing what can be done by practice. Our indefatigable friend attained to great skill in shooting his tracts and gospel pellets; in his line, he did as well as many a member of a rifle corps; making a good score upon coal waggons, market baskets, railway stations, and even through the hole of a street lamp, which the gasman had laid down for a moment, as it wanted some repairs. Wherever our friend saw any building going on, there he laid his tracts in the labourers' hods, and under bricks and slates which were sure to be moved. A new building was to him, much what a preserve is to a sportsman; eternity alone will tell the effect of what was found under the bricks. There are at the present moment some of our friend's tracts under hedge-side stones, which he does not expect to be found for some years; then he expects them to 'find,' as well as to 'be found.'

Surely we have no readers who are too timid to drop a tract upon the road; perhaps some one says, "but may be some one will pick it up and run after us?" Well! even if any one did, that would not hurt you; but we make every allowance for nerves; only we must not forget that nerves can be sent to school, and that if we begin at the alphabet of work, we may soon go on to something better. Let such an one begin to throw a tract when no one is in sight; then, when some one is coming on from a long distance; then, when some one is near; and so on; our friend in earnest, though feeble, will improve each day, and at last arrive at sufficient boldness to be able to get out, "May I beg your acceptance of this!"

"A minister was entertaining at his table another zealous minister of God—a young man, now very useful in France. He was desirous of knowing how his young friend had been led to Christ; as he had said that both his feelings and studies had kept him, for many years, far from the way of peace. 'The first impression made on my soul,' said the young minister, 'was, under God's grace, the effect of a small tract which I picked up from the highway side, near the village of Faong, in the Canton of Vaud, when I was returning from Germany.' 'Did that happen,' asked the master of the house, 'in 1826, and in the last week of October?' 'Precisely,' answered the minister, with astonishment; 'how do you know it?' 'Pray, were you dressed in a common travelling garb, with a knapsack on your shoulders, and a white cap?' 'Such was, indeed, my dress: but, again, how do you know it?' 'It was perhaps, also, that tract entitled 'L'épi Glané sur la Grande Route?' 'It was really: but I beg you to explain how——.' 'I will tell you, dear brother,' said the minister. 'I remember distinctly that at the foot of Faong hill, that very year, and the very week you speak of, as I was returning from Berne, I placed purposely, and with a prayer, the very tract mentioned on the left side of the road; hoping that a young man, whom I saw coming at some distance, would find it, and receive a benefit from it. And I remember that, as I was on the top of the ascent, I looked back, and saw the traveller bending, taking, and immediately reading the tract, and that I prayed again to the Lord that he would bless the reading.' 'Wonderful!' exclaimed the young man. 'How good is our Lord who prepared for us those spiritual ties; who has been pleased to show me my first unknown benefactor, and to encourage us to cast our bread upon the waters!'"

It is very true that if you pull out a little paper and offer some of its contents to your neighbour opposite you in the railway carriage, he will perhaps smile benignantly at you, if it contain sandwiches; and scowl unutterable things, if it contain divine truths; but remember, that where some refuse, some also take; and there is truth in what a tract distributor said, when he remarked, that if you offered tracts to people in a kind, and frank, above-board way, they seldom or never insulted you; but that people don't like tracts being given to them as though the person giving them were half ashamed of them himself. When a man has a genuine good article to dispose of, he is not ashamed of it; we know what we have to dispose of, even though it be by giving away; let us not be ashamed of it, as though it were some pinchback thing of little worth.

And here we may be permitted to express a wish that tracts were got up in a more attractive form than they often are; many an one will take a little book who will not take a tract; we also wish that where it can be conveniently dispensed with, tracts did not bear upon their very forehead their number and series. We believe that they would be much more likely to be effective if they came as isolated messengers, each complete in itself; many a man who gets hold of a tract marked, "Large Type Series, No. 8," or "Tracts to the Unconverted, No. 2," or "Wayside Leaves, No. 3," or some such inscription, feels that he is the victim of a system; he is not being grappled by a truth, or talked with by a friend; but he is being operated on by a system; and that he does not like.

Even hanging up a religious a'manac may catch a soul. "A question having arisen in a mess kitchen of the London police as to the date of some event, one of the men went to look at the almanac, but instead of answering the question, he by mistake read the text for the day. Its applicability struck some of them. It was talked about, and for a long time after some one was sure to call out at dinner time, 'What does the almanac say to-day?' The man in charge of the kitchen read the text. This often led to serious conversation, and eventually produced quite a reformation in the kitchen. So the almanac text proved a word in season."

It may seem unnecessary to speak here of *sermons* as gospel nets, to fish souls for heaven; partly because so few of our readers can fish in this way; and partly because the matter seems so self-evident. But alas! this great net is by no means as successful as it ought to be. The meshes of many a sermon are so wide that the fish can swim through them; the preacher is so vague and undefined that he misses laying hold of souls. This is the case even in the language that is used, especially where the knowledge of theological terms is assumed. On this subject Cecil spoke earnestly to Daniel Wilson, when he entered on his curacy.

"I particularly wish you would study hard to prepare yourself for this place. It is not enough that a man has good intentions. He needs also capacity, knowledge, aptitude, all which, you know, are greatly improved by study : and study itself much depends on method.

"Now, then, for the method. Go amongst the poorest and most illiterate of the people where you dwell, and let your subject of discourse to them be the solar system. Endeavour with great plainness to defend Copernicus against Tycho ; and make them thoroughly understand the difference and the superiority. Don't let one depart, until he is fully convinced that the sun must be placed in the centre. 'Stop,' say you, 'I shall never be able to make them understand my very terms.' 'No ?' Then invent new ones adapted to their capacity; for much easier is it to give people right notions of the solar system than of the gospel ; and far more willing will they be to let the SUN stand in his place there, than here. Pray, therefore, study hard : and in a way a college never teaches."

It is a great mistake to give even educated congregations absolute credit for a knowledge of such common terms as "justification" and "sanctification." It is easy to paraphrase these words, without any injury to composition ; and if any of our readers be in the ministry, and will only *try* how many of their congregations understand these terms ; they will, we are sure, see the need of keeping the *explanation* of them continually before their people.

It was the boast of the late Daniel O'Connell that he could drive a coach and four through any act of parliament that had ever been framed ; it may be boasted by

many congregations that they can go in and out through
the sermons they hear; the minister does not lay hold
of anyone, indeed he would be rather startled if he did.
Alas! how many ministers there are, who would be
amazed if some of their parishioners called upon them,
roused and startled by what they had heard from them
the previous day. Such would be almost as frightened
and flurried themselves, as their visitors are—they would
say to themselves, "What could I have said to make all
this disturbance? I'm sure, I did not mean to agitate
anyone"—the fact is, the sermon was never meant to
rouse anyone; and if the minister knew that it had such
explosive powers, he would have damped it down a little,
because he has a bad opinion of excitement in religion.
Preachers should ever have a fixed design in preaching;
aimless preaching will leave little result; they should
say to themselves, "what exactly have I tried to do to-
day; did I *aim* at rousing, restoring, or building up a
soul?*" In order successfully to make this sermon net, we

* The following answer might, alas! be only too truly given in the
present day. Dr. Sheldon, Archbishop of Canterbury, in 1675, on an
occasion when Betterton, the celebrated actor, was dining with him,
said, " Pray Mr. Betterton, inform me what is the reason you actors on
the stage can affect your audience with speaking of things imaginary ?"
" Why, my Lord," replied Betterton, " with submission to your Grace,
the reason is very plain : all lies in the power of enthusiasm. We
actors on the stage speak of things imaginary as if they were real;
and you in the pulpit speak coldly of things real as if they were
imaginary."

When the courtly Ridley complained of the little effect produced
by his sermons, old father Latimer told him that the fault lay in his
not speaking the *market* language, *i.e.*, what was understood by the
people.

must make the meshes close; and in order to use it, we must entirely forget self, in our earnest effort after what we can catch. What should we think of a man whose main anxiety was to show himself to the fish, and not to pull in the fish themselves? We should think him mad; but he would not be a whit more mad, than the minister who tries to get men to think of *him*, when he should be exerting himself to secure *them*.* And what should we think of a fisherman who purposely made his meshes so wide, that the fish could swim through; or who did not carefully close up every rent, so that none could possibly escape? Soul arresting, soul catching preaching is what we want. Let not the fishers of men be afraid of preaching a full law against impenitent sinners, and a full gospel for all penitent ones; let them show men their need of a physician, as well as the fact that the physician is at hand. Old Robert Flockart, who used to preach almost nightly in the streets of Edinburgh, and who was a persevering fisher of men, gives good advice to many preachers in this matter. "You never," said he, "saw a woman sewing without a needle! She would come but poor speed if she only sewed wi' the thread. So, I think, when we're dealing wi' sinners we maun aye put in the needle o' the law first; for the fact is, they're sleepin' sound, and they need to be awakened up wi' something sharp. But when we've got the needle o' the

---

* Such men sometimes come to grief. A story is told of a young minister, who ascended the pulpit full of self-possession and vanity; but, having been left to his own strength, quitted it humbled and hanging down his head; upon which an old woman whispered to him, "Ah, sir, if you had gone up into the pulpit as you came down, you might have come down as you went up."

law fairly in, we may draw as lang a thread as you like o' gospel consolation after it." There's many a man, who has clean made his escape from the ministry, because there were no law meshes to catch him. The gospel must be preached as all in all, but the gospel as made an imperative necessity by the law. It is a sense of the power of the law, that makes a man need the knowledge and power of the gospel. Take care, fisherman, that thy net be made of right materials, and woven with a close mesh, otherwise thy labour may be great, and yet thy fish be few.

And here it will be well to say a word or two upon the important subject of *mending our nets*.

We find in all earthly toil that no inconsiderable amount of time has to be spent in repairing the implements by which it is carried on. The mower spends one half his time in sharpening his scythe; the carpenter has often to stop to grind or sharpen his tools; the fisherman has to spend no little attention upon mending his nets. And as it is with them in their earthly, so is it with God's people in their spiritual toil; there is much to be done as it were in private, which if left undone, will cause the actual hours of toil to be without profit.

This is a point to which the attention of ministers might be profitably called in the present day. One of the chief characteristics of the present day is energy, action; ministers are compelled to head many parochial movements, to be up and doing in the various fields of charity and labour. To be here, there, and everywhere at one and the same time, is their duty, in the minds of unthinking, though perhaps pious and zealous men. The idea of "working" a parish is a good one in itself;

but it may, if carried too far, be productive of serious evil. And it *is* productive of evil. When ministers are always on their legs, and seldom on their knees; many times in the pulpit, few times in the study; continually talking, and not often thinking; always giving out, and seldom taking in; what can we expect but that they become blunt, like unsharpened tools, and ineffective, like unmended nets? A minister requires repairs as well as anybody, or anything else; the candle that is burnt at both ends, soon burns out.

But how shall we all mend our nets? most of this work is to be done upon our knees; the most tattered net can be made as good as new, if only we repair it on our knees. There, upon the knees, we get skill to piece in the old rent; and perhaps that piece will, when the net is next tried, turn out to be the strongest piece of all. We mend our nets also over our Bibles. Prepared work is generally effective work; we must not say of our materials "Anything will do." We mend them also by thoughtfulness over our miscarriages. It is by thinking over our faults, weaknesses, and failures, that we discern the flaws in our net; close them all up; and learn to avoid the like again. The time thus spent is well spent; for where this is neglected, then "the more haste, the worse speed." Let us think as well as act; pray as well as preach; prepare as well as work; the knees should prepare the way for the lips; the study should be the threshold of the pulpit; the net must be mended in quiet on shore, then it will stand the turmoil of the deep. Jesus Himself was much in prayer, and much alone; even in this respect His words hold good, "Follow Me, and I will make you fishers of men."

Those are weighty words of Cecil's. "I say every-where and to all, you must hold intercourse with God, or your soul will die. You must walk with God, or Satan will walk with you. You must grow in grace, or you will lose it; and you cannot do this but by appropriating to this object a due portion of your time, and diligently employing suitable means. I know not how it is," said he, "that some Christians can make so little of recollec-tion and retirement. I find the spirit of the world a strong assimilating principle. I find it hurrying my mind away in its vortex, and sinking me among the dregs and filth of a carnal nature. Even my ministerial employments would degenerate into a mere following of my trade, and crying of my wares. I am obliged to withdraw myself regularly, and to say to my heart, What are you doing? Where are you?'"

How can we more fitly close up this chapter, than by saying somewhat of the REWARD OF THE FISHERS.

There is a great variety and multitude of fish to be caught; "all sorts and conditions of men" lie before the fishers, to draw out from amongst them souls for Christ's glory and their own reward. Yes! look we where we will, we see fishes for the fisher's net.

Where will you cast your net? Down, deep into the dark abyss of vice, amid the almost unnameable outcasts of our race? Yes! there can be enclosed fishers for Christ; and thence can they be drawn, to increase for ever the wealth and glory of the fisher's joy. Courage, fishers in these deep dark waters! the records of the church are full of the experience of successful fishers, who have drawn forth these wonders of the deep. Even though you may have "toiled all night and caught nothing" nevertheless, at Christ's word let down your net for a draught, and you shall meet with great success. Who knows but that one rescued from such depths may be a mightier prey from the deep, than many who swam as it were in shoals hard by the gospel net? Let none persuade you, who are giving or working on behalf of these fallen ones, that because some fall back, none are saved; oh yes, they are; and from the harps of the redeemed there will be struck by their hands hereafter, perhaps some of their most wondrous tones; forgiven much, they love much; and their songs of praise have caught the tones of Him, who through our ministry spake to them in their sorrow, sin, and shame; and said, "Neither do I condemn thee, go and sin no more."

Where will you cast your net? Amid the vast multitude of fishes, and myriad shoals which gleam and glitter in the rippling waters, like silver spangles cast in lavish handfuls into the rising tide of life—amid the little children—those concerning whom the Saviour said, "Suffer the little children to come unto Me, and forbid them not, for of such is the kingdom of heaven?" Oh! God speed the fishers; there are great hauls for heaven to be made in these teeming waters. Little does it matter whether these children be ragged, destitute, and forlorn; little, that they be ill-taught, ill-tended, and ill-fed; they have that within them which is of amazing price; and lo! they are waiting as it were to be caught; and if you shoot wide your net—your close-meshed net —and encircle them for Christ, and draw them to shore for Him; oh; then shall you see how bright is your spoil; how well you are repaid. Myriads of children

shall doubtless be in the land of light, but amid those
myriads yours shall not be lost; that which you have
drawn forth from the deep for Christ shall be yours as
well as Christ's—His first, then yours; for your labour
shall not be in vain in the Lord.

Reader! vast depths teeming with life lie before
thee; cast thine hook, or shoot thy net into some of
them for Christ; if thou hast followed Him, it must be
to become a fisher of men. Fear not that exertions, or
money, or influence, will be ill-spent. The Lord's word
shall not return to Him void. How knowest thou, what
thou shalt catch? For aught that thou canst tell, thou
mayest bring to Christ some one who may consecrate a
great intellect, or great devotedness to His service. The
first young man reclaimed by a city missionary's instrumentality, from a very degraded and vicious life, after
spending several years in efforts to reclaim others, in
which he was much blessed, became a town missionary,
continued such for nine years, till his death; and was
followed to the grave by between 2000 and 3000 of
those he had visited; although numbers of them were
without shoes, and the snow at the time was ankle-deep
on the ground. His indeed was a funeral at once humble and yet noble, simple and yet grand; instead of
waving plumes, he had palpitating hearts; instead of
hired attendants, he had personal mourners; instead of
the wailing note of the cornet, and the boom of the
muffled drum, he had the cry of the sorrowing child, and
the sob of the stalwart man. No mourning coaches,
draped in black, ever left such a track behind them as
did the falls of the swollen, shoeless, livid feet of that
motley crowd in the yielding snow; no marble tablet

ever had recorded upon its fair white surface such a memorial as that snow had upon its downy breast! True! the first bright sun dispelled those foot-prints with his beams, (what need was there that they should tarry on the earth?) but the gratitude of which they were a record was sculptured indelibly in heaven; the types might well be broken up, seeing that a stereotype had been taken from them which could not be destroyed. Far be it from me to decry the splendid offering of a nation's gratitude in the public obsequies of the noble, the learned, or the brave; but when the time comes for me to be borne to my last home, let me not be followed by all the pomp and circumstance of woe, but by a sorrowing crowd like this; let me be laid in the earth, by those with whom I have affinities for heaven. Let my fellows' last farewell to me, be not the thundering of cannon, and the proclamation of the style and title of the deceased, but a silent look down into the grave saying, "We part with grief on earth;" and then a silent look upwards to the sky, saying, "We shall meet with joy in heaven!"

The "I Will" of Comfort.

—

JOHN xiv, 18.

JOHN xiv, 18.

"I will not leave you comfortless: [or, orphans,] I will come to you."

———◇———

ERE we have an "I will not," and an "I will," in close and significant conjunction. The one admits us into what me might, for our present purpose, call the passive, and the other into the active, side of Christ's love; the first gives us His knowledge, feeling, responsibility, &c., with regard to His people; and the second, the activity of His love. He will not leave them orphans, He will come unto them.

Reader, if you have become a disciple of Christ, peruse these pages, with reference to yourself, as well as those to whom the words we are now about to consider, were originally spoken. He who knows anything of the needs of the divine life will lay hold of such a promise as this, and take it in all its full teaching to himself.

And first, let us consider for awhile these blessed words, "I WILL NOT LEAVE YOU COMFORTLESS," or orphaned.

Look at the prospect that lay before the disciples;

whichever way we turn, it was a comfortless one: the loss of Christ was the loss of ALL—the loss of their head—the subtraction of the great object of life—the ·bereavement of themselves, so that they must be left in a condition of orphanage, with all the evils consequent on that helpless state. Jesus made a provision for all this gloomy prospect, when He promised that He would not leave them orphaned.

What a fearful loss would Christ have been to His disciples, had he gone away never to return any more! He was the head of this little family; to Him they had been accustomed to look up as Teacher, Lord, and All in All; in all their ignorances He was their adviser, in all their difficulties He was their helper; and although they were no doubt much to each other in holy brotherhood, still their relationship to each other was founded upon their common relationship to Him. Let Jesus be severed from them, let their bond with Him be broken up, and there remained nothing to bind them to each other. Oh! how sorely we miss the earthly head of a family, when he or she has filled up the headship in the way which God designed; we never know what such a head is to us, until it is lost; then, when the great void is made, and there is no one to look to for counsel, no one for action, when we are thrown back upon our own resources, we feel what it is really to be left *alone*.

Jesus knew well what would be the condition of His disciples if He left them thus headless; well did He know what He had been to them; He knew this, far better than they did; and, acting out of His own knowledge, He makes the promise, "I will not leave you comfortless." Is it not a comfort to us, also, that Christ acts towards us, even as He did towards those, His immediate disciples, out of His own knowledge. Jesus foreknows all that lies before His people, under such and such circumstances, and makes provision accordingly; it is as though Christ said, "I know what would happen if I were to leave you; do not fear, I will not hand you over to ruin."

Right thankful ought we to be, dear reader, that Jesus knows so much better than we do ourselves, what He is to us. We grow gradually into the knowledge of His headship—into the deep feeling of our own need of it; but He starts as it were with that knowledge, and He acts upon it, and is often acting in the power of His headship, when we are coming sadly short of acting in the power of our membership.

And it will not be amiss to pause for a moment, and ask ourselves, whether Christ be indeed our head; whether we feel Him in that relationship to us; whether, if He were removed, we should not altogether go to pieces. Are we amongst those who would sorely miss Christ, if He were to withdraw Himself and be gone? If we be, then we have this great comfort—Christ's knowledge always overpasses ours; He knows what He is to us, even better than we can know; and if we shudder at the thought of being left—left headless—our feeling about the matter is nothing compared with His.

But there was another very important point in which the disciples would have been left comfortless, had Jesus wholly departed from them; such a departure would have involved the *subtraction of the great object of their life;* the apostles must have been left aimless, objectless men. Christ had been the one prominent figure before them for many a long day; with Him they journeyed, with Him they rested; with Him they lived and moved and had their being, and every hope and thought were centred in Him. Mistaken though they were, about the immediate restoration of the kingdom of Israel, and their own consequent exaltation; still everything was connected with their great Master; and so to take Him away was to take all. Now we ourselves, perhaps, know in some measure, what it is to have a great object in life removed. Here is one who has planned, and laid out, and built for another; and now that other is gone; and the flower beds are colourless and scentless to him, and the rooms echo gloomily to the solitary footfall, and where every minute thing used to be of interest, now alas! everything oppresses; for the object for which all these things were, is gone. There is always some one object which is the mainspring of life; and when that is removed, the wheels stand still. The aimless, objectless man is generally a misery to himself.

Now, Christ foreknew what would be the misery of His disciples, thus left objectless in life. He knew that their nets could never be to them what they had been before, and that the receipt of custom had lost its exclusive charms; He knew, moreover, that it was He who had displaced these, as life's great object, substituting Himself in their place; and now, if He went away for ever, what remained for them but an aimless life and a miserable death. We cannot imagine Christ calmly contemplating this, without making provision for it. And all true-hearted disciples are very much in the position of those to whom our Lord here speaks. Jesus has become to them the great object in life; I do not say that He has taken away all life's interests, or that He has diminished the fondness of righteous affections, but He has placed Himself above them all; substituting Himself for whatever ruled the heart; and becoming THE object of that heart's affection, and that mind's thought; so that "they which live should not henceforth live unto themselves, but unto Him which died for them and rose again:" 2 Cor. v, 15.

Should these pages fall into the hands of any young persons, who fear that joining Christ in true discipleship involves great loss in the way of earthly interests; I would affectionately remind them, that Christ has effectually provided for this by *substitution*. He ever gives more than He takes; it is a fixed rule of the divine life, that none shall be a loser by Him. It is because they are ignorant of this substitution, that many are afraid of union with Jesus; nature abhors a vacuum, and they think only of what they shall lose, unmindful of what they shall gain. Just as the husband substitutes himself, and all his interests, and concerns, for the acquaintances and pursuits of unmarried life; and as this is no loss but a gain—again—when the husband is worth loving, so Christ substitutes Himself and all His interests and concerns, for that which formerly absorbed the heart; and when He does this, it must be to our gain. Now, the very fact of Christ's doing this, is in itself an argument against His so departing from His people, as to leave them comfortless; deliberately to make Himself all this to the soul, and then deliberately to go away, would be cruelty indeed; we are slow in raising expectations which we are not certain of being able to answer; shall Christ be less thoughtful than we? Not so. He substi-

tutes Himself, the imperishable One, for all that passeth
away. He gives Himself to His people as He is, "the
same yesterday, and to-day, and for ever."

Did not the blessed Lord Jesus Christ see also the
helpless condition of His disciples if He left them alone
in the world, to return to them no more? We know
that none are so helpless as the orphan: all the little
needs of daily life are seldom thought of by any save a
parent's head, all the little sorrows of life are but feebly
felt for, except by a parent's heart; and thus helpless
must the disciples have been, if their connexion with
Christ were now to be broken off by death. For who in
the world could supply their need, even supposing that
need were known? The wants of the disciples were
such as the world had no stores to meet; and this Jesus
knew; the aspect of a friendless, helpless family was
that which met His view, if His people were permanently
despoiled of Him. This is the picture which a deserted
people present even now to Jesus; this picture He will
never allow to become a reality, in the case of even the
weakest, and most friendless, of those who have cast in
their lot with Him. Be not afraid, dear reader, of ever
becoming a poor forlorn creature, if you embrace Christ;
friends, perhaps, threaten to desert; you may feel that
even in your own family circle you must stand alone;
Satan may work this thought in your mind, and say,
'How can you ever stand such a trial as this?' our
answer is that of the apostle, "I can do all things,
through Christ which strengtheneth me;" it is this, 'We
take the promise of Jesus to ourselves; we are His disciples;
His promise is to us also, as well as to the apostles,
"I will not leave you comfortless, I will come unto you."

Now let us look at this dreary prospect of orphaned disciples, *in its relation to the Lord Jesus Christ personally.*

Their Master was, if we might so speak, bound to take care of them, as He had influenced them to give up all for Him. We are ready to grant that that 'all' was very little; still it was 'all' to them; and God looks at all things relatively, as well as absolutely; He estimates that which is given according to the capacity of the one who gives. It is a very comforting thought that God looks at things in this light: that He puts His own and not man's value upon the two mites; that He knows our feelings, and what it may cost us to do, or give, or give up, anything for Him.

Whoever makes any sacrifice for Christ, comes forthwith into relation with Him in reference to that sacrifice; Jesus puts Himself in the place of all that we have given up; we have ventured in obedience to His word; it would be a horrible scandal throughout eternity, if any could point out a man who had been a loser by Christ. Christ will not disavow the consequences of the great act, by which we give up all for Him; He will never say, 'Your act was right, but as these are only the natural consequences of it, I have nothing to do with them;' oh no! Christ links Himself to the consequences of the great act, even as He is unalterably linked to the act itself. Whenever we can clearly trace a connection between our suffering, and the One for whom we suffer, we may always rest assured, that that One will never leave us nor forsake us.

And, surely, it has been the experience of God's people that Jesus has amply made up to them for any-

thing that they have given up for Him.   Hewitson gave
up every earthly prospect for Christ—the world, and the
things of the world; and what was his testimony?   " I
never have a moment's peace, when I return in the
slightest degree to conformity with the world; but I
always have great peace when my soul returns home to
its ' city of refuge,' the Lord Jesus Christ.   Communion
with Christ is the only source of satisfying, the only
source of lasting enjoyment.   I have enjoyed even more,
this morning, from beholding the loveliness and glory of
Christ, as revealed to me by the Spirit, than I have from
the world, during the whole of my life past."   And in one
of his letters to a college friend, he gives such a plain
testimony to the all-sufficiency of Jesus, as a supplier of
any void that is made for His sake, that we shall insert
it here.   " Do you recollect," writes he, " what converse we
often had together at —— on religious subjects?   That
converse was pleasant to me, and yet painful, for I was
seeking Jesus then, but I had not found Him.   I was too
ambitious of human honour, too fond of the world, to seek
anything else in Jesus, than a deliverer from the guilt
of sin.   I did not hate sin itself—I did not seek Jesus,
that I might be delivered from the power and dominion
of sin.   There was a vehement controversy between the
Holy Spirit, and my carnal nature in those days!   He
often drew me with loving kindness, but my neck was an
iron sinew, and I still willingly lay in chains of darkness, a slave to the beggarly elements of this world's enjoyments.   I did not lay to heart these words of Jesus,
' How can ye believe, who receive honour one of another,
and seek not the honour that cometh from God only?
I sought to believe, but the pursuit, or rather the thirst

of worldly honour made faith impossible. Glad enough
I would have been, if I could have followed Jesus, without being obliged to deny myself, and to take up the
cross. I was labouring under a strange delusion, for I
did not know that if only I were willing to leave all and
follow Christ, He would make the cross not heavy to be
borne, but a delight, more pleasant than to the miser is
his load of gold, or to the earthly monarch are his insignia
of power. I did not know what these words meant, 'My
yoke is easy and My burden is light.' Now I understand, that if we only be willing to give up all for Christ,
He is willing to give us more happiness, ten thousand
fold, than we give up for His sake."*

Jesus amply made up to Hewitson for all he gave up
for Him.

"Out of 365 religions in the world," said a highly
educated Jew one day to his beloved child, an accomplished and lovely girl of nineteen, as she was urging
upon him the wonderful graciousness of that Divine
Saviour whom she had found in the crucified Nazarene,
"I don't think yours the easiest; people have to work
so hard, and be so distressingly earnest, and so awfully
solemn; it makes me ill to think of it." "Ah!" replied
the youthful convert, "this religion is a very happy and
a very easy one. I have an inward peace and joy which
is unspeakable.   Jesus is precious; He is heaven;
He blesses me every moment. Oh! His boundless love
to me!"†

Jesus amply made up to this girl for everything she
had to give up for Him !

* "Memoir of Rev. W. H. Hewitson," p. 55.
† See "Memoirs of Adelaide Newton."

The truth is, the love of Christ as realized, is in itself an immense compensation for all we have to give up; yes, more than this, it has an expulsive power, so that it and the world cannot consort together; and hence we should always seek to win the young to give up the world, not by imposing upon them a system of prohibitions, but by bringing them into personal contact with Christ, by shewing them that Jesus will be better to them than all beside; that He will never allow them to say, "The old way was better; my new pursuit is a failure; Jesus is not as good as the world." "I cannot help thinking," writes Adelaide Newton to a schoolfellow, "that if you are much occupied with thoughts of heaven, of holiness, of the meek and lowly Jesus, and how he lived and walked on earth, you will feel a secret shrinking from worldly society, which will make balls, &c., very painful to you. God has left no positive commands upon things of this sort, for He knows that where the heart is given to Him, the life will assuredly be given too. And the motive of gospel obedience is not so much duty, as love. The child that loves its parents devotedly, or its friends, does what will please them at any cost."

This witness is true; the world is to be given up because of love; and that love supplies the great compensation for the world,—Jesus substitutes Himself.

"I can never be thankful enough," says Mrs. Hawkes, "that I am not obliged to waste my time in visiting and receiving visits. There was a season when I was as fond of doing so as anyone, but thanks be to my gracious Saviour, who has given me a new taste, new objects, new pursuits, new and true enjoyments. With my books I never find the day long enough, and the week is gone before I am ready for the end."

The time thus taken from the world was not given up as a prey to *ennui;* the gracious Saviour was present in the new tastes and new pursuits. Christ knows what anyone gives up for Him, and he knows also how to fill the void.

We must also bear in mind, that Jesus knew what would happen to these disciples, if they were left to themselves; they, the sheep, must be scattered abroad, if He, the Shepherd, were permanently removed. Now, Jesus knew well what lay before His disciples in their *upward* and *onward* struggle—a struggle on which He Himself had set them—a struggle for which they were wholly incompetent apart from Him. From Him they had received the mighty impulses of the new life; from Him, the visions of a noble future; they, like others, had through much tribulation to enter into the kingdom of God: and which of them were, in themselves, sufficient for these things? They needed their leader as well as their teacher, and Jesus would never leave them unled.

Let us contemplate also the difficulty which these disciples would have had in retaining their union with Him. When He had been taken from them by an ignominious death; when all the world hooted at them as the followers of a dead malefactor, how could they, by any mere force of natural character, have clung to Him? The trial would have been too much for human nature; it would have failed. In the religion of Christ we have to cling not only to a system, but to an individual—not only to a creed, but to a man; and if

the person were wholly taken away from the disciples,
what would have become of them?

Now Jesus well knows the difficulties which beset
His people in retaining their union with Him; He
knows also that the being linked to an abstraction—
a system of truth—will never carry them whither He
would have them be; and so He provides for His personal union with us now. We retain our union in the
power of a *personal* attachment to a living Being *personally* attached to us. Christ is the vine and we are
the branches; there must not only be vitality in us to
cling to Him, but there must be vitality in Him to
inject sap into us.

Remember then, dear reader, as you survey this side
of the subject, that separation from the world does not
involve a thoroughly orphaned or comfortless condition.
If you have broken off affinities with it, you have
become connected with higher affinities in Christ; ye
have meat to eat which the world knows not of. We
are told in Matt. ix, 25, that "when the people were
put forth, He went in and took her by the hand, and
the maid arose." How apt a picture is this of what we
are considering now; the putting forth of those who
can do us no good; the incoming of the One who
can. Only remember, that by our own fault we may
for a season be left comfortless; we may hide out our
spiritual affinity with our Saviour; we may not see
the One who lives for us, and still is ours, though
our eyes are so dimmed, that we know not He is
near.

Such a state of discomfort has ofttimes fallen upon
the people of God, but they have not been left in it

by Jesus; they have gone into it themselves. His promise is unbroken, though we are suffering from our sin. "Suffering! comfortless!" Yes, happy is he who is suffering and comfortless without his Lord, his cries and griefs are a witness that he lives. The existence of life may be manifested by a tear, as well as by a smile; by the voice of weeping, as well as by the voice of joy.

And now comes the promise of our Lord, "I will come unto you," or as it is in the Greek, "I am coming to you," for He would be so short a time away, that His future is as it were present.

What is this coming?

Whatever other meanings may attach to this promise, we must hold that the primary one has reference to Christ's personal appearance after the resurrection. The grief of the disciples was connected with the departure of their Lord; and that grief was primarily to be dispelled by His coming to them in person again.

We can easily understand how this reappearance of their Lord would comfort the disciples' hearts. Now first, *the great loneliness would be done away.* Death brings with it the most saddening loneliness which falls to the lot of man; and in proportion as we have allowed ourselves to be bound up in a single object, in that proportion comes the desolation of loneliness when that object is removed. Now Jesus had been all to the disciples; and as we have already seen, when they lost Him, they lost all; when He returned, they got all back again.

And this suggests a solemn inquiry to us; would the loss or absence of Jesus cause the great loneliness in our heart? Have we so companied with Him; so been

willing to give up all for Him; so had Him as the
prominent object of our heart, that if He were taken
away our heart would be lonely indeed?

If this be our condition, ours is the unspeakable
comfort of knowing, that we shall never have the long
loneliness which so often falls to the poor heart, whose
one absorbing object was some human love. We may
have a lesser loneliness; we too may have to look upon
an empty chair, and to eat our morsel alone; but the
great, the enduring loneliness of being eternally bereft
of Christ shall never fall to our lot. Lesser stars may
fall from their courses, yea, some of them of the first
magnitude as stars; but the Sun of Righteousness,
which is the centre of our system, shall never be
removed.

For, be it remembered, that it is *as an eternal source
of comfort that our Lord comes.* "Christ dieth now no
more. Death hath no more dominion over Him." "I am
He that liveth, and was dead; and, behold, I am alive
for evermore:" Rev. i, 18.

It was in resurrection life that Jesus would come; a
life which they could understand; a life with which they
could have a connection, for Jesus was to return to them
in a body again. It was in that body they saw Jesus
ascend to heaven, to His Father, and their Father; and
henceforth they had no more to do with a dead, but
with a living Christ. An *eternal* source of comfort had
thus come to the disciples; a source with which death
could never again interfere, which nothing could break or
dry up any more. And thus is Jesus to His people now
an eternal source of comfort; we need never be afraid
that the world can take Him from us; He is far beyond

the world's reach. Here we outlive our comforts; we see them fade and perish almost before our very eyes, but Christ holds out to the very end.

One stormy winter day, when Rev. Mr. Young was visiting one of his people, an old man, who lived in great poverty in a lonely cottage a few miles from Jedburgh; he found him sitting with his Bible open on his knees, but in outward circumstances of great discomfort; the snow drifting through the roof, and under the door, and scarce any fire on the hearth. "What are you about to-day, John?" was Mr. Young's question on entering. "Ah! sir," said the happy saint, "I'm sitting under His shadow with great delight!" The old man was not left comfortless, the Saviour had come to him. And so was He also with that other old man of the same minister's congregation, who was hourly looking for his last change. "How do you feel yourself to-day?" asked the minister. "Very weel, sir," was the answer, "very weel, but just a wee confused in 'the flittin.'" Through the last broken circumstances of life in the one case, and on the point of death in the other, enduring even unto the end, the source of comfort did not fail!

And let us mark this inexpressible comfort, which the disciples received by the returning of Jesus to them again. *They now had* HIM *still to live for;* they had the highest motive in life; they need not slip back again to living only for their earthly interests; He was alive, and could be served, and pleased; the great object of life was restored to them again.

This comfort belongs now to all true disciples of the risen Saviour; they have Him to live for, evermore; they need never slip back to the world, to find objects of

interest and attraction, to win them to activity; Jesus
lives; His disciples must live for Him.

Yes, *for* Him. Shall we be willing to live *in* Him,
and *by* Him, so as to derive all personal benefit *from*
Him, and shall we not be willing to live *for* Him also?
Why this listlessness, this *ennui*, in many in the Christian
world? Why this frequent slipping down to earthly
vanities, as though there were not enough in Christ
abundantly to draw out our highest energies? It is
because men are not living in the power of a living
Christ—One, who has come unto them, and comforted
them, and shewn them that His connection with them is
unsevered, that they are serving a personal, living Lord.

Let us lay firm hold of this great idea; we are not
merely fulfilling a law, we are serving a person; we are
not only under the obligations of duty, we are also
under the constrainings of love; we are to live for the
One who is walking amid the seven golden candle-
sticks, and noting all that His people do. We should
be ever rising higher and higher above the world, as the
supplier of our objects of interest; all the interests connected with a dying world are perishing; all connected
with a risen Christ are eternal.

As long as we realize that we have Christ to live for,
we shall never feel that *all* is lost, even when the worst
calamities and bereavements of life have fallen upon us.
We shall not want to hide ourselves with a grief which
devours us; nor feel a morbid pleasure in being eaten
into by its corroding tooth. Oh! we shall grieve if we
lose our dear ones; we shall weep and feel lonely, and
we shall taste of that desolation which sin by death has
brought into the world; but we shall also feel, that the

living Christ rises, in His great claims, above the dead
friend; we shall go forth to our work, it may be men of
sterner mould, hardened in the fires of sorrow against
the blandishments of the world; but we shall not surrender ourselves a prey to aught that belongs to death;
for we shall feel that we have to answer the claims of a
living Lord. We may have close to us the ashes of the
past, but we may nevertheless burn upon the hearth with
a brilliant glow; we also consuming in our service, and
dying daily while we live.

Having declared our belief, that whatever other
advents may be included in the "I will," which we are
considering; this, the appearing of our Lord in His
resurrection body is the first and chief, and *that* indeed
upon which all else must hang; let us now turn to the
fulfilment of His promise, an account of which we have
given to us by St. Luke. The disciples are assembled
at Jerusalem—a company of troubled ones; with them
things have been going hard indeed; without are fight-
ings, and within are fears; good cause have they for
trouble; they were weak in faith; their leader was
away; they were half stupefied by all that had occurred;
they had just gone through a terrible past; before them
lay an unknown future; they seem, inasmuch as some
of their company had walked with the One that had
been crucified, to have come into awful proximity to the
mysteries beyond the grave; the one cure for all their
sorrow was Christ's manifestation to them, as their own
Christ, once more; and so, He stands in the midst of
them, and says unto them "Peace be unto you;" and
when they are terrified and affrighted, supposing that

they had seen a spirit, He says unto them, "Why are ye troubled, and why do thoughts arise in your hearts? Behold my hands and my feet, that it is I myself; handle me, and see; for a spirit hath not flesh and bones, as ye see me have. And when He had thus spoken, He shewed them His hands and His feet. And while they yet believed not for joy, and wondered, He said unto them, have ye here any meat? And they gave Him a piece of a broiled fish, and of an honeycomb. And He took it, and did eat before them:" Luke xxiv, 38—43.

Christ's manifestation of Himself is the great cure for the troubled soul.

Think, O wounded heart, on this great truth; think it into thy very being; it is a simple, but withal a mighty truth; it is a truth that will save thee a world of trouble in inquiring "How am I to be comforted?" Thou art to be comforted by Christ's manifesting Himself with special plainness to thee; by His saying "Behold my hands and my feet, that it is I myself; handle me and see."

But let us see what we can gather for ourselves from the sorrows of the disciples, and from the manifestation of their Lord.

We see that *troubles may come on those who have companied long with Christ.* It is true that the disciples, though farther advanced than any upon earth, were as yet but little advanced in real knowledge of their Lord; but still they had been long with Him, and He Himself acknowledges this; for He says, "Ye are they which have continued with me in my temptations:" Luke xxii, 28. Upon these old companions and followers of Jesus deep trouble had now come. It may be that we think that we are to be exempt from all trouble, because we have long been followers of Jesus Christ; but, perhaps, we are like these disciples, long following, and yet but little advanced; if this be the case, we shall have all the spiritual disquietude and sorrow which are incidental to those who have to face trial in such a state. But we must not, on this account, allow ourselves to think, that we have not been followers of Christ at all; we may be true disciples, yea, even old disciples of Jesus, and yet be very deficient, "Have I been so long time with you, and yet hast thou not known me, Philip?" John xiv, 9. The Evil One will draw no distinction between a man's being a weak disciple, and not being one at all. Oh! that we may not only company long with Jesus, but advance far into the knowledge of Him; trouble loses half its power, if suffered with or for, a well known Christ.

But perhaps the reader is a *privileged* believer; and says, "Am I, with all my privileges, still to be subject to sorrow?" Were not all the disciples privileged? Who had such privileges as they; and yet what greater trouble could any have had, than that which now filled their hearts? Had the disciples used their privileges aright, they would probably have escaped the trouble which came upon them now—trouble, from not being able plainly to discern Jesus; but no amount of privilege, even if made the most of, will save from trial of every kind. We must use our privileges to carry us through trial, not to procure exemption from it; "for, whom the Lord loveth He chasteneth, and scourgeth every son whom He receiveth. If ye endure chastening, God dealeth with you as with sons; for what son is he

whom the father chasteneth not? But if ye be without
chastisement, whereof all are partakers, then are ye
bastards and not sons:" Heb. xii, 6—9. Dear reader,
do not deny your privileges, because you cannot deny
your trials; never listen to your great enemy, when he
says, "If you were a child of God, you would never have
been thus tried;" this was how the Evil One assaulted
Job, when he said, "Put forth thine hand now, and touch
his bone and his flesh, and he will curse thee to thy
face:" Job ii, 5.

Let us enquire, however, into
SOME OF THE CAUSES OF THE DISCIPLES' TROUBLE,
which Jesus dispelled by the performance of His promise, "I will come unto you." "Behold my hands and
my feet, that it is I myself."

A part of their troubles arose from *imperfect apprehension of the truth.* They cannot apprehend the
resurrection of the body as yet. They believed, no doubt,
in a future life, but the resurrection of the body was a
mystery to them. And from this very source come
many of our troubles; we know a part of a truth, but we
fail in taking in the whole; and then, when events
occur, which can be explained only by our knowledge
of that part of the truth which we have failed to learn,
we are confused, perhaps confounded, and brought into
great trouble. If we have but a very imperfect apprehension of the great truth that "God is love;" then
when His love is shewn in sorrowful dispensations, we
do not perceive that there is love in them, and we are
amazed. If we had fully grasped the truth, then we
should have known that let what will come, love must
be in it—must come with it—and the fulness of our

knowledge of Divine love would keep us in perfect peace.

It is a great thing to have our apprehension of truth made more perfect; to be growing in knowledge which will keep us from disagreeable surprises in the Divine life. Had the disciples apprehended more fully the resurrection of the body, that which at first proved to them a disagreeable surprise (disagreeable, inasmuch as it affrighted them) would have proved a most agreeable one—yes, the most agreeable they could possibly have had. If we enter fully into the teachings of Jesus, we shall have no disagreeable surprises, we shall have many most agreeable ones; for we shall in all behold Him, that it is He Himself.

Another part of the disciples' trouble arose from an *unaccustomed manifestation.* One who had been dead and buried came amongst them alive again. But why should they have been so amazingly astonished at this? Jairus's daughter, and the nobleman's, and the widow's son, and Lazarus, had been raised from the dead; might they not have remembered these, and so have been less troubled when they saw the Lord Himself? In the first place, death and resurrection came more home to themselves now, than they had done on any previous occasion; this was a matter in which they were personally concerned; and in the next place, on all previous occasions those who had been restored to life, lived again in the old bodies, the same that they ever had, and not in resurrection bodies at all. They had bodies which belonged to this life, the same as before; Christ had a body which belonged to this world no more. Jesus could prove the identity of His body, for He says, "Behold my hands and my feet, that it is I myself; handle me, and see; for a spirit hath not flesh and bones as ye see me have;" but it was now the body of the resurrection, and to the manifestation of such a body, they were wholly unaccustomed.

And are we to expect that we are never to travel out of the beaten road of *accustomed* manifestations? If this be the case, we can never make great advance in the Divine life. It is by going on to new problems that the mathematician perfects himself in science; it is by copying new scenes that the artist perfects himself in art; it is by practising new pieces that the musician perfects himself in song; and it is by new manifestations of Jesus that the believer also makes his advances. Surely we shall lead a miserable life, if every un-accustomed, every new aspect, in which Jesus presents Himself to us, is to bring us consternation and misery. May we so apprehend Christ's teachings by the Spirit, that when He manifests Himself *in any way*, we may not be troubled, but say, "I discern His hands and feet; it is He Himself."

There is another aspect in which this trouble of the disciples must be surveyed. *They were all in trouble together;* they could not help the one the other. The stoutest of the apostles—Peter—was as much terrified as any of the rest, and so was the most loving,—John; as they looked in each other's face, they could see nothing to calm and re-assure; all was consternation, terror, and distress. They were just as helpless as they had been in the storm on the lake, when they saw Jesus, and thinking that it was a spirit, cried out for fear.

There are seasons of trouble, when no one on earth

can help us; when we find old familiar spiritual friends quite unable to bring us comfort; when they themselves are as much astonished and perplexed as we are. The child of God is sometimes like one in a family, where death has made an awful chasm; he looks in every one's face for comfort, but each one looks as mournful and comfortless as he does himself. Have not some of us experienced this; have we not been amongst many who would have comforted us, but they could not? The lack was in their power, and not their will. Christian families, and Christian communities, and churches, have been like the disciples—the whole body confused, terror stricken, and distressed.

All this is very terrible; but, perhaps, we must be taught the nothingness of man in this form, as well as others; it may be that God would speak to us and say, "Your comfort, your peace lie not in the many, any more than they do in the few; you will find these blessings not amongst many of your fellow men, or from their countenance and ministry, but from one man, even Christ Jesus, His countenance, and His ministry, and that alone."

Yes! the revelation of Jesus Christ Himself is the solution of trouble. Jesus knew this when He gave His disciples the promise, "I will come unto you!" He proved it when He now appeared; and it was on the full manifestation of His identity that they obtained peace. "*I* will come unto you;" everything hung upon the identification of their Lord.

Now this fulfilment of Christ's promise has much to do with ourselves; we also are greatly concerned in the identity of Christ. For, when this identity is es-

tablished, we know that we have to do with One whose
*new life is connected with previous well-known life, that
previous well-known life being identical with our own.*
This idea, amongst others, underlies the words of our
Lord to St. John, when He appeared to him, in, not only
a resurrection, but also a glorified body; thus He
comforted the apostle who fell prostrate at the sight.
"And He laid His right hand upon me, saying unto
me, Fear not; I am the first and the last: I am He
that liveth and was dead, and behold, I am alive for evermore. Amen:" Rev. i, 17, 18.   "I am He that liveth and
was dead." It is by bringing the past and present
together that the Lord, declaring His identity, comforts
the affrighted man.

What can comfort us more than the knowledge that
our Lord, now in union with us, although in glory,
remembers vividly His former life upon the earth? What
that life was, we know full well; in it met all the
sorrows of humanity in the highest form; none endured
such pain as He; none wept such tears as He; none
were so isolated in loneliness as He; none were so
maligned, insulted, wronged as He; His life was like
an hour glass, every sand-grain in which represented a
sorrow,—one upon another do they heap with deep
broad base and tapering point,—the base made up of
the falling together of many a sharp point, until at
last there remains not a grain to fall—not a sorrow to
be endured; He had exhausted the sum total of human
woe! Then came the turning of the glass: behold for
Him all things are made new; in resurrection life He
receives glory for all the sufferings of the past; but it
is no part of His glory to forget the past.   To forget

the past would be to destroy human sympathy—to blot out all that it has to do with mediation, comfort, and support. "This [man] because He continueth ever, hath an unchangeable priesthood:" Heb. vii, 24. But what kind of priesthood? The priesthood of the *man* Christ Jesus: "For verily He took not on Him the nature of angels; but He took on Him the seed of Abraham. Wherefore in all things it behoved Him to be made like unto His brethren, that He might be a merciful and faithful High Priest in things pertaining to God, to make reconciliation for the sins of the people. For in that He Himself hath suffered being tempted, He is able to succour them that are tempted:" Heb. ii, 16—18.

In this well-known passage, the great comforting point is the identity of the Christ on earth with the Christ in heaven—the oneness of 'the suffering' and 'the glorified' One—the carrying out, in fact, to its legitimate result, the promise, "I will come unto you." It involves the retention and exercise of the power of human memory—the power of throwing one's self into the past, with all its circumstances and feelings, and then acting in the vividness of that recollection. How little do we know of this! We have memories, but they are imperfect; we recall facts, but we cannot recall the feelings connected with facts in their original power; but Jesus recalls feelings and facts together, and acts in the power of both. When Jesus said, "I will come unto you," that promise linked itself to all the future trials of His Church, from the spilling of the martyrs' blood, down to the breathing of the half unconscious sigh; with that golden chain He bound Himself as the "Man Christ Jesus" to His Church, in the weakness of its suffering humanity, and pledged Himself to be a man with men; one of them, even after having passed through death—the great severer of human ties. Jesus lives at present surrounded with the memories of the past; His coming in human form to the apostles was but a preliminary step to His after visitations by the Spirit. It is such a Christ that we must take as our own, hearing Him say to us no other than what He said to the apostles of old, "I will not leave you comfortless, I will come unto you."

But this is not all. When Jesus fulfilled His promise to His disciples, He brought them peace as regards the world beyond, by the convincing proof of a bodily human life which had gone through and survived death. This body had wounds; and whatever aspect these wounds might have worn, when He hung upon the cross and lay in the tomb, as the tokens of the power of the violated law, avenging itself on Him; the aspect which they wear, as Christ comes now in this same living body, to fulfil His promise to His disciples, is one of victory. These wounds were the proofs of His triumph over death; they were "peace-tokens connected with His death;"* in His very body Jesus brought the

* "The Lord showeth His wounds not merely as the tokens of His crucifixion, for the identity of His body; but evidently also as the tokens of victory, the proofs of His triumph over death, and therefore also—and this is its deepest meaning—as pertaining to His introductory greeting! as the peace token of His sacrificial death, of His accomplished atonement. This had reference, indeed, rather to the future understanding of the disciples (which soon followed in the opening of Scripture), in the symbolical meaning of this His revelation for His whole future Church; yet we may, as Diez says, expound it as historically true, that 'they began to have a presentiment of the

elements of comfort; the marks of suffering all spake, and said, "Peace be unto you;" 'ye are not left comfortless, I have come unto you.' "We will have no Saviour," says St. Martin, "without the prints of the wounds;" so say we; for these are speaking wounds, and their utterance is, "peace."

Should these lines be read by anyone who is taking this world as his portion, I would say to such a one: 'this is a comfortless world apart from Christ.' Sooner or later, what you think to be springs of comfort will dry up; what you think to be gold and wealth will become ashes and dross; and then, perhaps, for you there will be no friendly comforting Christ. Alas! for you there will remain no promises, no sympathies, and this your desolation will come upon you by your own rejection, by your own fault. A visiting Christ bodes no good to you —no good—but evil—deep dark evil of the most fearful

mysterious connexion between this peace and the wounds of Jesus.' This is the true token, by which He comforts the terrified conscience and heart.........That He retained in the resurrection these marks of His wounds on the body which was to be exalted to heaven (marks which otherwise, as the concomitant of death, might or should have been abolished); and that He retains them till now, and for eternity, as the glorious tokens of His victory and atonement, is of great and blessed significance for our faith. It was as assuredly the Lord's will, as we see, to appear Himself to His disciples as 'the crucified,' as the angel in the empty sepulchre termed Him; and *thereby* to manifest His *glory*, *thereby* to seal His *peace*. To this referred that suggestive legend of Satan's appearance in the form of the glorified Saviour, when St. Martin repelled him by asking him for the prints of the wounds. No φαντασμα *(phantasm)* could counterfeit these wounds, for these were chosen and sanctified by the Lord of glory as the tokens and marks by which He would be known." See Stier's "Words of the Lord Jesus," vol. viii.

kind. "Behold, He cometh with clouds; and every eye
shall see Him, and they also that pierced Him: and all
kindreds of the earth shall wail because of Him:" Rev.
i, 7. Ah! poor fellow sinner, where will you be then?
Where will you secrete yourself? What cave will open its
mouth to hide you in its stony breast? What mountain
will fall upon you, to crush you with its ponderous
weight? For you there will be no hope; for you there
will remain nothing, but an eternity of deep and dark
despair. May such a fearful doom be averted by a
speedy closing with the offers of the Lord; amongst the
true disciples of Jeses, the comforted and the blest,
"yet—yet—there is room."

And to the Lord's people I would add this comforting
word.

(1.) Look not at yourself as isolated, as the sparrow
upon the housetop, as one friendless, homeless, belonging
indeed to Christ, but having no affinity, no relationship
with anyone else. You are one of a family, of a family
like that of the disciples, made up of one gathered from
this quarter, and another from that; you have first the
great affinity with Christ, and then that with His people;
you have relations; there are those with whom you have
a common interest; those to whom Jesus says, "I will
not leave you comfortless, I will come unto you." Be
cheerful in the thought; you have friends, both in
heaven and on earth.

And (2.) Never permit yourself for one moment to
consider that you are cut off from the benefits of Christ's
personality. If you do, vagueness and indistinctness
will characterise your spiritual life; and you will lose
yourself in the surrounding haze.

It is the privilege of the believer to have to do with a substantial Christ; thrice happy he who knows what it is to live, and move, and speak with a personal, living Lord. Jesus fulfilled His promise to His disciples. Let us also grasp the "I will" which He spake to them, and He will fulfil it to our peace.

The following extract, from one of Captain Hedley Vicars' letters, gives us a touching instance of the comfort given by the presence of Christ, in cheerless daily life.

"It is a very gloomy day, the sky black and lowering, and the rain descending in torrents. I was meditating just now on this bleak scene of cheerless solitude—my only companion a little quail!—and thinking over the strange and often appalling sights my eyes have looked upon, in the realities of death and the grave, since God called me here. As these ideas floated through my mind, the train of my thoughts suddenly changed, and the dismal view without, and the cold and dreary room I occupy, brought before me 'the man of sorrows'—Jesus —who once weathered the stormy tempest for you and for me; and of whom it may be said, from the manger to the grave, that He had not 'where to lay His head.' It is so soothing to the soul, in seasons of cloud and distress, to know that Jesus hath 'borne our griefs, and carried our sorrows,' and to rest on the tender kindness of Him who has said, 'As one whom his mother comforteth, so will I comfort you.'"

The troubled ones form a large portion of the great family of God. There are many mourning garments, many sorrowful countenances, many depressed hearts amongst His children; all tears are not yet wiped away from the eyes of the people of the Lord. It may be that we are sad because of our own fault; or perhaps, without any fault of ours, simply because we are under discipline; but whatever the cause, amongst us the sadness is often to be found. Some are sitting silent, some solitary, some perplexed, some weeping, some doubting; there are different kinds and different degrees of woe.

But, for all these, there is the one Christ, uttering now the self-same words;

"I will not leave you comfortless, I will come unto you."

The "I Will" of Disposal.

John xxi, 22.

JOHN xxi, 22.

"Jesus saith unto him, If I will that he tarry till I come, what is that to thee? follow thou me."

———◇◇◇———

PETER'S discipleship involved his education! Jesus was not only the Master whom he was to follow, but the One also by whom he was to be taught. On many different occasions we find him thus being instructed in the school of Christ. On one occasion, he will make human affection thrust itself forward, so as to come in conflict with the Divine will; and he receives the severest reproof which was ever inflicted upon any of the apostolic band; our Lord said to him, "Get thee behind me, Satan: thou art an offence unto me: for thou savourest not the things that be of God, but those that be of men:" Matt. xvi, 23. On another occasion, he will go beyond his faith; and his Master shews him what was in him, rescuing him indeed from a watery grave, but saying, "O thou of little faith, wherefore didst thou doubt?" Matt. xiv, 31. On farther in his career, when he draws the sword, and will rescue with a temporal blade the spiritual king, he

is taught forbearance, and the mind of Jesus towards
man, by the healing of Malchus' ear; for Jesus came to
be wounded and not to wound, "to give His life a
ransom for many." Yet again, our Lord, first by word
of caution—and when that was unheeded, and disastrous
results ensued, then by a piercing look, taught him—the
vaunting and self-confident one—that distrust of self,
which is in the Christian character no element of weakness, but rather of amazing strength. And now, here, at
the very end of Jesus' earthly career, we find Him teaching still; for the words, "If I will that he tarry till I
come, what is that to thee?" contain at once a sharp
rebuke, and instructive lessons for the apostle; and for
us as well as him.

What some at least of these lessons are, we shall now
proceed to consider; they will be found of no small
value in our daily spiritual life.

And first of all, we see here, how *Christ is the
sovereign Disposer of His disciples.*

In Peter and John we have represented to us the
three great parts of the church's work, viz., *working, suffering,* and *watching,* and our Lord here distributes to
every man severally as He will. Jesus is the Captain of
our salvation, therefore He has a right to dispose of us,
His soldiers, in the line of battle, as He will. He is the
Shepherd of the sheep, therefore He has a right to
appoint to each one of the flock where it is to feed. He
is the Master of the house, therefore He has a right to
appoint every man his work, and to command the porter
to watch. (Mark xiii, 34.)

Now, it is an important question; do we recognise

this disposing power in Christ? And, having recognised it, do we willingly yield ourselves to it? Do we say to Him, "Just do with me as Thou wilt, O my Lord; I am absolutely at Thy command." Are we ready to let Him change, unchallenged, His dispensations towards us? upset our plans—spread before us a new and unexpected path—take into account only the thoughts of His own mind, and not those of ours at all? Is there not sometimes in us, a little of the spirit of Ananias and Sapphira; we will vow all, and yet give but part? Christ has often to teach His disciples the completeness of His disposing power; and never can they have perfect peace in all that may betide them in life, until they have said in truth, "Do with me as Thou wilt." But we shall meet by and bye with more of this subjugation of the will.

We are further taught here, that *we are not to trouble ourselves about the arrangements of our Lord.*

Now, when we do not act upon this principle, a serious stumbling block is very often put in our way; our attempts to unravel what is too complicated for us, lead us into perplexity and doubt; we vex our spirits needlessly about what is really no affair of ours.

And this not leaving all in the hands of the Lord, will frequently lead us to sinful complainings about our own lot. Forgetful that our duty is simply to stand in the spot where our Lord puts us, and to move in the orbit which He has appointed to us; we vex ourselves as to why we are put there, and why we were not put somewhere else; and perhaps we begin to think, 'Can't we change our sphere, we see one that will suit us much better?' we must needs order the pillar and the cloud, instead of simply following wherever they lead. If the Lord

wills, this, or that, it is no affair of ours; our duty is to
let Him arrange, unquestioned, all that He would have
us do, or be. A questioning spirit is always a troubled
one; God "giveth not account of any of His matters:"
Job xxxiii, 13. And there is no reason why He should
help us out of our trouble, by yielding to our infirmity.
Nay, rather must we overcome the infirmity, bringing
our minds, by His grace, into unquestioning obedience
to His mind; our only words being these, "Speak, Lord,
for Thy servant heareth." The centurion says to one of
his soldiers, "Go, and he goeth, and to another, come,
and he cometh; and to his servant, do this, and he
doeth it:" Matt. viii, 9. Shall we, soldiers and servants
of the great Captain, and the great Lord, do less than
those who yielded unquestioning obedience to an earthly
chief?

And shall we not be then most happy, when we just
commit everything simply into our Lord's hands?—when
we leave all arrangements with the One who knows what
bearing circumstances have the one upon another; who
can control, overrule, appoint, and dove-tail all things,
so that they may turn out most for His own glory, and
therefore best for us? Let us for a moment picture to
ourselves the frightful consequences of the effectual
entrance of some great disturbing body into the planet-
ary system; the universe itself would feel the shock;
but what would this be, compared with the successful
intrusion of man's will into the complicated arrangements of the will of God? Then would arise confusion
indeed; and out of that confusion we should emerge a
mere shattered wreck, our will would have proved our
ruin, the perdition both of body and soul.

Alas! that we recognise so little the existence of this great superior "I will" so little, our own position of simple obedience; that we do not see that our Lord's orderings are no business of ours. Could we but say "He wills," and that is enough for me, we should receive no rebuke, and we should enjoy sweet calm and peace.

What best becomes us is to believe deeply that our Lord acts evermore, out of secret depths known to Himself, and Himself alone; His way "is in the sea, and His path in the great waters, and His footsteps are not known:" Psa. lxxvii, 19. And can we not see, in a moment, how this would bring us peace? What a world of speculation, and doubt, and discontent, we should be saved? When we could not see to the bottom of this or that strange thing, how should we comfort ourselves with the thought, "My Lord sees to the bottom of it;" "Thou wilt keep him in perfect peace, whose mind is stayed upon Thee; because he trusteth in Thee:" Isa. xxvi, 3.

And as we are not to trouble ourselves about the arrangements of the Lord, so,

We are to mind our own business. This is all important to us. And I may be permitted to observe, that this will generally give us as much as we can possibly do. If we find that it does not give us enough to do, to mind our own business, it is because we have not taken up the position fully which God has pointed out to us. Our Lord does not leave any one in a position, where there is nothing to be done. If any one think that He does, let him seriously set to work, and try and

find out whether there be not something that he can do
for Christ; and if he find that there is, and that he has
not done it, then let him complain no more that he has
nothing appointed to him of the Lord. It is for idle
minds, that "Satan finds some mischief still to do."

We may rest assured, that we are not following our
Lord fully, when we thus turn about, and meddle with
other persons' matters; yea, meddle with the arrangements
which He makes. And we may also rest assured, that
when we "turn about" and leave our own "following" of
the Lord, we are getting out of the path of duty, and
very near rebuke; what can we say, when we bring it
upon ourselves?

This 'not minding our own business' involves the loss
of concentration; and wherever there is a loss of concentration there is a loss of power. Peter, it seems,
"turned about;" he probably did something more than
merely turn his head; most likely he turned his whole
body; but under any circumstances he was hindered in
carrying out the command which he had just received,
to follow Christ. We all know how seriously we are
delayed by very small stoppings, or even by turning to
look round; if another be walking with us, who does
not thus stop and turn, he gets several paces in advance
of us, and we may find it very hard to catch him up
again. Eternity alone will tell how much is lost by
turning, and stopping, to meddle it may be with that
which does not belong to us at all, as is the case with
Peter now. And be it observed, that it by no means
follows that these turnings and stoppings are necessarily
connected with worldly things.   Alas! we have sad experiences of turnings, and stoppings, to look at the peep

shows which the world has at every corner of the streets; we need the intense energy and concentration of the hero of "Excelsior," to stop our ears, and avert our eyes from that which would beguile and hinder us on our way; we fritter away our power, by spending part of it upon what has no claim upon it at all; something, it may be, that was not immediately presented to us, but which we turned round to, and thereby made ourselves amenable to rebuke. We dilute our strength by these turnings; at every turning Delilah pulls out a hair, though she cannot entirely shave the head.

We can never go out of our own place of simple following without the ensuing of evil, or confusion of some kind; and in such evil and confusion, we shall not have the comfort which we can have in the trials with which we meet, when closely following our Lord. There is a great difference between self-made, and providential trials; in the first we throw ourselves out of the sympathy of Christ; in the second, we may be sure that that sympathy is ours.

Trials while *following* are light—we have Jesus *before* us; trials while *turning* are heavy—we have Jesus *behind* us.

Observe also, *how different oftentimes are Christ's answers to our expectations.*

Peter had just had assigned to him a two-fold position, to which was attached honour of the very highest kind. In verses 15—19, he has a position of activity appointed to him; he is constituted a feeder of Christ's lambs and sheep. It may be that by first directing his attention to the lambs, the Lord would

not only shew His own special care of the weak ones ;
but He would also point out to the once aspiring
apostle, that the highest energies of which he was possessed, would be worthily expended upon even the
very least in the kingdom of God. The prophet Isaiah
[xl, 2] declared, that Jesus should "feed His flock like
a shepherd;" that He should "gather the lambs with
His arm, and carry them in His bosom;" and it was
very meet and right that He, the Great Shepherd, should
give especial charge to an under shepherd, to be careful
of those for whom He deigned to make His own bosom
a fold.

In this shepherding of the lambs and sheep, a
position of great activity was assigned to Peter; it may
be that he now expected to hear the like appointed to
John. Christ's answer was entirely different to what
he looked for; instead of telling him about this other,
He recalled him by a sharp rebuke to his own duty.
Now, had Peter, while following, put some needful
question to Jesus with reference to himself—one asking
for direction, there is little doubt but that he would
have received a gracious answer; the needful questions
of followers are always graciously answered; but this
was the question of a turner, and the answer was a
rebuke. Many a time has the Christian put himself
into Peter's position, and fared as Peter did. And let
us not forget that high personal position will not
save us from such rebuke. Peter had just accepted the
laborious office of a shepherd, and accepted, moreover,
the sufferings which were implied in his being girded
and carried where he would not. But all this does
not save him from rebuke when he goes astray. Is it

not ever thus? Will not the Lord always deal with us according to each short-coming? Perhaps the very height of the apostle's position brought upon him this exceeding sharpness of rebuke. "Open rebuke is better than secret love:" Prov. xxvii, 5. "As many as I love, I rebuke and chasten:" Rev. iii, 19. It might seem to us but a small thing to turn for a moment; this was, as we should think, but a little fault in the great apostle; but it was in the very presence of the Lord; it was while His words, "Follow me," were still almost ringing in his very ears.

Is it not well for us, dear reader, that Jesus does not permit Himself to be swayed by our expectations? Ah! how foolish are earthly parents and friends in this particular; often you cannot bear to disappoint the expectations of a child, or of a friend, when they expect you will do for them what you feel you ought not. Such is the weakness of love; and very fearful are the evils which the weakness of love has inflicted on the world. But there is none of this in Christ,— false expectations are not honoured by Him. We cannot be too thankful that a turning Peter met with a rebuking Christ.

And now let us learn further, that *the will of Christ may be very strongly manifested in a comparatively uneventful career.* " If I will that he tarry."

Shepherding and martyrdom had just been appointed to Peter; "tarrying" is all that is marked out for John.

How do we know what is involved in many apparently uneventful careers? Uneventful careers are such only in our forms of speech, and in our eyes; there

are really none in the spiritual world. The heroes of
that world are not those only who are associated in our
minds with fire and sword, with dungeon and with rack;
these indeed are mighty heroes; we stand aside in the
shade, as they defile in long procession, with all the
symbols of martyrs, before our eyes; we look upon them,
and then say of ourselves, "What are we?" but we
believe that in the last day of great account, there will
be found many whose career has been as strange as
theirs. Now, he who swims down the stream, may
have an uneventful career, but he who breasts it will not;
he who is content to tarry in his dungeon may have an
uneventful career, but he who makes his escape will not;
and in many a country hamlet, leading, to all outward
appearances, calm and unruffled lives, are such heroes
and heroines of the cross; the battle field deep hidden
in their own hearts; the fire burning, and the falchion
glittering there. Man racks his brain for stories of
romance; and fearful lest his tale should flag, brings
actor after actor in quick succession on the scene; the
deed of violence, the craft of knavery, the soft tender-
nesses of love, he crowds upon his page; but amazed
perhaps will these men be, when they find that their
imagination has been outstripped by reality; that they
have painted in but washy tintings—scenes, which in all
the intensity of deepest colouring have been enacted
within the Christian's heart—scenes in which the
"murderer from the beginning" attempted murder
again; in which the deceiver swore, and lied, to cheat
a soul of heaven; in which the "love that passeth
knowledge" won the victory at last.

I hold that there is no such thing as an uneventful

life in the spiritual world, except it be for those who are
"dead in trespasses and sins;" they no doubt have some
events in their life, just as a body in the grave has its
events in its progress to decay; but in them there is
no spiritual vitality, and Satan leaves his own alone.
And let this address itself to those who are panting for
large spheres of labour, or great opportunities of devotion, who want to prove their devotion by facts; and let
it say, "Hast thou so proved thy devotion in this inward
sphere, and so fully followed Christ therein, that thou
hast exhausted there all opportunities of life for Christ,
and must go forth to find vent for the mighty impulses
within?" Who can say that he has followed Christ to
the full, amid the many windings even of his own
naughty heart? Not one! There never was a man who
availed himself of every inch of ground which was
afforded him in his own heart, for winning glory to his
Lord. When we are called to outward service, right
cheerfully let us enter upon it; but if to us there be
manifestly appointed the still path, then let us walk
cheerfully therein, being assured that it also is not
uneventful, and that in it, as well as in a more crowded
road, we may live and move for God.

And here arises an important question; viz., Is what
we call our uneventful path, that which God has marked
out for us, or is it one of our own choosing? Have we
it as our own portion by Divine arrangement, or by our
rejection of the turning point, which might have led us
to a more eventful career? It is highly possible that
some one on reflection, may be able to see, that such
turning points were presented to him in his past life, but
he turned off the rail and ran up a siding, and there he

has remained even to the present day; while trains fast and slow are passing by, there he is, in the same place now, that he was many years ago. There are, unquestionably, many turning points in our spiritual career— turning points as regards the destiny of our usefulness, and even as regards our spirituality; and to fail in taking advantage of these, is a serious error indeed; should the reader unhappily have left such a turning point of usefulness unimproved, let him now confess his fault; let him simply put himself in the hands of God again; let him say, "Here am I, do with me as thou wilt;" then with fire as it were rekindled, and steam got up; with wheel and piston oiled and bright, let him keep looking earnestly for a signal to tell him to move on. When the right time has come, an instrument will always be found to turn the switches, and you will find yourself upon the line; in glorious action for the Lord whom you would serve.

In saying this, there are of course two points which we assume; the one is that waiting is not the *distinctive* lot appointed to us of God; the other is, that it is His Spirit who gives us the gracious thoughts of which we have been speaking. And fully are we persuaded, that if any to whom this distinctive work of waiting is not appointed, and who have nevertheless been unoccupied for God, because of their own shortcoming, will now yield themselves unreservedly into the hand of God, they shall find that their sphere will be appointed to them ere long; an humble one indeed it may be, but still it will be a real one; an honourable service, in which there will be a great reward.

Nor would we part from this portion of our subject

without availing ourselves of the privilege of saying a word to those, who are by the Divine arrangement distinctly placed in the position of tarrying ones; and who are perhaps inclined to envy those who have had assigned to them a more active sphere. You, dear friends, do not aspire to driving an express at high pressure for the Lord; you would be content unnoticed to do hard work, like the luggage train that rumbles along through the night quite unobserved, with a heavy weight of uninteresting trucks behind it; anything would satisfy you, so as only you were in action.

Do not fall into the mistake, of not being able to discern the will of God except through your own activities; must He depend upon anything in you, for evidence of the working of His will? Ah! is not this putting *ourselves* forward; was the action of Christ's will to be discerned only in the shepherding and the martyrdom of Peter, and not at all in the tarrying of John? Be persuaded, that in lying upon a sick bed; or in moving on noiselessly through some manifestly appointed humble sphere; or in recognising the will of God in your being kept back from the activities of work, you are fulfilling that very will. To be still, requires as much grace, sometimes, as to be active; oh! for such a heart as would seek, whether in activity or retirement, in shepherding, martyrdom, or tarrying, only to discern, and try to carry out, the will of God in Christ.

And now we come to see how *antecedents develop themselves in an entirely different way from what we should have supposed.*

It needs no great philosophy to be able to perceive,

that in the abstract, causes and effects are linked together; indeed in the natural world we may go even further, and from certain causes invariably predict certain effects; but it is not so in the spiritual world. There also the cause and effect are linked together, but we do not always see the connection; circumstances are found to develop themselves in a different way from what we should have supposed. Of this we may be sure, that in the hand of God all circumstances develop themselves aright.

Now look at the antecedents of John; and with none but human rules to guide us, should we not have supposed that some extraordinary sphere would have been appointed to him? He was the choice apostle of love; he was the one who leaned on Jesu's breast at supper; and that ventured to ask Him who it was that should betray Him; what more reasonable than to suppose, that some especially wonderful work would be appointed to him? But it was not so. God "seeth not as man seeth!" our thoughts are not as His thoughts, neither are our ways like His ways; and unless we believe this, we shall often be offended and perplexed.

Let us mark this well in our own spiritual career; we are very apt to be offended, if the folded bud does not develop into the exact flower we have pictured in our minds; if the figures which lie before us do not add up exactly to the amount that we expected. If we know our own place, as being in subjection to the Divine will, we shall not only look to God with reference to circumstances, but with reference to their development also. Look at that young man, with a noble intellect and a consecrated heart, where is his fitting sphere?

You destine him for the pulpit—for a great career of active usefulness; his early piety gives promise of this development; but perhaps God's development is altogether different; it may be that with blasted health, he is to become a simple tarrier for Jesus, or for aught we know, he is going to be removed altogether, and to find his development and expansion in heaven. Or look at that young woman, whose heart is early given to the Lord; would not she have made a helpful wife to some toiling man of God? would it not have been a boon to the world, to have her character, and energy, and holy principles reproduced in a family, all of them devoted likewise to the Lord ?—so thinks man—but lo! she too is touched with illness, and pines for many a long year; or her lot is one of patient waiting upon another; perhaps it is one of poverty, simply struggling to live; but whatever it be, it is not what we had marked out; and have this one's antecedents been belied in her destiny? Not so; they may have found their most worthy development in that lot; and heaven's records of how divine problems were worked out, will one day shew us this.

But we need not always wait for the revelations of eternity; we can in many instances trace the dealings of God in time. For, let us look at this very case of John; this great love of his for his Master may have been necessary for his "living dying,"—his long wearing out life—the loneliness of being left the last of all the apostolic band. Who can tell what it was to him to have his righteous soul vexed from day to day with the unlawful deeds of evil; what it was to be exiled into Patmos; what it was to be continuing long in a world with which he had little sympathy, except such a sympathy as it rejected—a sympathy with its woe. Perhaps, so far as spiritual instrumentality goes, nothing short of these antecedents of which we have been speaking, would have carried him through. And oftentimes it happens that spiritual performances, which we despise as not being brilliant, rest upon a deep substratum of love to Christ; there may be that in them which nothing less than such a substratum would hold up. It may seem a small thing to us for a person day by day patiently to eat a crust; and yet that contentment may be resting on the perception of that love of Jesus, which ever provides aright. Perhaps we think little of a person's resignation when all friends are gone, and he is left alone; and yet nothing short of a long and well tried love of Jesus might have sufficed to close an otherwise murmuring lip for many a long year. We may be almost certain that all spiritual trainings are connected with important results; it is the preservation of proportion between the wide spreading root and the wide spreading branch—the branch whose leaves do not wither, and which bringeth forth its fruit in its season.

This waiting was John's mission; as much his, as shepherding and martyrdom were Peter's; his previous love developed in the performance of that mission; love was as much needed for tarrying, as for death.

We must look at John, however, as *a waiter in connection with Jesus.* "If I will that he tarry till I come." How often do we, dazzled by appearances, forget the true position of God's waiters. "They also serve who only stand and wait." We can understand the connec

tion between Christ and the martyr; and between Christ
and the worker; we often fail to see it between Christ
and the waiter. And hence the true Church of God
appears numerically much smaller than it really is; we
do not see the hidden ones who are in connection with
Him; we see the Elijahs as they smite Baal, but not
the seven thousand who are reserved, who in connection
with their God do not bow the knee to him.

If you, dear reader, in the providence of God, be one
of the waiters, and if you feel that you are Christ's,
then cheer up your spirits with that blessed thought.
Say to yourself, "I also am joined unto the Lord! I
also am standing in my place! I am acting in the power
of love! I day by day 'lead the life I now live in the
flesh,' in simple union with my Lord." Oh! what an
inestimable comfort must it have been to the apostle,
to feel that he was day by day fulfilling the will of
Christ. Surely he realized his position,—his hope
through all the long waiting time was fixed on *Him;*
—day rose after day—night fell after night; and though
he doubtless would have taken the wings of a dove,
and flown away and been at rest, if he had only his
own pleasure to consult; yet ever was he sustained by
this one thought, *it is His will.*

Observe lastly—

The directions of concentration. "Follow *thou* me."
Peter had turned himself after having been told to
follow, and hence this stern rebuke, and also this re-
iterated command. In this second command our Lord
recalls the apostle to *personal* obedience, fixing his
attention upon himself, his own duty, and, moreover,
the need of doing it at once. And this is the very

300 THE "I WILL" OF DISPOSAL.

direction which we so often need; we want to be taught that we are out of the path of personal obedience, and to be brought back to it again. It is as though our Lord said, "Be thou engaged in thy personal obedience, and that is my will with regard to thee." It was the same direction repeated; as though the Lord would shew the apostle that what He wills is the reparation of a fault, not the destruction or casting off of the one who commits it. Peter had already been restored, and the great sin of his denial forgiven; how soon he needs restoration and forgiveness again! This is just our history; our gracious Master has to rebuke us and restore us too; He does all; He pours in both oil and wine—that which will cleanse the wound, and that which will make it whole.

What now remains but to ask the reader what is his position at this very time? Let each one question himself, "Am *I* following? Am I following HIM? Is my mind concentrated upon obedience to His command?"

Compare the explicitness of "Follow thou me," with the hypothetic "If;" and in that explicitness mark the determination of the Saviour's will.

Reader! whatever may be the will of Christ with regard to others, what is that to thee? His will concerning thee is plain,—"Follow thou Me."

The "I Will" of Subjection.

———

MATTHEW xxvi, 39.   MARK xiv, 36.

MATTHEW xxvi, 39.

"Nevertheless not as I will, but as Thou wilt."

MARK xiv, 36

" Nevertheless not what I will, but what Thou wilt."

F we could only see, with these our mortal eyes, that which is going on in the spiritual world, we should be amazed at its deep reality, at its terrible intensity. By the spiritual world, we do not here mean the angelic, whether good or bad, but men's spiritual being, with all the action of spiritual agents upon them, for good or evil.

Were our eyes thus opened, here should we see a soul pressed down under heavy weights, the like of which, if placed upon the frame, would crush its vitality in a moment; and there, should we behold a soul fettered and manacled with chains, the like of which, if binding any human body, would effectually prevent its ever getting free. On one side should we behold men driven on to the brink of precipices which they see not, imagining that they are upon a smooth and easy road, the end of which is Paradise—and .on another, men driven on to those same precipices, seeing them, and yet unable to avoid them; and as we looked on all these real sights, we should then perhaps believe, that the spirit world is as real as this in which we live and move, and touch and eat.

But it is not evil only that by such an opening of our eyes would be revealed to us, we should also be shewn good—"good," beautiful in its calm sweetness—"good," beautiful in its terrific sublimity. For example: here is a soul in which the will is conformed in great measure to the will of God; and whether it be the will of God, that there should be a day of toil to be borne, or that the night of death should now close in; in either case there is an even calm; just as there is in the long day's early twilight, when the day is about to break, or in its shadowy eventide, when it is about to close.

But all good sights would not be like this. We should see strife and crucifixion, we should hear sounds of sorrow and of pain. Battles would be seen going on in the souls of some, as real as are fought upon the fields of earth; crucifixions as real as that which took place on Calvary. Men, under the generalship of God, would be seen fighting their evil selves—cutting, thrusting their own evil wills; and although we can imagine but little sublimity about a cross which was the malefactor's death-spot—the end of his life of ignominy and shame; yet, forasmuch as Jesus raised even the cross into the regions of the sublime, so also can the followers of Jesus; and when a man is seen binding his will to the cross, nailing it, crucifying it, piercing it, hearkening not to its cries; what is this but the sublime? No! not the sublime in the eyes of those who see with unsanctified eyes—but the sublime in the eyes of the Father, and of the Son and of the Holy Ghost.

There is nothing harder than the crucifixion of the will; the highest stage of Christian attainment is the sanctification of the will. There are many triumphs to be won in the spiritual warfare; many points of progress to be made in the spiritual journey; many evidences of our having learned specific lessons to be obtained in the spiritual school; but they all sink into comparative nothingness, when compared with the great attainment of all—the sanctification of the will.

Let it be distinctly observed, that we do not undervalue any spiritual triumph, progress, or attainment. God forbid! each has its own specific worth, and its relative worth also, we trust, as an evidence of a measure of sanctification of the will; but the sanctification of the will itself, that inner root work in the very depth and mystery of our being, is the great point of all. This is fountain work, and lo! the streams will flow as clear as crystal; this is root work, and lo! the flowers and fruits will bloom and ripen to perfection; this is heart work, and lo! the whole system will partake of the health of the vital organ—a sanctified will is the very kernel of spiritual life.

Let us, with all reverence, ponder awhile the human will of our blessed Lord; and then bethink us of our own wills, alas! so unlike His; but yet capable of being made like thereto, by the gracious influences of the Holy Ghost.

Jesus Christ commenced, passed through, and ended His life with a sanctified human will.

Our Lord, as being in all points like unto us, with the

exception of sin, had a true human will; it was, I
suppose, in no particular different from our wills, with
this exception, that it was ever sanctified, even from the
womb—that it never had any bias towards the commis-
sion of evil, or rebellion against God. I believe that
Jesus, the second man, had the same free will that Adam,
the first man, had in Paradise; and if He had not that
free will, I do not see how He could have been "tempted
in all points," like unto ourselves. If He had so willed
it, He might have cast Himself down from the pinnacle
of the temple; or commanded the stones to be made
bread; or have refused the bitter cup of Gethsemane,
and the bitter anguish of Calvary. What the consequences of His so doing would have been, so far as we
are concerned, we can easily see; all we desire to say is,
that such things might have been done. Christ was
born with a real, but a sinless human will.

And we find the blessed Saviour living in a perfect
sanctification of this human will; we have indications in
Scripture of how this holy will interpenetrated His
whole life; it was a part of His very being, therefore
its actings were everywhere to be found. Let us gather
up some of the Scripture teachings which we have concerning it.

In John iv, He is represented to us as sitting upon
Jacob's well, weary with His journey. While there, all
weary as He was, He enters into conversation with the
Samaritan woman, penetrating her conscience, enlightening her mind, and enunciating, in His declaration of
God's intense spirituality, one of the highest forms of
spiritual truth. His disciples come to Him, and bringing
provisions with them, pray Him, saying, "Master, eat."

" But He said unto them, I have meat to eat that ye know not of. Therefore said the disciples one to another, Hath any man brought Him ought to eat? Jesus saith unto them, My meat is to do the will of Him that sent me, and to finish His work." The Lord does here, what He does on so many occasions—takes a passing word or fact, and either grounds upon it or teaches from it some wondrous truth. Whilst the disciples thought of nothing but the lower need of hunger, Jesus felt the higher need of hungering after the fulfilment of His Father's will, in the enlightening of a soul; while they thought of no means of supplying hunger but by bread, He discerned a higher nourishment, the fulfilment of His Father's will.

Now, how was it meat to Jesus, to fulfil His Father's will? We can easily imagine His being *spent* in doing that will, but not so easily, His being *nourished* therein. We can learn something on this point from our own experiences. When we work out the determinations of our own evil wills, do we not thereby confirm and strengthen those wills in evil? do we not nourish them for becoming stronger to will fresh evil? and is it not thus that sinners become ever harder and more confirmed in sin? Our will strengthens itself by its own acts, just as the banyan tree, which drops its branches to the ground, and forms from each branch a stem, increases itself, by the spending of its energies. And hence is it not a marvel of grace, that the evil will, which we have so strengthened, and fed, from earliest youth, should be controlled, and overruled, and actually changed, by the influences of the Holy Ghost? Jesus' holy will was nourished by its own acts, yet was it perfect even from the beginning, just as Adam's body was fed upon the fruits of Paradise, though it came perfect from its Maker's hands. There is a sustaining power in holy action, when that action is the result of sanctified will; and that sustaining power was enjoyed by Jesus, as the man Christ Jesus, with a perfect human will; He had it as a natural consequence; and thus, as in many other ways, it was meat to Him to do His Father's will. Thus much appears to us to be upon the surface; the depths of the mystery of the interpenetration of Christ's human will, by the Father's Divine will, we presume not to attempt to sound.

Although we shall have to consider specifically our own wills, a little further on; yet we must not leave these various Scripture indications of Christ's will, without drawing from them what instruction we can for ourselves; for He, the man Christ Jesus, must be our teacher and example in the matter of the human will, as in all else.

Now (1.) what kind of a will have we been nourishing? Has the reader been simply gratifying his own will; has he, by every act, been confirming himself in selfishness, in obstinacy, in such like sins; or has he been nourishing a will in unison with God's will, by holy obedience, after the example of his Lord? Remember that if your acts flow forth from your will, they re-act upon that will also. And this is how many persons are lost; by carrying out their wills in acts of worldliness and fleshliness, those wills become stronger and stronger against God, and stronger and stronger for the service of Satan. Of course Divine interferences can do anything with a man; but this is the legitimate result. Well might the will of the flesh, and of man, be set aside by the apostle, when he tells us who are the sons of God. "But as many as received Him, to them gave He power to become the sons of God, even to them that believe on His name: which were born, not of blood, nor of the will of the flesh, nor of the will of man, but of God." John i, 12, 13.

Does not this show us (2.) the immense importance of a holy life? We complain of the strength of our evil wills—alas! have not we ourselves fed them? We complain of the weakness of our good wills—alas! have not we ourselves starved them? We are as much bound to nourish the life of a holy will, given to us of the Spirit, as we are to nourish the life of the body; we, like Jesus, should have meat to eat which the world knows not of.

And in truth, this meat would nourish us in a wonderful way; we should rise above the world; we should become a mystery perhaps to our very own, as the Lord did to His disciples. A life for God has not its influences confined simply to the judgment day; it is a mighty engine acting upon our own characters, penetrating, I am persuaded, even to having reflex effect upon our wills. Alas! how profoundly do we, by writing such things, shame ourselves, but this we believe to be the truth.

Mark also, how this sanctified will *entered into Christ's pursuit in life.* In John v, 30, He tells us, "I seek not mine own will, but the will of the Father which hath sent me." The one absorbing aim of life with Jesus was the performance of His Father's will; He did not merely take up that will when it crossed His

path, but He pursued it. "He went about doing good."
His life was one long labour in fulfilling His Father's
will. And in this pursuit, we can easily perceive, how
many opportunities there were for the giving up of the
mere natural will to the higher will of the Father, as
evidenced in the path plainly outstretched by Him
before His Son. The human will of Jesus would never
have led Him to the temptation of the desert—never to
fastings and reproaches; He would as naturally have
shrunk from these things as ourselves. And He *could*
have shrunk from them. He might have retired into
private life; He might have shunned the "contradiction
of sinners," but He must pursue His Father's will,
in every place, at every time; and so, forth He came
again and again in His self-denying ministry to
man. The *energy* of the Divine will was seen in His
will to pursue God's work, whenever it was to be
done.

Alas! here also we have to feel profoundly the
difference between our Lord and us. What *sought* He?
What *seek* we? What know we of the energy of pursuit, in doing the will of God? Do we not *seek* our own
wills, even though we be so far sanctified as to *yield* to
God's will, when He shows it? It is a solemn inquiry;
Whose will do I pursue?

Then, mark *the affections of our Lord.* We are told
in Mark iii, that His brethren and mother (after the
flesh) came and sought him; and when the multitude
told Him of it, He said, "Who is my mother, or my
brethren? And He looked round about on them which
sat about Him, and said, Behold my mother, and my
brethren! For whosoever shall do the will of God, the

same is my brother, and my sister, and mother." Mere human affection would have centred the heart's longings upon the relatives after the flesh; Jesus, in fulness of union with the will of His Father, saw in the performers of this will, those who were by the law of spiritual affinity nearest relatives to Himself; "the same," said He, "is my brother, and sister, and mother." Jesus did not ignore the relationships of earth, but He showed that the truest and highest relationship was not that of the flesh, but of the spirit; and men were to take place according to their spirit life, in fulfilling the will of God.

It is a comfortable thought that there will be recognition for brethren and sisters—for those who carry out the will of God in the bold actings of manhood; and those who carry it out in the tender sympathies of womanhood; yea, for such as are mothers to the weak ones of Christ's church, servers of the least of the brethren of Jesus; and so, doing unto Him. Here our Lord lets us into the secret of how interwoven into His heart, was the desire for the performance of His Father's will. There is something more than the judgment that it is the best that can be done; something more than the stern determination that it shall be done; there is the fact that all His sympathies are wrapped up in those who do it; in thus doing the will, they and He are in close relationship. How perfect must have been the sanctification of Christ's will, when it thus overpasses all the claims of nature, and institutes a new relationship, in which all depends upon doing the will of God.

It will surely be worth our while to ask ourselves,

whether we, in our daily life, are admitting the existence
of this relationship. Are we swallowed up in the selfishness of earthly wife and child love? Have we a heart
only for our kith and kin? Is the tie of blood everything
to us? There is many a one that would rather give £1000
to a thirty-fifth cousin after the flesh, than £1 to a brother
or sister in the Lord. Surely either the spiritual relationship does not exist at all, or we have not as yet arrived
at Christ's method of estimating such relationship; we
do not love on the same principle as He did. Let us
remember, how precious in His eyes were those who did
the will of His Father; precious, from the power of
sympathy; and may such be precious in our eyes also.
But we cannot now enlarge on this; the point which we
must now especially note, is the amazing worth of His
Father's will in His eyes, seeing that its performance by
others involved even relationship with Himself.

Yet once again: let us look at *the Saviour's joy.* We
know what His portion was on earth; sorrow and distress of every kind; it was the fulfilment of the pro-
phecy which went before, that He should be "a man of
sorrows and acquainted with grief," but He was not destitute of joy; only His joy, like His food, was such as
the world knew not of. What that joy was, we find in
Psa. xl, 8, "I delight to do Thy will, O my God, yea, Thy
law is within my heart." And this was indeed our
Lord's joy, through a world which, so far as its pleasures
were concerned, was a joyless world to Him. That
which excited the hopes and expectations of the young,
had no excitement for Him; that which moved the
mirth of the joyous and the gay, won no smile from
Him; earth's sins and sorrows lay too heavily upon His

heart for any of its joys to sparkle there. We are told He wept, we never read that He laughed. But Jesus was not without joy; He had joy over the one sinner that repented, He had joy over every pang of suffering that He removed—over every tear that He caught and dried up ere it fell—over the great prospects of the victory of holiness, which lay before Him in His death. He was the revealer, as well as the doer of the Father's will, and when we do find Him rejoicing, what is it that excites His joy? (Luke x, 21.) "In that hour Jesus rejoiced in spirit, and said, I thank Thee, O Father, Lord of heaven and earth, that Thou hast hid these things from the wise and prudent, and hast revealed them unto babes; even so, Father; for so it seemed good in Thy sight. All things are delivered to Me of My Father; and no man knoweth who the Son is, but the Father; and who the Father is, but the Son, and he to whom the Son will reveal Him. Even so, Father, for so it seemed good in Thy sight"—that was God's will; and then Jesus declares how He carried out that will; and therein He found His joy.

These are some of the Scripture indications of how Jesus was one with the Father, in the perfect sanctification of His will.

At last the time came for Christ to die; then it was that He spake the words, which above all others shew us the subjection of His will, "He went forward a little and fell on the ground, and prayed that, if it were possible, the hour might pass from Him; and He said, Abba, Father, all things are possible unto Thee, take away this cup from me, nevertheless, not what I will, but what Thou wilt·" Mark xiv, 35, 36.

Let us, with deep reverence, contemplate for awhile the *action*, and yet the *abnegation*, of this human will of Christ.

When our Lord says, "Not what I will," He doubtless referred to His human will; that which He had as the man Christ Jesus; that which, in His true humanity, He has in common with us. This will was now in *natural action ;* in no otherwise than yours and mine would have been, under similar circumstances, shrinking from agony and death, and that death a death of shame. To Jesus, such a death involved much more than it could possibly have done to you or me, had we been led to the cross; but it was the human will that shrank from all the suffering.

"Now," says Bishop Hall, "before these eyes, this Sun begins to be over-cast with clouds; He began to be sorrowful and very heavy : Many sad thoughts, for mankinde, had He secretly hatched, and yet smothered in his owne brest, now, His griefe is too great to keep in ; My soule is exceeding sorrowful, even unto death : O Saviour, what must Thou needes feele, when Thou saidst so ? Feeble minds are apt to bemone themselves upon light occasions ; the griefe must needs be violent that causeth a strong heart to break forth into passionate complaint; Wo is Me; what a word is this for the Son of God ? where is that Comforter, which Thou promisedst to send to others ? where is that Thy Father of all mercies, and God of all comfort ; in whose presence is the fulnesse of joy, and at whose right hand there are pleasures for evermore ? where are those constant and cheerful resolutions of a fearelesse walking through the valley of the shadow of death ? Alas ! if that face were not hid from Thee, whose essence could not be disunited; these pangs could not have beene; the Sun was withdrawne awhile that there might be a coole, though not a dark night, as in the world, so in Thy brest, withdrawne, in respect of sight, not of being: it was the hardest part of Thy sufferings, that Thou must be disconsolate. Every one of these words is both sharpe, and edged; My soule is exceeding sorrowful, even unto death; what humane soule is capable of the conceit of the least of those sorrows that oppressed Thine? It was not Thy body that suffered now: the paine of body is but as the body of paine; the anguish of the soule, is as the soule of anguish. That, and in that Thou sufferedst; where are they that dare so far disparage Thy sorrow, as to say Thy soule suffered only in sympathy with Thy body; not immediately, but by participation; not in its selfe, but in its partnere? Thou best knewest what Thou felt'st, and Thou that felt'st Thine own paine, can'st cry out of Thy soule. Neither did'st Thou say, My soule is troubled; so it often was, even to teares; but My soule is sorrowfull; as if it had been before assaulted; now possessed with griefe. Nor yet this in any tolerable moderation; changes of passion are incident to every humane soule, but exceeding sorrowful. Yet, there are degrees in the very extremities of evils; those that are most vehement, may yet be capable of a remedy, at least, a relaxation; Thine was past these hopes; exceeding sorrowful unto death.

"What was it? What could it be? O Saviour, that lay thus heavy upon Thy Divine soule? Was it the feare of death? Was it the fore-felt paine, shame, torment of Thine ensuing crucifixion? Oh! poore and

base thoughts of the narrow hearts of cowardly and
impotent mortality! How many thousands of Thy blessed martyrs have welcomed no lesse tortures with
smiles and gratulations? And have made a sport of
those exquisite cruelties, which their very tyrants
thought unsufferable? Whence had they this strength
but from Thee? If their weaknesse were thus un-
daunted and prevalent, what was Thy power? No! No!
it was the sad weight of the sinne of mankind; it was
the heavy burden of Thy Father's wrath for our sin that
thus pressed Thy soule, and wrung from Thee those
bitter expressions.

"What can it availe Thee, O Saviour, to tell Thy
griefe to men? Who can ease Thee but He of whom
Thou saidst, 'My Father is greater than I?' loe! to
Him Thou turnest: 'O Father, if it be possible, let
this cup passe from mee.'

"Was not this that prayer (O deare Christ) which
in the dayes of Thy flesh Thou offeredst up with strong
crying and teares, to Him that was able to save Thee
from death? Surely this was it; never was cry so
strong; never was God thus solicited. How could
heaven choose but shake at such a prayer from the
power that made it? How can my heart but tremble
to heare this suit from the Captaine of our salvation?
O Thou that saidst, 'I and my Father are one,' dost
Thou suffer ought from Thy Father but what Thou
wouldest—what Thou determinedst? Was this cup of
Thine either casual, or forced? Wouldst Thou wish
for what Thou knewest Thou wouldst not have possible? Farre, farre be these mis-raised thoughts of
our ignorance and frailty; Thou cam'st to suffer, and

Thou wouldst do what Thou cam'st for; yet, since Thou wouldst be a man, Thou wouldst take all of man, save sin. It is but humane (and not sinfull) to be loath to suffer what we may avoid; in this velleity of Thine, Thou wouldest shew what that nature of ours, which Thou hadst assumed, could incline to wish; but in Thy resolution Thou wouldst show us what Thy victorious thoughts raised and assisted by Thy Divine power, had determinately pitched upon; never-thelesse, 'not as I will, but as Thou wilt.' As man Thou hadst a wille of Thine owne; no humane soule can be perfect without that maine faculty; that will, which naturally could be content to incline towards an exemption from miseries; gladly vailes to that Divine will, whereby thou art designed to the chastise-ments of our peace; those paines, which in themselves were grievous, Thou embracest as decreed; so as Thy feare hath given place to Thy love and obedience. How should wee have knowne these evills so formidable, if Thou hadst not in halfe a thought inclined to depre-cate them? How could we have avoided so formidable and deadly evils, if Thou hadst not willingly undergone them? We acknowledge Thine holy feare; we adore Thy Divine fortitude."

And this will was also in *sinless action*,—there was no sin in that shrinking; it was a purely natural act; had there been the smallest speck of sin in it, it would have made Jesus unfit for sacrifice—He would then have been a spotted and blemished lamb.

And hence may we not gather, with what eye God looks upon our shrinkings, albeit we be prepared that in us His great will should be carried out? We have

such shrinkings—they are the natural and sinless
motions of our very nature; sin begins when our will
must have its own way—when it will not put itself
at the disposal of God's will—when, perhaps, even worse,
it will not succumb to the pressure of it. Now the
Father never had to bring pressure to bear upon the
will of Christ; that will was ever at the disposal of the
Father's will; it acknowledged its existence, "what I
will," but it held itself at the Father's command—"not
what I will, but what Thou wilt." We may have shrinkings without sin; *obedient*, not *unfeeling*, human nature
is what God desires. The very shrinkings of Jesus
formed, no doubt, an ingredient in His cup of suffering
—they were a part of the dark valley of death—they
were almost the first pangs of His now present disso-
lution. He was to be taken as a *human* sacrifice;
therefore with all that belonged to sinless humanity,
its shrinkings, and all beside.

Ah! what heart shrinkings and flesh shrinkings
we have, when times of trial draw near; shall we say
that God is angry with us because of them—that He
counts them sin? I do not think so; I believe He
pities us in them, and sends us some messenger to
strengthen us; "He knoweth whereof we are made;"
"Like as a father pitieth his children, so the Lord
pitieth them that fear Him;" a consecrated will, and
yet a shrinking will, may exist in one and the same
person. Truly God is no hard God, waiting for an
opportunity to strike, but patient and gentle; He en-
courages our wills, so that we also are taught to say
with our Lord, "Nevertheless, not as I will, but as
Thou wilt."

We may pause for a moment to ask what this human will of Jesus could have done apart from the will of the Father? It could have willed not to suffer, —it could have willed this sinlessly; had Jesus pleased to surrender the salvation of the world, what was there to hinder Him? But His will and the Father's were one for atonement—so He died.

It may be that we can easily understand how the will of Jesus suffered a rude assault in Gethsemane, and perhaps also on Calvary; and possibly we think, that the trial, though quick and sharp, was soon over; but His will had other trials besides these.

This sanctified will of Jesus met with opposition, where, humanly speaking, we should have least expected it, *i.e.*, in the bosom of His own family—the apostolic band. "Then Peter took Him, and began to rebuke Him, saying, Be it far from Thee, Lord: this shall not be unto Thee; but He turned, and said unto Peter, Get thee behind Me, Satan; thou art an offence unto Me; for thou savourest not the things that be of God, but those that be of men:" Matt. xvi, 22, 23. Now, these were very sharp words to utter to a zealous and beloved disciple, whose only apparent feeling was deep sympathy with his Lord—a love too great to hear Him talk of suffering and death, without being moved. Such words had never before fallen from the lips of Jesus towards any one of His apostles, nor had they been said even to the worst of His adversaries; the nearest approach to them, being what we find in John viii, where He says to the cavilling Jews, "Ye are of your father the Devil, and the lusts of your father you will do."

There must have been a profound depth of sin in

Peter's remonstrance with his Lord, to call forth this in-
dignant rebuke—the like of which we do not find in the
previous history of Jesus; no, nor afterwards, when in
the upper chamber, He held forth His pierced hands to
the doubting Thomas; nor yet, when from the discovered
radiance of another world, He spake to the persecuting
Saul. Such being the case, we may expect something
more than ordinary in these verses, which exhibit Jesus
in an attitude so energetic, and Peter in a character so
dark; and in truth we shall not be disappointed, for
through the instrumentality of an apostle, the wicked
one here ventures very close to Christ, presuming to try
to interfere with, and to unsanctify His will; and endeavouring by the hand and voice of friendship to arrest the
salvation of man. It is true that the apostle was personally guilty; he had mingled selfishness with love; he
could not part with his visions of worldly power which
he still entertained, and which made him believe that he
should receive great temporal things from the Christ the
Son of the living God; he was under the darkness and
the sin of an earthly heart; but it was not earthliness
alone that was rebuked, it was also misguided affection
—Satanic will hidden under the mask of human love—
a temptation which was calculated to be a peculiar
hindrance to the great work which the Saviour was to
do. We know that as a man, the Lord shrank from
death; and now, when the voice of love without strengthened the feelings of the heart within, Christ saw a peculiar manifestation of the Devil, and rebuked it in these
fearful words. The words of Peter, when looked at in
the original, seem to throw yet further light upon this
matter. We can scarce imagine, that however bold the

apostle might have been, he would have presumed to rebuke the Lord in the way in which one man rebukes another. After all the displays of Christ's power which he had witnessed, we can hardly think of his having ventured so far; nor did he; the words used imply "an affectionate chiding." "And Peter took Him, and began affectionately to chide Him, saying, 'Pity Thyself,' (mark here the disturbing influence brought to bear upon Christ's will,) this shall not be unto Thee. Then Christ turned and said unto Peter, Get thee behind Me, Satan, *i.e.*, 'adversary,' thou art an offence, an obstacle unto Me, thou art not well affected to the things of God, but to those that be of men."

Let us suppose for a moment that Peter had been altogether untinged with any earthly aim; that he scorned all worldly advancement; that he was even at that very moment ready to shed his blood for Christ— that he would have stamped the gold of an earthly crown to powder beneath his feet—that he had altogether forgotten 'self' in Jesus; even though it were thus, what mistaken kindness was it to endeavour to hold back the Lord from the accomplishment of His high aim—an aim which involved at once our salvation and His glory, and to attain which, suffering must be undergone. The executioner that nailed the hands of Jesus to the accursed tree, the soldier who pierced His tender side, the scoffing rabble who railed upon and cursed Him—array all these together, and not one of them was such an adversary to Jesus as the apostle who said to Him, "Pity Thyself; this shall not be unto Thee."

Thus was Jesu's holy will tried severely—we have seen what that will was able to do in itself; now let us

look at it for a moment in connection with the will of
the Father. What position did it occupy with reference to that? It was a will not overruled by necessity,
(as ours, alas! too often is,) but drawn *with* all human
shrinkings into perfect unison with the Father's. There is
no reason for supposing that Jesus ever lost any of His
shrinkings from death; He remained the man Christ Jesus
to the very end; and it was the triumph of His holy will,
that it entered even with all flesh-shrinkings into the
will of God. It is not sin in us, nor is it the least dete-
rioration from the purity of our will, to carry our flesh-
shrinkings into our trials with us; the spirit may be
willing and the flesh be weak—excision of feeling is by
no means essential to sanctification of the will. What
comfort does this supply to some, whose natural man is
faint, but whose spiritual man is strong in time of trial.

And now, before we turn from this contemplation of
Christ's will, let us observe where these words were
spoken—in Gethsemane—Gethsemane was the place of
truest and greatest conflict; it was the last place of trial
and decision; it was with human shrinkings, but no
longer with an expressing human will that Jesus went to
Calvary. "It is finished" might have been said in one
sense, in the garden, as well as on the cross. We too
have our place and time of decision, often preliminary
to that of suffering; thrice happy are we if we pass as
victors out of the first conflict into the second, victorious
in the second conflict, because we have been victorious
in the first.

We descend now from this higher subject of Christ's
will, concerning which we write with great restraint, as

being one too high for us to venture far into, down to man's
will, a subject with which we are alas! only too familiar in
its dark aspects of waywardness, unconsecration, and
selfishness. What darker subject of contemplation can
any man have, than his own will? And yet, the subject
is, we trust, not altogether full of gloom; are there not
some streaks of light? Yea, perhaps, it may be said of
the reader, that even though it be only as a twilight,
still there is a *pervading* light, which shall shine more
and more unto the perfect day? Now, first, what is the
condition of our wills by nature? We have inherited
sinful wills, and one part of their sinfulness consists
in our very self-will, our standing out for independence
—our saying, "'Who is Lord over us?' we will be
lord unto ourselves." The Devil tempted man to independence, "For God doth know that in the day ye eat
thereof then your eyes shall be opened, and ye shall be
as gods, knowing good and evil:" Gen. iii, 5; and that
independence is now the main characteristic of the
natural will. The pride of the natural heart will hear of
no subjection; its own will must be its law.

"In disowning God's will as a rule, we disown all
those attributes which flow from His will, as goodness,
righteousness, and truth. As an act of the Divine
understanding is supposed to precede the act of the
Divine will; so we slight the infinite reason of God.
Every law, though it proceed from the will of the law-
giver, and doth formally consist in an act of His will,
yet it doth presuppose an act of the understanding. If
the commandment be holy, just, and good, as it is,
(Rom. vii, 12,) if it be the image of God's holiness, a
transcript of His righteousness, and the efflux of His

goodness; then, in every breach of it, dirt is cast upon
those attributes which shine in it, and a slight of all the
regards he hath to His own honour, and all the provisions He makes for His creation."*

It was not so in Adam when he was created; it was
not so in the sinless man Christ Jesus; it is so in us;
we begin our life with a will contrary to the will of
God. If we were only to sin, when drawn into it by
grievous temptation, bad as our case would be, it would
be good compared with what it is now; for now man
sins out of an ingrained evil will, pervading his whole
life, and cursing him more or less in every act. His
depraved will, is a law within him, which is contrary to
the law of God. And this will is not something that
can be idle; its very nature is activity; it is the great
impulsive power of our nature; it sets all else in motion
to accomplish its determinations; it must of necessity
keep up a continual rebellion against God.

"We make an idol of our own wills," says Charnock, "and as much as self is exalted, God is deposed;
the more we esteem our own wills, the more we endeavour to annihilate the will of God; account nothing
of Him, the more we account of ourselves; and endeavour to render ourselves His superiors, by exalting our
own wills. No prince but would look upon his authority
as invaded, his royalty derided, if a subject should
resolve to be a law to himself, in opposition to his
known will; true piety is to hate ourselves, deny ourselves, and cleave solely to the service of God. To
make ourselves our own rule, and the object of our
chiefest love, is atheism. If self-denial be the greatest

* " Charnock on the Divine Attributes."—Art. Practical Atheism.

part of godliness, the great letter in the alphabet of religion; self-love is the great letter in the alphabet of practical atheism. * * * Self-love is so far from bending to the righteous will of the Creator, that it would have the eternal will of God stoop to the humour and unrighteous will of a creature; and this is the ground of contention between the flesh and the spirit in the heart of a renewed man; flesh wars for the godhead of self, and spirit fights for the godhead of God; the one would settle the throne of the Creator, and the other maintain a law of covetousness, ambition, envy, lust, in the stead of God."

In connexion with the last days of Jesus' life, wherein we find His holy will submissive to the will of His Father, we find a horrible development of the will of man. We are told in Luke xxiii, 25, that Pilate delivered Jesus to *their will*. He who was, so to speak, the very incarnation of the will of God, is put into the power of the will of man, and how does that will act? It develops itself in hatred to the light, quenching the beams which shone upon it, determining to kill Jesus at any cost. It stops the warning voice, which should have been all the more powerful as coming from a heathen's lips, "Shall I crucify your king?" It wreaks its vengeance on Christ; a vengeance long stored up; a vengeance connected with the thwarting of its will, by the whole life and teaching of the Lord. The will of man was capable of doing this dreadful deed long before; it was ever seeking the way to work out this deadly end, but the restraining hand of the Lord was upon it, it could do nothing until that restraint was removed.

And have we not here a doleful suggestion as to what the will of man shall be in hell? All its activity will remain in full force, and the restraint now on it will be taken away. Oh! what a horrible prospect is thus in store for the lost. Oh! what must it be to dwell for ever amongst unrestrained evil wills; there are few more fearful subjects than that of "the activities of hell!"

It is to this, now unrestrained will, that Jesus is delivered; everything in the way of reason, justice, and thought, is overborne; man's wicked will works out its own desire to the uttermost; and Jesus dies.

And after all, what have we here? is it anything strange or unnatural? No! it is only the full natural development of an evil will. This is what we have in us; our will, if left to work out its evil bent, would crucify the Son of God afresh, and put Him to an open shame.

But it is earnestly hoped that the reader is not altogether under the power of an evil will—that he knows something of the work of sanctification upon that will; so that in the matter of his will, as of all else, he feels, "I am not mine own, I am bought with a price, therefore I must glorify God with my body and my spirit which are His."

It is to the subject of *the condition of our will during the process of sanctification*, that we must now turn for awhile.

The will of man undergoes *a progressive change*. We do not by any means come into immediate conformity with the will of God in all things, when we embrace

the cross, and are washed in the justifying blood of the
Lord Jesus Christ. Sore disappointment does this cause
to many true hearted beginners in the divine life; they
thought that the blood of Jesus would immediately
make them holy in themselves, even as it certainly
made them accepted before God; but lo! even after conversion they found self-will, and that self-will in direct
opposition sometimes to the will of God. At times, this
will shewed itself by refusing to go with the will of
God; and at times, by wanting to go in a course diame-
trically opposed to it. But no matter how it shewed
itself, it was an unsanctified will, and acted simply out
of its own nature, as such.

Does not Satan often perplex, and sorely cast down
young believers, by arguing upon this their as yet un-
tutored will? Does he not tell them that they cannot
be the children of God—that they cannot have received
Christ in love—that it is all a make-believe of grace
with them? We know he often argues thus, and almost
succeeds in drawing poor, weak, and young believers,
down into the very depths of despair. Would that
such could see, how that even in the most advanced
believers—old grey-headed saints—there is still a progressive work going on with reference to the will; they
would then know that this is no strange thing which is
happening to them; they would not be surprised, at not
being, at the beginning of their course, perfect in that
which is the very last thing to be perfected in the saints
of God.

Our will by no means succumbs willingly and all at
once. Is it natural that it should do so? After having
had all its own way for so long a time, is it accord-

328 THE "I WILL" OF SUBJECTION.

ing to the usual order of things, that it should enter
with willingness upon a new arrangement, in which
it becomes, as it were, nothing? The reason may be
convinced, the affection may be won; and yet the 'evil
will' want to work out its own desires; and hence come
some of those fierce strifes, and rendings of the inner
man, which make the believer cry, "O wretched man
that I am, who shall deliver me from the body of this
death?" Rom. vii, 24. Surely all of us, who know anything of the divine life, have felt, that the reason has not
had power over the will; our reason may have been
convinced, but the will was urging hither or thither,
irrespective of reason! a new influence had to come in—
it was the power of the Holy Ghost—we were taught
that God's people shall be willing in the day of His
power. (Psa. cx, 3.)

To such as are aiming after this entire sanctification of
the will, a few words of caution may not be out of place.

Let us beware of mistaking *apathy* for active consent to the will of God; it is possible to fall into the
fatalism of the Turk, while desiring to carry out the
highest life of the Christian.

The sanctification of the will has made but little
progress, if the utmost we have attained to be the
feeling 'we can't help it, and therefore, we may as well
make the best of it, and resign ourselves to the will of
God.' Might it not be well said, "What thank is there
to you for that? 'You can't help it, and therefore you
are making the best of it,' *i.e.*, you are treating the
will of God just as you would a bad debt; you are
making a virtue of necessity." God knows the pressure

of the necessity, and He will not give such a one credit for the virtue. There may be little or no difference between the man who struggles against God's will, and the one who sulkily, or sleepily, or slavishly lies down under it. "Resignation" is a word that is greatly abused as regards moral position before God; in many a case, if it were paraphrased, it would run thus: "I don't rebel, for there's no use." Let us beware of this kind of conformity of our will with God's will, under circumstances of worldly loss, and especially of bereavement. We must aim not merely at a crushed assent, but at a living consent with the will of our Father who is in heaven,—we must try to enter individually into the words we utter, "Thy will be done in earth as it is in heaven." Oh! how little "life of the will" really exists in much of what we call resignation; assent, and not consent, is the highest to which we can attain.

The harmony of the human will is essential to God's glory; when this harmony does not exist, the service is of constraint. Now constrained service is not what God desires; *that* He can have simply by the power of the bridle, and the lash, keeping back or urging on by irresistible force. This was the kind of service He took out of Balaam; this is what He unquestionably takes out of many a one now; it is not the service claimed by a Father, but that exacted by a Lord. The apostle shews us in 2 Cor. ix, 7, the kind of service in which God delights—a willing service. "Every man according as he purposeth in his heart, so let him give; not grudgingly or of necessity, for God loveth a cheerful giver."

In our times of great bereavement let us be alive, by God's grace, to the need of the harmony of our will with the divine will; let us seek after the active principle in our obedience; there is rarely happiness in mere resignation.

No doubt this is very, very hard; but the Holy Spirit, who is the Sanctifier of our wills, can do this for us; thus we may become "as sorrowful, yet always rejoicing."

And now, it will doubtless encourage us much to seek this sanctification of the will, if we see plainly the special advantage which we shall have from having our will in unison with the will of God.

The harmony of our human with the Divine will, will bring us calmness of mind. *The rebellious element of antagonism will be removed*, and we shall have the peace of God which passeth all understanding. When wind and tide are contrary to each other, then the waves arise; but when they go together, though the tide be running strong and the wind be blowing fresh, there are harmless riplets instead of angry waves.

Then, there will be *less cause for chastening discipline*. We bring much chastening and corrective discipline upon ourselves, in immediate connection with our wills. We are not chastened because we *did* such and such a thing, or left such and such a thing undone—the doing, or the leaving undone were, we will allow, the proper course of action; it is with the spirit at work in that course of action that God is dealing now; many a time is the child of God chastened for his will, and not for his deed at all.

There is, however, another kind of discipline besides

that which is corrective, *viz., instructive;* and this we
cannot under any circumstances hope to escape,—nor
indeed, should we wish so to do. The will cannot
advance in sanctification without Divine dealings upon
it, and exercises of it—without its being crossed. The
crossing of our wills by providential dispensations and
teachings, draws out their inward corruption; it shews
us the evil that is within us; it superinduces the
exercise of struggling with the will; it is in crossings
of the will that we learn to overcome the will. No mere
precept will accomplish this; it can only be brought
about through the discipline of facts. And this will,
perhaps, account for many of the thwartings with
which we have met in our daily life; we were under
instructive discipline, though we knew it not; and hence,
perhaps it is, that some one trial has been continued
for a long time; and that oftentimes, when we thought
we were upon the point of escaping from it, we were
put back and obliged to remain exactly where we were
before; and hence, also, that the same trial assumed new
phases, or complicated itself with other trials; or returned, after it seemed to have taken its departure for
ever. Our wills were being drilled—they were under
discipline—they were being taught the word of command. Watch the motions of a regiment on parade:
now they form in line, now in column; now they are
broken up into sections; at one moment they are
charging at the double, at the next they are standing
immovable in a square; now the rifles discharge a
volley, now it is file-firing that falls upon the ear, as
up and down the flashes run along the line. Here, we
see varied positions taken up, in response to the will

of a single man; and that which the men are being taught is to give quick and precise obedience to that will. What else are we being taught by the instructive discipline of the Divine dealing with these too wayward wills of ours?

But to return to the special advantage of having our will in unison with the will of God; this will give us calmness of mind *under changes of providential arrangement.* Man never continueth in one stay; when we have settled down into comfortable conformity with the will of God in some one position, we think we are in conformity in everything: then comes a change of providential arrangement, and it remains to be seen whether the will be ready, not for some one act of obedience, but for any which may be required.

It is highly possible that the mind may be so torn with temptation, and the body so racked with anguish, that all that can be done is to hold fast to the will of God, come what may. But this is a great achievement. With the afflictive dispensation comes the Satanic temptation; and to hold unwavering to the will of God, as the rule of our will, is the effect of its sanctification by the Holy Ghost.

Let us look at two eminent children of God under deeply afflictive circumstances, and see in each, the sanctification of the will.

The first of these is Mrs. Fletcher, of Madeley. Her change from the height of human happiness to the depth of human misery was sudden; it came upon her when she was weakened with fever; Satan took advantage of her state; she seemed to lose all except a close clinging to the will of God; but in retaining this she kept—how much! We turn to the journal for a history of her trial.

"For a good while past, my dear husband has joined with me in prayer in an uncommon manner. We are led to offer ourselves to do and suffer all the will of God. Something seems to tell me I must have more of the bitter cup; and these words are much to me, 'That I may stand in the evil day, and having done all, stand.' My prayer is, that the evil day may be before death—not at the last. But Lord, Thy will, Thy whole will be done. Certainly I have now scarce any cross. Thou hast made my cup to run over! Yea! Thou hast made me to forget all my sorrows. It seems as if I had never suffered anything. There is not a comfort I can wish for which I have not; but Lord, I want more grace.

"Oct. 25.—When I wrote last (July 26) I was indeed arrived at the summit of human felicity! My cup did indeed run over! I often said, Lord, how is this? Am I indeed one of those of whom it is said 'These are they who came out of great tribulation.' My way is strewed with roses; I am ready to say with Joseph, 'The Lord hath made me to forget all my afflictions, and all my father's house.' But oh! how shall I write it? on the 14th of August, 1785, the dreadful moment came. The sun of my earthly joys for ever set, and the cloud arose which casts the sable on all my future life. At half-past ten that Sabbath night, I closed the eyes of my beloved! What a change! The whole creation wears a new face to me. The posture of my mind at this season I will not trust my memory to describe.

"On the Tuesday before my love died, when those words were applied to my mind, 'Where I am, there

shall my servants be, that they may behold my glory,"
I felt such a power in them, as seemed in a great degree
to take away the bitterness even of that dreadful cup.
'To behold my glory!' That thought would for moments
swallow up all, and I seemed to lose myself in the desire
of His glory being manifested. But that awful night!
when I had hung over my dear husband for many hours
expecting every breath to be his last, and during which
time he could not speak to, nor take any notice of me,
a flood of unspeakable sorrow overspread my heart, and
quite overwhelmed my spirit. I was scarcely in my
senses; and such a fear seized my soul, lest I should say
or do anything displeasing to the Lord, that I was torn
as it were a thousand ways at once.

"My fatigue had been great. I was barely recovered of
my fever, and this stroke so tore my nerves, that it was
an inlet to much temptation. In former parts of my life,
I have felt deep sorrow; but such were now my feelings,
that no words I am able to think of can convey an ade-
quate idea thereof. The next morning,—O, my God!
what a cup didst Thou put into my hand! Not only my
beloved husband, but it appeared to me my Saviour too
was torn from me! Clouds and darkness surrounded both
soul and body! The sins even of my infancy came before
me, and assaulted me as thick as hail! I seemed to have
no love, no faith, no light—and yet I could not doubt
but I should see the smiling face of God in glory! Yea,
that heaven would terminate all my sufferings! There
did not seem one doubt thrown at my *final* salvation.
An unshaken belief that Christ would bring me through
all, was my great support; and it seemed to me that I
must have been annihilated had I been moved from that

anchor. No finite creature could have supported it. My agonized soul seemed to sweat blood, and I felt the meaning of these words, 'The pains of hell gat hold upon me!' What, said I, is this the soul that but a few days ago delighted in the thought of His glory! But now He hath entered into judgment with me! My soul was amazed, and in deep anguish; and literally my life drew nigh to the grave.

"When formerly I have read accounts like this I have thought,—these persons have a strong way of expressing themselves; but alas! I solemnly declare, no expression appears to me strong enough for what I felt; that word passed my mind several times,

> 'Even to His Father did he look
> In vain—His Father Him forsook!'

"A host of fears seemed to surround me, and I was (as it appeared to me) given into their hands. Those words came often to my mind 'To know Him, and the power of His resurrection, and the fellowship of His sufferings.' Sometimes I remembered that expression, 'My God! My God! why hast thou forsaken me.' I cast my mournful eyes towards the 'Man of sorrows,' who spoke them, but there seemed no answer. All was horror and darkness.

"Many times a day I visited my lovely corpse, remembering as I knelt beside him how he used to say, 'Ah! my dear Polly, must I ever see thee laid out on this bed!' But alas! he could no more speak to me, no more express his tender sympathy! Now 'I trod the winepress alone,' and truly, 'There was none with me.' The rest of the day I sat mostly alone in the next room, where my window presented to my view the grave digging, and the churchyard visited by numbers to look at the vault!

"My anguish was extreme. All outward support seemed to be withdrawn; appetite and sleep quite failed me; and even the air, I often thought, had entirely lost all its vivifying powers. As I never before had any conception of the bitter anguish which the Lord saw good to visit me with at this season; so I can give no just description of it. 'Known unto God are all His ways;' and I was assured, even in the midst of my trouble, that all He did was well, and that there was a needs be for this heavy trial. But what bound all my other trials upon me was, I felt continually the keenest accusations from Satan, constraining me by every possible suggestion to look at my extreme sensibility in suffering, as being deeply sinful! What, thought I, has made this change? If Jesus was my all, should I not feel as keenly the sense of His having suffered for me, as I do in the thought of my dear husband's kindness, and in the dreadful feeling of my separation from him? And because I could feel but very faint touches of sensible communion with God, I was torn as it were in pieces. All my religion seemed shrunk into one point; *viz.*, a constant cry, 'Thy will be done!' *I will, yes, I will glorify Thee! even in this fire.*

"Yet it seemed to me I did not glorify Him; and so afraid was I of turning to any human comfort, or stopping short of all the Lord would have me to do or be, that in the midst of this terrible furnace, I can say, that at every moment my conscience was 'quick as the apple of an eye, the slightest touch of sin to feel.' Yea, my spirit was all eye to discern its most distant approach. Yet in everything I seemed to be accused, and also condemned! so that 'my soul was' indeed 'sorrowful even unto death.'"

And now let us look at Madame Guyon's trials.

"It would be difficult for me," said she, "to enumerate all the acts of unkindness and cruelty which were practised towards me. The little garden near my cottage, I had put in order. Persons came at night and tore it all up, broke down the arbour, and overturned everything in it; so that it appeared as if it had been ravaged by a body of soldiers. My windows were broken. They were dashed through with stones, which fell at my own feet. All the night long persons were around the house, making a great noise, threatening to break it in, and uttering personal abuse. I have learned since who put these persons upon their wicked work.

"It was at this time that notice reached me, *that I must go out of the diocese.* The good which God had enabled me to do, was condemned more than the greatest crimes. Crimes were tolerated; but the work of God, resulting in the conversion and sanctification of souls, could not be endured. All this while I had no uneasiness of mind. My soul found rest in God; I never repented that I had left all to do what seemed to me to be His will. I believed that God had a design in everything which took place; and I left all in His hands, both the sorrow and the joy."

Under these circumstances, it is obvious that she could no longer remain. "I saw," she says, "that there was nothing for me to do here, so long as the bishop should be against me. I did what I could to gain his good will; but it was impossible to do it on any other terms than the engagement which he demanded of me, and which I knew it to be my duty not to make." The union of priests, bishop, and people against her, she regarded as an obvious indication of Providence, that, in the language of scripture, she must "shake off the dust of her feet against them," and go to another city.

And what were the feelings under which she was thus compelled, for a second time, to leave her field of labour, and go again, she knew not whither? "My soul," she says, "leaving all to God, continued to rest in a quiet and peaceable habitation. O Thou, the great, the sole object of my love! If there were no other reward for the little services which we are able to perform, than this calm and fixed state, above the vicissitudes of the world, would it not be enough? The senses, indeed, are sometimes ready to start aside, and to run off like truants; but every trouble flies before the soul which is entirely subjected to God.

"By speaking of a fixed state, I do not mean one *which can never decline or fall,* that being only in heaven. I call it fixed and permanent, in comparison with the states which have preceded it, which, being in the mixed life, and without an entire and exclusive devotedness to God, are full of vicissitudes and variations. Such a soul, one which is wholly the Lord's, may be troubled; but the sufferings which it is called to endure, affect only the outside, without reaching and disturbing the centre. Neither men nor devils, though they discharge all their fury against it, can permanently harm a soul that is free from selfishness, and is in union with the Divine will. No sufferings whatever could ever affect it, neither more

nor less, neither within nor without, *were it not permitted
for wise purposes from above.*"

We shall have this calmness of mind in petty circumstances also.   According to the trite aphorism,
"Life is made up of little things," and the mind that
will accept the will of God in great matters and not in
small, must have some out of the way sphere appointed
to it, if it be conformed to this will at all.   Let us take
care how we provoke the Lord to appoint us out of the
way spheres; they may shake us with terrible rendings;
the lack of humility displayed in not accepting the
Divine will in little things, will surely make the Lord
deal with us with the rod.   He who refuses the discipline of the crook, shall certainly get the discipline of
the rod.

And let us mark the great advantage which we shall
get in an *increased rectitude of judgment.*   Our will
now biases our judgment; it comes in as a disturbing
influence; if it do not kick the beam, it at least holds
the balance unevenly; it ceases to be "what should be,"
and becomes "what we would have it be."   The bias of
the will is often fatal to the rectitude of the judgment.
But if our wills be conformed to the will of God; if we
cease to wish to have a will of our own, we shall allow
all arguments and facts to have their due weight with
us; and we shall judge righteous judgment.   Even the
natural judgment will find its great advantage, in the
subservience of the will; that subservience will produce
quiescence; and the heart being stilled, the will of God
will speak.

And now, lastly, how much this sanctification of the

will comes home to us, in the matter of our *own personal happiness.*

When we have given up our will to God's will, we shall enjoy the peace of being in the path of duty. The consciousness of being in the path of duty sweetens many bitter trials; lightens many heavy depressions; and gives stability in many slippery places. We know that all must be right and well, seeing that it comes in the order of the working out of God's will, and we are at peace.

See what contentment it will give us when others increase and we decrease; when we are put low, or kept low; for it is all according to the will of God.

Oh! that such a consecration of the will may be abundantly vouchsafed to the readers and the writer of this book; may we be able to pray from the heart's core, "Thy will be done in earth as it is in heaven:" may we be able to say, "Nevertheless, not as I will but as Thou wilt." We, in our *small* measures, have our Gethsemane and Calvary, our garden, and our cross; oh! that the utterance of our consecrated, though bleeding, hearts may be this, "Nevertheless, not what I will, but what Thou wilt."

The "I Will" of Glorification.

———

JOHN xvii, 24.

JOHN xvii, 24.

"Father, I will that they also, whom Thou hast given Me, be with Me
where I am; that they may behold My glory, which Thou hast
given Me: for Thou lovedst Me before the foundation of the
world."

⟶⟩⟨⟵

NOW precious are family gatherings on earth!
When the Christmas log blazes upon the
fire; and it may be, three generations meet
together; and they are all one, in common
blood, from the grandsire who leans upon his staff, down
to the infant that lies slumbering in its cradle, how
genial is the glow that diffuses itself through the heart;
a glow, not from the Christmas log, but from the still
hotter fire of human love.

And what efforts are made to accomplish such
family gatherings as these! The old man has tottered
a long way upon his staff, the young man has worked
harder than his wont, to pay for daintier fare. And what
efforts are made that this shall be a day of enjoyment;
and that it may be so, the old man determines to forget
his pains, and the young man his labours, and the
anxious mother her cares; alas! that there should be

generally so much toil to secure a little joy; we squeeze out in slow and laboured drops, what flowed in gushing streams in Paradise.

And then, when with difficulty and labour, we accomplish such large gatherings on earth; how swiftly, to use the poet's simile, does "sorrow tread upon the heels of joy." Solemn thoughts gather in the minds of thinking men; even whilst the enjoyment is going on, the time of dispersion is drawing near, and, will that company ever meet together on earth again? It may be that before Christmas comes once more, that old man will have calmly heard the voice of the messenger, and gone away to the distant land; or, perhaps, that young man will be broken up in some of life's tempests, and the fragments of his shattered home be tossed hither and thither, to be seized and appropriated by the lawless wrecker's hand; who knows but that the young mother's soft lullaby may be stilled for ever; or that the little babe, ere it lisps on earth, may be taken to sing in heaven? The sword of Damocles is suspended over every heart, the dead fly is in every pot of ointment, the cloud no bigger than a man's hand is in every sky. On earth we gather, but to be dispersed; life is a garden in which the bud blossoms but to decay; it is a dissolving view in which the smile melts away into a tear.

But turn we to God's great family gathering, of which all earthly family gatherings are but broken and imperfect types, and here we shall find that for which the heart so earnestly pants; a scene of joy which shall be unbroken; a meeting of dear friends which shall never be dispersed. "Gather my saints together; those that have made a covenant with me by sacrifice:" and in final fulfilment of that pregnant word, they shall come from the east and the west, and from the north and the south, and sit down in the kingdom of God.

What a noble family gathering will that be, where millions upon millions assemble in one vast home; all relations; all loving, all pure, all fresh in health and strength, all with common interest, all meeting never to part again. I pray God that every reader of this book may be present at the Great Father's feast; God their Father, and heaven their home!

And for this gathering great efforts are now being made. By efforts, we mean puttings forth of Divine power; for strictly speaking, God need never make any effort; He has but to give His command, and what He wills must be done. But, we may say, efforts are being put forth, if we look at the means by which God works, and by which He has providentially ordered that His will shall be carried out. Down in dark cellars city missionaries are diving; up lofty attics are they climbing; away over the seas are foreign missionaries speeding; the iron missionary labours from morning to night throwing off its printed sheets of warning, instruction, and invitation; Bible women, colporteurs, district visitors, sabbath school teachers, and many such are gathering together the family of God: and with that gathering there are none but glorious thoughts connected; its brightness shall never be dimmed; its unity never broken up.

The unity of the church of God is connected with the glory of Christ,—to break up that unity would be to hurt His glory—His people are to behold His glory, and that glory is to be eternal; they must behold it not only in its degree, but in its duration—for ever and for ever. "Father, I will that they also whom Thou hast given me, be with me where I am; that they may behold my glory, which Thou hast given me; for Thou lovedst me before the foundation of the world."

Now first of all, let us direct our attention to the *prominent position which this 'will' occupied in the mind of Christ.*

We see it in His *labouring.* Christ's life was one of labour; and this labour, whilst fulfilling the will of His Father, had an ulterior object, viz., the gathering together of His Church. Jesus knew that He had to teach His people, if they were to be made fit for glory— that He had to leave them an example—that the church would enter into His labours in after years; all true believers striving to fashion themselves after the model which He set. Jesus underwent a vast amount of labour before He suffered on the cross, but He knew that He was God's workman, with a surety of the harvest before Him, and with joy unutterable in His future rest, from the church present with Him in glory—the Church for which He wrought. I apprehend that Jesus was as God's servant, a man of the future as well as the present. He was a man of the present inasmuch as He seized all present opportunities, and performed with all His might all present duties, undergoing also all present toil; but He was a man of the future also, because He lived in the consciousness of the great recompense before Him, when He entered into His rest.

And Jesus had this will prominently before Him in *suffering* also. We are told by the apostle, that "for the joy that was set before Him, He endured the cross, despising the shame :" Heb. xii, 2. We err if we suppose that all Christ's suffering was in the garden and on the cross; temptation was suffering to Him; contact with evil, albeit He was undefiled thereby, was suffering; and so was the endurance of the waywardness and heaviness of His disciples; the cross was but the culminating point of accumulated suffering; no doubt the cross has its own grand distinctiveness, and this above all, that in that particular suffering of Jesus we find our life; but the cross stands as it were upon a pyramid, composed of the many sufferings of previous years. In all this we believe that Jesus kept steadily before Him the purchase and future possession of His Church. "Husbands," says the apostle in Eph. v, 25, &c., ... "love your wives, even as Christ also loved the Church, and gave Himself for it; that He might sanctify and cleanse it with the washing of water by the word; that He might present it to Himself a glorious Church, not having spot or wrinkle, or any such thing, but that it should be holy and without blemish." Christ had no visions of isolated glory; He had isolated glory without leaving the bosom of the Father at all.

This will was also strongly before His mind *in providing them with the Holy Ghost.* Well did Jesus know what His people would need, before they were fitted for being with Him, where He was. He knew they could not take their sinful natures, any more than their sins themselves, into heaven; and so, he provided that they should be sanctified as well as cleansed. It will be well for us when we think of Christ's determination to have His people with Himself, not to forget *how* He means to have

them also; His is no arbitrary will that overrides all
moral necessities; it is necessary that they who are to be
in glory should be holy, and that which is in Christ's
mind is not the determination to drag them to heaven
without any reference to sanctification, but rather to
sanctify them, and so fit them for being with Him there.

But this will of Christ had also a prominent place as
regards *personal feeling*. Jesus had such a personal interest in His people that He willed that they should get
the best. Now where was the best to be had? Was it
not with Himself, in His glory; in the place where He
was to enjoy what was pre-eminently His given glory—
i.e., the glory connected with the redemption of man?
Jesus knew the glory that awaited Himself, but He did
not, as selfish man too often does, think only of Himself;
He would make His people partakers of the best which
it was possible for them to have. Such is the interest
that our blessed Lord has in all His people now; these
words belong to us as well as to the apostles, and we may
fully take them to ourselves. And what a peace-giving
thought it should be to the heart, that we may leave all
our interests in our Lord's hands, as being abundantly
cared for by Him. He will have us in no less a place
than that in which He is Himself. We, with our poor
human love, know what it is to try and get the best we
can for those we love; we toil to be able abundantly to
provide for them; if there be anything worth seeing, we
try to show it to them; if anything specially fit for
them to have, we try to get it for them; we are but poor
scholars in the school of love, unless this be our experience. But Jesus is the Great Master in the school of

love; it is from His perfect lips that we gather up our poor lisping accents of love; and He carries out the natural impulses of love in getting the very best for His people. And Jesus has not to try, and fail, as we too often do; we have often felt sorrowful because we could not accomplish what our heart desired. Jesus receives from the Father all the desires of His heart; so that His people shall have throughout eternity everything that he desires for them. And if my Lord desire I should have the best, how entirely may I leave all belonging to eternity with Him. Yes! and all belonging to time also; if I trust Him with the greater, surely I may with the lesser also; if He care for me in heaven, He will care for me also upon earth. And thus will the world grow less and less; the best that it can give will be viewed side by side with even the least of the joys which Christ will give, and the light of heaven shall eclipse the light of earth.

And let us further mark, how the prominence of this will of Christ in personal feeling shews us that *His enjoyment is bound up in His people.* He is to have glory from the Father. He wills that that glory should be seen by His people. The closest connection which Jesus shall have through eternity, next after that which subsists between His Father and Him, will be that which shall subsist between Himself and His church. The damned will be His prisoners, and the angels His servants; but the church will be His bride, one with Himself in the closest and tenderest of unions for ever. Now, this is as though our Lord said, "I do not wish to keep all this glory to myself; I wish those to whom I have the tenderest feelings to enjoy it; my heart finds its pleasure in benevolence, in outflowings, in givings away; let my church, my spouse, be with me to behold and to rejoice in my glory."

And as we believe that Christ's enjoyment will be bound up in His people, so also do we believe that *their enjoyment will be bound up in Him.* They will know how He won His mediatorial glory; their own hearts will tell them the history of the jewels in His mediatorial crown; and however varied may be the joys, and however delightful the companionships of heaven, HE will continue the main attraction for ever and ever.

And this "I will" of Christ shews us that His connection with His people shall be not merely temporal but eternal. Death is the great severer of all human relationships; the closest bonds it snaps as though they were but a thread of tow. But none shall take away Jesus from the eyes of the heavenly beholders; none shall take away the beholders from Him; until the relationship be broken, the results flowing from it cannot be cut off, and so this "I will" secures to Christ's people an eternity of bliss.

Shall not this thought comfort us much, under the sore bereavements which we have to endure on earth? As wound after wound is inflicted upon our hearts, and friend after friend drops by our side; until at last a whole row of empty chairs stands in our room, shall not we find solace in this blessed thought,—the highest (oh! may we also ever be able to say, 'the dearest') of my relationships is unbroken. All these rendings are but for a season; soon I shall be with my Lord; and then, forasmuch as I am to be where He is, and He is all in all, I shall know such pangs as these no more.

Oh! these earthly separations from those we love, how terribly do they scald and wear the heart! day by day to see those things laid out, as it were, in such stony death-like forms, which used to lie about here and there, in the sweet abandonment of daily life. Oh! the misery of that order, where everything is in exactly its proper place, because there is no living hand to touch and move it; oh! that some one would come unawares and scatter those chairs about the room, and bid them not stand motionless like funeral mutes against the wall; oh! that some one would take those pens out of the inkstand, and drop them carelessly upon the table, as though some living hand had been using them; oh! for a wrinkle in that smooth and close drawn cloth; as smooth almost as the strained covering of the coffin lid; so that we might fancy that some one (*the* some one) had been leaning upon it, or using it in some of the work of daily life! Yes! all this comes of separation—the great separation—but take courage, Christian; thou shalt have a home in which there shall be the great separation no more.

But is it only the great separation that wrings the heart? ah! the lesser ones wring the heart strings too. What a feeling of heart-sinking comes over us, as we go into the room, which a dear friend has inhabited in our house, and from which he is just gone; look at those torn letters, look at that tossed and tumbled bed, from which life seems to have so recently fled; oh! that something had been left behind, that we could lay hold of, to connect the whole scene with the activities of life again; and have not we felt these heart-sinkings; the low murmurings of the voice which saith, "Man never continueth in one stay." "Arise ye and depart, for this is not your rest."

Well, dear reader, has it been observed, that next to a funeral, a wedding is often one of the saddest occasions on earth. Far be it from me to add one drop to the gall and bitterness of life—or to cause to pass even the most fleeting cloud across the wedding day's bright sky : but are there none to whom that day brings thoughts of sadness ? Does the mother shed no tear as she gives up her child ? does the father part with that which is bone of his bone, without feeling the wrench ? do not tears come into sisters' eyes as they say good bye ? and is there not an awkward silence when the carriage wheels are rolling from the door ? And when all is over, and the guests are gone, and the fragments of the feast lie neglected upon the festive board, and you stand and look, and think for a moment, how it all fleeted by like a dream ; of what froth can your heart be made, if there steals not into it one solemn thought—there has been a separation—a bud has been cut from the parent tree—'tis true, the sun shone upon the blade that severed it—and summer breezes, with soft and perfumed breath, sang merrily the marriage chant—but with all the brightness, all the music, the deed is done—the tree is cut—the bud is gone.

We too can rejoice with them that do rejoice, as well as weep with them that weep ; we make it almost a point of conscience to open our caskets, and bring out whatever jewels we possess for this festive day ; we try to drink into the spirit of Him who turned the water into wine : but we see in this, which is presumed to be the happiest of earth's days, what we see in the rose which is called the fairest of earth's flowers, the traces of the great separation between man and God—(the separation, which has borne as its fruit all other separations)—the one sad cause mars the beauty of the fairest flower, and dashes with a drop of bitterness the highest festivity of life.

But there shall be no more of this by and bye. Jesus shall hereafter be the great object of His people's love, companionship, and delight; and "where He is, there they shall be also." Nor shall there be any separation amongst the redeemed. We believe fully in the activities of heaven; we do not believe in the pictures which represent the redeemed as hanging midway in the air, with harps in their hands surrounding a Being, who is hanging there also. This to us is not the beatific vision. The infidel who saw a picture of it said, "If this be your heaven you may keep it to yourself." Our beatific vision takes a wider range than this; we believe it probable that the universe itself will be open to the activities of the redeemed, that there will be diverse spheres of service for the Lord—the rulership over ten cities and over five—but there shall be no separations, such as we experience upon earth. The whole body of the redeemed shall be gathered up into Jesus, as the folds of a garment are gathered up into one band; they shall be in union with Him as the myriad rays of the sun are with the one bright orb; they shall each perform their several functions, but they shall all be members of the one body of which He is the head.

And seeing that all this blessing is linked to connection with Jesus, how great is the need of clinging to Him! "If any man serve me, let him follow me and where I am, there shall also my servant be: if any man serve me, him will my Father honour:" John xii, 26. Let us link ourselves to that which seems the most enduring upon earth, and we shall find that it will crumble or dissolve; its very nature is, that either its relationship with us, or ours with it, cannot endure; but let us be linked to Christ, and we shall find that though heaven and earth pass away, His words shall not pass away, we shall be in unbroken relationship with Him for ever; His words shall be fulfilled, "Father, I will that they also whom Thou hast given me, be with me where I am, that they may behold my glory; for Thou lovedst me before the foundation of the the world."

We now come finally to consider, so far as we are led to do by this verse, a part of *the blessing of the redeemed*. It is spoken of here as "beholding the glory of Christ." This beholding will not be a mere "looking at," just as we look at some spectacle now— ourselves having no interest in the matter, except the pleasure which we may derive from the sight. The saints have a greater interest in the glory of Christ than this; "If we suffer we shall also reign with Him:" 2 Tim. ii, 12. "To him that overcometh will I grant to sit with me in my throne, even as I also overcame, and am set down with my Father in His throne:" Rev. iii, 21. Nor shall this beholding be merely transitory, for the apostle tells us in 1 Thess. iv, 17, that His people shall be ever with Him, "And so shall we ever be with the Lord."

We can easily understand how much more delight

the saints will experience in beholding the glory of their
Lord, when they themselves have an interest in it, than
they would have had if Jesus were one simply to be
admired, but wholly out of connection with themselves.
It may be that the devils will have some considerable
knowledge of the glory of Christ; perhaps as Dives
knew something of the happiness of Lazarus in Abraham's bosom, so the lost ones will have some consciousness at least of the glory of the Lord. But such a
consciousness will only increase their misery. He is
no Saviour, no friend, no glorifier to them. Will not
the personal love of the redeemed to their Lord make
them intensely happy in beholding His glory, even
apart from any actual reflection of that glory upon
themselves? We think it will, and that the analogy
of earthly relationship holds good here. When the
conqueror returns to his own country, victorious over
all His foes, and laden with their spoils; and when in
triumphant procession he enters the city amid the
clang of martial music, the waving of banners, and the
loud acclamations of thousands; who feels proudest of
him? whose eye dwells with greatest satisfaction upon
him? who feels personal honour in his honour, personal triumph in his triumph, personal gain in every
shout of the multitude, and boom of the thundering
gun? Surely we can think of but one—it is his
spouse, she with whom he is one, and who from her
very connection with him, feeble and unworthy though
she be, must in some measure share his glory. From
all such earthly triumphs we ascend to those yet
higher; and who in heaven will have the most joy
and interest in beholding the glory of the triumphant

Saviour? Is it the angels? Nay, they are not the spouse of Christ; and, moreover, they have never been redeemed through Christ. Who then? The Church; these of whom Christ speaks in the passage before us now. And would, that even now we perceived this our interest in Christ, as readily as we perceive His interest in us; then should we be more ready than we are to take a share in the conflict; as He will in the power of relationship share His glory with us; so should we in the power of relationship give our energies to Him. Alas! how one-sided are the best of us; we expect to get, we are unwilling to give. We should remember that as relationship involves giving, it involves receiving too. It is thus that the Church will behold, and in the power of relationship share the glory of her Lord.

But we may proceed yet a little farther into this matter; the redeemed shall behold the glory of their Lord with a great power of *comprehension*. Of course, they never can either fully scale the heights or sound the depths of the glory of Christ; vast as is the capacity of the saints it is finite still, nevertheless they shall know much about this. For the saints shall hereafter have great power of comprehension; now they see as through a glass darkly, but then they shall see face to face; now they know in part, but then shall they know even as they are known. The increased power of comprehension, wherewith the saints shall behold the glory of their Lord, shall form no small part of their happiness in heaven. They shall behold Him then, with the understanding which *personal experience* gives.

It is true we now, I hope, have some personal experience of our Lord; but it is an experience clogged with adverse circumstances. Jesus cannot now let the fulness of His glory flow forth to the individual soul; such flowings forth would be stopped by either the deadness or the evil within us, as we know that they have already frequently been. But when Christ's people are with Him, where He is, all these impediments shall be removed; they shall have full power to receive Him; they shall be able to make use of the revelations which He will give; all prejudice, all blindness, all mental cloggings will be removed, and they shall be able to enjoy the splendour which, in Christ, is outstretched before them. In glory, the capacity of the creature shall be increased, and he who recognises some brightness in Jesus now, shall then behold Him brighter than the sun; there will no doubt be Divine revelations of the wonders of the cross, to suit the expanded comprehension of the redeemed; and then, so far as He can be, by still finite beings, Christ shall be understood. What wonders of Divine *wisdom* will then meet our eyes, when we find that our Shepherd led us by ways that we knew not; we shall then know that it was Jesus guided us by such and such a path; and we shall see that He led us away from the beetling precipice, away from the shifting quicksand, away from the treacherous bog with its deceptive phosphorescent lights; it will be a part of the glory of Christ to have led His sheep through all these dangers to the fold, and we shall know it, and shall mingle wonder with our love. What wonders of divine *endurance* will then open out before our minds, when we ascertain how much the Saviour bare from us; how long He bare with us. Now, we know not the glory of His character, because we know not the

instances in which it is exemplified; but we shall know
it then; Jesus will shine forth in heaven, not only
with the glory of what He is, but with that of what He
has done; and with what eyes shall we behold Him when
we think, "Thus He endured for me"? What wonders of
divine *triumph* will then meet our eyes, when we have
unveiled to us many of the mysteries of Christ's agony
in the garden, and death upon the cross; when we see
how the councils of hell were thwarted, and the assaults
of hell repelled; and how those words, "It is finished,"
scattered the powers of darkness, and opened up the
great highway to the realms of light! What can we poor
dull creatures understand of all this now? We just grasp
the truth that Jesus died, in order that by it we may
be saved, but we cannot see far into it; we tarry as it
were in its outer courts, while there is a holy of holies
into which we shall be admitted by and bye. Cannot we
imagine how the hearts of the saints will be enraptured,
as they see and comprehend all these wonders in their
Lord? The astronomer, as he surveys the vast expanse of
heaven through his telescope, has his admiration drawn
out as it never could have been if he surveyed it only
with the naked eye; and he who examines a flower
through a microscope, rises from his steady gaze, and
strong light, and high magnifying power, which has let
him into nature's secrets, with an enthusiasm which otherwise he never could have felt; but neither telescope nor
microscope ever admitted any philosophers into such
secrets in the natural world as those to which this "I will"
of Jesus shall admit his glorified people in the spiritual
world. "On His head are many crowns," (Rev. xix, 12)
and they shall see them all—yea, not only the crowns—

but also the jewels in the crowns; what precious stones are there, and what their wondrous worth.

It may be that the redeemed will be admitted into many of the deep mysteries of God. This possibly is hinted at in the words, " For Thou lovedst me before the foundation of the world." Perhaps, their understanding something of this truth will give them the truest insight into the mysteries of the cross. The Father's love before the foundation of the world, will probably shew them in truest colours the price of the salvation of a soul. Thus, and thus only, can they know the cost at which their souls were redeemed; the value which was put upon those souls by God; the love which dictated a sacrifice so great. The Father's love to the Son *before* the foundation of the world, will be the greatest exponent of His love to mankind *in* the world.

As we think of these exceeding glories of the future, do we not see how vast is the difference between the pleasures and pursuits of Christ's people, and the world's, both now and hereafter?

The people of the world are toiling for honour, which cannot permanently ennoble them—for wealth, which cannot permanently enrich them—for health, which cannot permanently remain with them; no portion have they in the grand future of the saints; for they have none in Him by whom that future is made. When they lay down the coronets of earth, they have no crowns to take up in heaven; when they are severed from earthly wealth, they have no bags which wax not old; when they are unclothed of this their mortal flesh, they have no prospect of being clothed with a body like their Lord's. They may die with weeping, because they

have to part from their earthly things, as that great
actress, who had her jewels spread upon her coverlet,
and wept because she must "leave all these;" or, as that
unhappy creature whose spirit fleeted from her, while
her eye was fixed immovably upon a chest in the
corner of the room, where afterwards it was found that
her money was stored up; or in decent resignation they
may turn their face to the wall, and leave not even a
wrinkle upon their brows; but for them there is no
bright home beyond, for they care not for the presence
of Jesus, by whom that home's chief brightness is
made.

But for the saints all is bright, because they are
going to be with Him, whom their soul loveth. "I am
going to Him," said Dr. Owen, "whom my soul has
loved, or rather who has loved me with an everlasting
love, which is the sole ground of all my consolation."
When Mr. Payne said to him, "Doctor, I have just been
putting your book on '*The Glory of Christ*,' to the press,"
he answered, "I am glad to hear it; but, oh! brother
Payne, the long looked for day is come at last, in which
I shall see that glory in another manner than I have
ever done yet; or was capable of doing in this world."
What a death was that which was only a going forth to
meet One whom the soul loved. "I desire to depart
and to be with Christ, which is far better," said the Rev.
John Brown, of Haddington, "and though I have lived
sixty years very comfortably in the world, yet I would
turn my back upon you all to be with Christ. Oh!
commend Jesus, there is none like Christ, none like Christ.
I have been looking at Him these many years, and never
yet could find a fault in Him, but was of my own making,

though He has seen ten thousand faults in me. Many a comely person have I seen, but none so comely as Christ. I am weak, but it is delightful to feel one's self in the everlasting arms. Oh! what must He be in Himself, when it is He that sweetens heaven, sweetens scriptures, sweetens ordinances, sweetens earth, sweetens trials?" And when Rowland Hill was dying, all his thoughts were centred on beholding the person of his Lord, and being where He was. "I do believe," said the dying man, "that for the first ten thousand years after we enter the kingdom of glory, it will be all surprise." "But will this surprise never end?" "Never, while we behold the person of our Lord." "You are going to be with Jesus, and to see Him as He is," said a friend. "Yes!" replied Mr. Hill, with emphasis, "and I shall be like Him, that is the crowning point." Thus upon the dying bed, did these saints enter into the mind of Christ; thus did His "I will" pervade their wills, so that they were ready "to depart and be with Christ:" Phil. i, 23. For them death had no terrors, the unclothing of the spirit no discomforts, the silence of the grave no loneliness; for they knew that they were in Christ, and that soon they should be with Christ; they heard, they leant upon His words, "Father, I will that they also whom Thou hast given me, be with me where I am, that they may behold my glory which Thou hast given me; for Thou lovedst me before the foundation of the world."

And now we draw this volume to a close. In it we have heard the sweet voice of *invitation*, and Jesus has been presented to us as "willing" that all weary ones should come to Him for rest. In it, we have also heard

His solemn promise. He has been presented to us as irrevocably pledged "willingly" to *receive* every man who on his part will receive His grace. Thus inviting, thus receiving, the Holy One has been seen in His mighty work *cleansing* the poor leprous soul, for it is indeed His deepest "will" that it should be clean. Then, we have marked how cleansed ones are *made confessors* for their Lord, and how He "will" confess them before His Father in heaven. Yet, before that glorious time can come, we have heard what is appointed to many of us to do—to go forth and win souls to Christ; each one in his sphere "will" He make *a fisher of men.* Nor, thus confessing, thus working, shall any of us be left uncheered; Jesus Himself is with us in our toil; He "will" *not leave us comfortless,* He "will" come unto us. In these pages also have we read, how that every follower of Christ must be at His *disposal,* for toil or rest, for martyrdom or life; that it is His "I will," that must determine His people's lot. And very solemn is the inquiry which has been here suggested to us, concerning the *sanctification of our wills,* that highest point of Christian life, as from the deep shade of Gethsemane, we hear the voice of that sweet submissive human will, "Nevertheless, not as 'I will,' but as Thou wilt." Thus did Jesus "will" to suffer Himself, that He might be able to "will" in covenant power, *the glory of His people;* saying, "Father, 'I will' that they also whom Thou hast given me, be with me where I am, that they may behold my glory, which Thou hast given me, for Thou lovedst me before the foundation of the world."

APPENDIX.

MARTIN LUTHER.

As Luther is going from his father's house, at Mansfeldt, to Erfurth, he is overtaken by a violent storm, the lightning flashes, the bolt falls at his feet. Luther throws himself upon his knees; his hour is perhaps come. Death, the judgment, and eternity summon him with all their terrors, and he hears a voice which he can no longer resist. Encompassed with the anguish and terror of death, as he says himself, he makes a vow, if the Lord delivers him from this danger, to abandon the world, and devote himself entirely to God. After rising from the ground, having still present to him that death which must one day overtake him, he examines himself seriously, and asks himself what he ought to do. The thoughts that once agitated him now return with greater force. He has endeavoured, it is true, to fulfil all his duties, but what is the state of his soul? Can he appear before the tribunal of a terrible God with an impure heart? He must become holy. He has now as great a thirst for holiness, as he had formerly for knowledge. But where can he find it, or how can he attain it? The university provided him with the means of satisfying his first desires. Who shall calm that anguish, who shall quench the fire that now consumes him? To what school of holiness shall he direct his steps? He will enter a cloister, the monastic life will save him; oftentimes had he heard speak of its powers to transform the heart, to sanctify the sinner, to make man perfect. He will enter a monastic order. He will there become holy; thus will he secure eternal life.

Luther enters the monastery, and to mark his complete

separation from the world, sends back to the university his
ring of Master of Arts; there, in that monastery, he endures
the greatest humiliations; he is made the mendicant of the
order; but he stoops to all; for he is in search of holiness
and peace, and to disobey would in his mind be sin.   When
Luther had become a reformer, and had declared that heaven
was not to be obtained by such means as mortifications,
fastings, and watchings, he knew very well what he was
saying, "I was indeed a pious monk," he wrote to Duke
George of Saxony, "and followed the rules of my order more
strictly than I can express. If ever monk could obtain heaven
by his monkish works, I should certainly have been entitled
to it. Of this all the friars who have known me can testify.
If it had continued much longer I should have carried my
mortifications even to death, by means of my watchings,
prayers, reading, and other labours."   Luther did not find in
the tranquility of the cloister, and in monkish perfection, that
peace of mind which he had looked for there.   He wished to
have the assurance of his salvation—this was the great want
of his soul.   Without it there was no repose for him.   But
the fears that had agitated him in the world pursue him to
his cell.   Nay, they were increased.   The faintest cry of his
heart re-echoed loud beneath the silent arches of the cloister.
God had led him thither that he might know himself, and to
despair of his own strength and virtue.   His conscience,
enlightened by the Divine word, told him what it was to be
holy, but he was filled with terror at finding, neither in his
heart nor in his life, that image of holiness which he had
contemplated in the Word of God.   The monks and divines of
the day encouraged him to satisfy the Divine righteousness by
meritorious works.   But what works, thought he, can come
from a heart like mine?   How can I stand before the holiness
of my judge with works polluted in their very source?   I
saw that I was a great sinner in the eyes of God," said he,
"and I did not think it possible for me to propitiate Him by
my own merits."   A tender conscience inclined Luther to
regard the slightest fault as a great sin.   He had hardly discovered it before he endeavoured to expiate it by the severest
mortifications, which only served to point out to him the
inutility of all human remedies, "I tortured myself almost to
death," said he, "to procure peace with God for my troubled

heart and agitated conscience, but surrounded with thick darkness, I found peace nowhere."

So fierce was this inward strife, that on one occasion Luther, overwhelmed with sorrow, shut himself up in his cell; and for several days and nights allowed no one to approach him. One of his friends, Lucas Edemberger, feeling anxious about the unhappy monk, and having a presentiment of the condition in which he was, took with him some boys who were in the habit of singing in the choirs, and knocked at the door of his cell. No one opens, no one answers. The good Edemberger, still more alarmed, breaks open the door. Luther lies insensible upon the floor, and giving no signs of life; his friend strives in vain to recall him to his senses; he is still motionless. Then the choristers begin to sing a sweet hymn. Their clear voices act like a charm on the poor monk, to whom music was ever one of the greatest pleasures; gradually he recovers his strength, his consciousness, his life.

While this fierce struggle was going on, there comes a new actor upon the scene, this is John Staupitz, vicar-general of the Augustines for all Germany. This man who had undergone much the same course of conflict as Luther, although probably not with such severity, had found peace to his soul in simple faith in Christ; he is now destined to help Luther on to the peace of God, though an humbler instrument is designed to complete the work. Staupitz comes to the convent of Erfurth to make the usual inspection; when there, he exhibited much kindness to those monks who were under his authority. One of these brothers soon attracted his attention; he was a young man of middle height, whom study, fasting, and prolonged vigils had so wasted away, that all his bones might be counted. His eyes that in after years were compared to a falcon's, were sunken; his manner was dejected; his countenance betrayed an agitated mind, the prey of a thousand struggles, but yet strong and resolute; his whole appearance was grave, melancholy, and solemn. Staupitz, whose discernment had been exercised by long experience, easily discovered what was passing in his mind, and distinguished the youthful monk above all who surrounded him. He had had to struggle like Luther, and therefore could understand him above all; he could point out to him the road to peace which he himself had found......Luther's heart found an echo in that of Staupitz. The vicar-general under stood him, and the monk felt a confidence towards him that he had as yet experienced for none. He unbosomed to him the cause of his dejection, described the horrible thoughts that perplexed him; and then began in the cloister of Erfurth those conversations so full of wisdom and of instruction. Up to this time no one understood Luther. One day, when at table in the refectory, the young monk, dejected, and silent, scarcely touched his food. Staupitz, who looked earnestly at him, said at last, "Why are you so sad, brother Martin?" "Ah," replied he, with a deep sigh, "I do not know what will become of me." "These temptations," resumed Staupitz, "are more necessary to you than eating or drinking." These two men did not stop there; and ere long, in the silence of the cloister, took place that intimate intercourse which powerfully contributed to lead forth the future reformer from his state of darkness.

"It is in vain," said Luther, despondingly to Staupitz, "that I make promises to God; sin is ever the strongest."

"O my friend," replied the vicar-general, looking back on his own experience, "more than a thousand times have I sworn to our holy God to live piously, and I have never kept my vows. Now, I swear no longer, for I know I cannot keep my solemn promises. If God will not be merciful toward me for the love of Christ, and grant me a happy departure, when I must quit this world, I shall never, with the aid of all my vows, and all my good works, stand before Him; I must perish."

The young monk is terrified at the thought of Divine justice. He lays open all his fears to the vicar-general. He is alarmed at the unspeakable holiness of God, and His sovereign majesty. "Who may abide the day of His coming. and who shall stand, when He appeareth?"

Staupitz resumes; he knows where he had found peace, and he will point it out to the young man. "Why," said he, "do you torment yourself with all these speculations and these high thoughts? Look at the wounds of Jesus, to the blood He has shed for you: it is there that God's grace will appear to you. Instead of torturing yourself on account of your sins, throw yourself into the Redeemer's arms. Trust in Him—in the righteousness of His life—in the atonement of His death. Do not shrink back. God is not angry with you, it is you who are angry with God. Listen to the Son of God, He became man to give you the assurance of divine favour. He says to you, 'You are my sheep, you hear my voice; no man shall pluck you out of my hand.'"

But Luther does not find in himself the repentance which he thinks necessary for salvation, and replies : "How can I dare believe in the favour of God, so long as there is no real conversion in me? I must be changed, before He will accept me."

His venerable guide shews him that there can be no real conversion so long as man fears God, as a severe judge; "What will He say then," asks Luther, "to so many consciences to which a thousand insupportable tasks are prescribed in order that they may gain heaven?"

Then he hears this reply of the vicar-general, or rather he does not believe that it comes from man; it seems to him like a voice from heaven, "There is no real repentance except that which begins with the love of God, and of righteousness. What others imagine to be the end and accomplishment of repentance is, on the contrary, only its beginning. In order that you may be filled with the love of what is good, you must first be filled with love for God. If you desire to be converted, do not be curious about all these mortifications, and all these tortures. Love Him who first loved you!"

Luther listens—he listens again. These consolations fill him with joy till then unknown, and impart new light. "It is Jesus Christ," thinks he in his heart. "Yes, it is Jesus Christ Himself, who so wonderfully consoles me by these sweet and healing words." These words indeed penetrated to the bottom of the young monk's heart, like the sharp arrow of a strong man. Guided by this new light he begins to compare the Scriptures. He looks out all the passages that treat of repentance and conversion. These words till then so dreaded, to use his own expression, "are become to him an agreeable pastime, and the sweetest of recreations. All the passages of Scripture that used to alarm him, seem now to run to him from every part, to smile and sport around him." "Hitherto," exclaims he, "although I carefully dissembled the state of my soul before God, and endeavoured to express towards Him a love which was a mere constraint and a fiction, there was no expression in Scripture so bitter to me as that of repentance. But now there is none so sweet or more acceptable."

Although Luther had been consoled by Staupitz' words, he nevertheless fell sometimes into despondency. Sin was again felt in his timid conscience, and then all his previous despair banished the joy of salvation. "O my sin! my sin! my sin!" cried the young monk one day in the presence of the vicar-general, with a tone of profound anguish. "Well! would you only be a sinner in appearance," replied the latter, "and have also a Saviour in appearance?" "Know," replied Staupitz, with authority, "Know that Jesus Christ is the Saviour even of those who are great, real sinners, and deserving of utter condemnation."

It was not alone the sin he discovered in his heart that agitated Luther: the troubles of his conscience were augmented by those of reason. If the holy precepts of the Bible alarmed him, some of the doctrines of that Divine book still more increased his tortures. The truth which is the great medium by which God confers peace on man, must necessarily begin by taking away from him the false security that destroys him. The doctrine of Election particularly disturbed the young man, and launched him into a boundless field of inquiry. Must he believe that it was man who first chose God for his portion, or that God first elected man? He wished to penetrate into the secret counsels of God, unveil His mysteries, see the Invisible, and comprehend the Incomprehensible. Staupitz checked him; he told him not to presume to fathom the hidden God, but to confine himself to what He has manifested to us in Jesus Christ. "Look at Christ's wounds," said he, "and then you will see God's counsel towards man shine brightly forth. We cannot understand God out of Jesus Christ. In Him, the Lord has said, you will find what I am, and what I require. Nowhere else, neither in heaven, nor in earth, will you discover it."

The vicar-general did still more. He shewed Luther the paternal designs of Providence in permitting these temptations and these various struggles that his soul was to undergo. He made him view them in a light well calculated to revive his courage. "It is not in vain," said he to him, "that God exercises you in so many conflicts: you will see that He will employ you as His servant for great purposes."

Thus the struggles of Luther prepared his heart to understand the Word of God. The soil had been ploughed deep, and the incorruptible seed sank into it with power. When Staupitz quitted Erfurth, a new dawn had risen upon Luther!

But the work was not yet finished. The vicar-general had prepared the way: God reserved its accomplishment for an humbler instrument. The conscience of the young Augustine had not yet found repose. His body gave way at last under the conflict and the tension of his soul. He was attacked by an illness, that brought him to the brink of the grave. This was in the second year of his abode in the convent. All his distresses, and all his fears were aroused at the approach of death. His own impurity, and the holiness of God again disturbed his mind. One day, as he lay overwhelmed with despair, an aged monk entered his cell, and addressed a few words of comfort to him. Luther opened his heart to him, and made known the fears by which he was tormented. The venerable old man was incapable of following up that soul in all its doubts as Staupitz had done; but he knew his *Credo*, and had found in it much consolation to his heart. He will therefore apply the same remedy to his young brother. Leading him back to that Apostle's creed which Luther had learnt in early childhood at the school of Mansfeldt, the aged monk repeated this article with kind good nature: "*I believe in the forgiveness of sins.*" These simple words, which the pious brother pronounced with sincerity in this decisive moment, diffused great consolation in Luther's heart. "I believe!" he repeated to himself ere long on his bed of sickness, "I believe in the forgiveness of sins!" "Ah!" said the monk, "you must believe not only in the forgiveness of David's and Peter's sins, for this even the devils believe. It is God's command that we believe our own sins are forgiven us." How delightful did this commandment seem to poor Luther! "Hear what St. Bernard says in his discourse on the Annunciation," added the aged brother: "The testimony of the Holy Ghost in thy heart is this: 'Thy sins are forgiven thee.'"

From this moment light sprung up in the heart of the young monk of Erfurth. The word of grace had been pronounced, he had believed in it. He disclaims all merit of salvation, and resigns himself confidingly to the grace of God, in Jesus Christ. *From D'Aubigne's History of the Reformation.*

DAVID BRAINERD.

SOMETIME in the winter of 1732 I was something roused
out of carnal security, by I scarce know what means at first;
but was much excited by the prevailing of a mortal sickness
in Haddam. I was frequent, constant, and sometimes much
melted in duties, and took great delight in the performance of
them; and I sometimes hoped that I was converted, or at
least in a good and hopeful way for heaven and happiness,
not knowing what conversion was. The Spirit of God at this
time proceeded far with me; I was remarkably dead to the
world, and my thoughts were almost wholly employed about
my soul's concerns; and I may indeed say, "Almost I was
persuaded to be a Christian." I was exceedingly distressed
and melancholy at the death of my mother, in March, 1732,
but afterwards my religious concern began to decline, and I
by degrees fell back into a considerable degree of security,
though I still attended secret prayer frequently.

About the 15th of April, 1732, I removed from my
father's house to East Haddam, where I spent four years, but
"still without God in the world;" though for the most part I
went a round of secret duty. I was not exceedingly addicted
to young company, or frolicking, as it is called. But this I
know, that when I did go into company, I never returned
from a frolic in my life with so good a conscience as I went
with; it always added new guilt to me, and made me afraid
to come to the throne of grace, and spoiled those good frames
I was wont sometimes to please myself with. But, alas! all
my good frames were but self-righteousness, not bottomed on
a desire for the glory of God.

About the latter end of April, 1737, I removed to
Durham, and began to work on my farm, frequently longing,
from a natural inclination, after a liberal education. I became
very strict and watchful over my thoughts, words, and
actions; and thought I must be sober indeed because I
designed to devote myself to the ministry, and imagined I
did dedicate myself to the Lord.

Sometime in April, 1738, I went to Mr. Fiske's, the pastor of the church at Haddam, and lived with him during his life. And I remember he advised me wholly to abandon young company, and associate myself with grave elderly people, which counsel I followed! and my manner of life was now exceeding regular, and full of religion, such as it was; for I read my Bible more than twice through in less than a year; I spent much time every day in secret prayer and other secret duties; I gave great attention to the word preached, and endeavoured to my utmost to retain it. So much concerned was I about religion, that I agreed with some young persons to meet privately on Sabbath evenings for religious exercises, and thought myself sincere in these duties; and after our meeting was ended I used to repeat the discourses of the day to myself, and recollect what I could, though sometimes it was very late in the night. Again on Monday mornings I used sometimes to recollect the same sermons. And I had sometimes considerable movings of affections in duties, and much pleasure, and had many thoughts of joining the church. In short, I had a very good outside, and rested entirely on my duties, though I was not sensible of it.

After Mr. Fiske's death I proceeded in my learning with my brother; and was still very constant in religious duties, and often wondered at the levity of professors; it was a trouble to me that they were so careless in religious matters. Thus I proceeded a considerable length on a self-righteous foundation; and should have been entirely lost and undone, had not the mere mercy of God prevented.

Sometime in the beginning of winter, 1738, it pleased God on one sabbath day morning, as I was walking out for some secret duties, as I remember, to give me on a sudden such a sense of my danger and of the wrath of God, that I stood amazed, and my former good frames that I had pleased myself with all presently vanished; and from the view that I had of my sin and vileness, I was much distressed all that day, fearing the vengeance of God would soon overtake me; I was much dejected, and kept much alone, and sometimes begrudged the birds and beasts their happiness, because they were not exposed to eternal misery, as I evidently saw I was. And thus I lived from day to day, being frequently in great distress; sometimes there appeared mountains before me to obstruct my hopes of mercy; and the work of conversion appeared so great, I thought I should never be the subject of it; but used, however, to pray and cry to God, and perform other duties with great earnestness, and hoped by some means to make the case better. And though I hundreds of times renounced all pretences of any worth in my duties, as I thought, even in the season of the performance of them, and often confessed to God that I deserved nothing for the very best of them but eternal condemnation; yet still I had a secret latent hope of recommending myself to God by my religious duties; and when I prayed affectionately, and my heart seemed in some measure to melt, I hoped God would be thereby moved to pity me; my prayers then looked with some appearance of goodness in them, and I seemed to mourn for sin: and then I could in some measure venture on the mercy of God in Christ, as I thought, though the preponderating thought and foundation of my hope was some imagination of goodness in my heart-meltings, and flowing of affections in duty, and sometimes extraordinary enlargements therein.

Sometime in February, 1738—9, I set apart a day for secret fasting and prayer, and spent the day in almost incessant cries to God for mercy, that He would open my eyes to see the evil of sin, and the way of life by Jesus Christ. And God was pleased that day to make considerable discoveries of my heart to me. But still I trusted in all the duties I performed, though there was no manner of goodness in those duties, there being no respect to the glory of God in them, nor any such principle in my heart; yet God was pleased to make my endeavours that day a means to show me my helplessness in some measure.

Sometimes I was greatly encouraged, and imagined that God loved me, and was pleased with me, and thought I should soon be fully reconciled to God: while the whole was founded on mere presumption, arising from enlargement in duty, or flowing of affections, or some good resolutions, and the like. And when, at times, great distress began to arise, on a sight of my vileness, and nakedness, and inability to deliver myself from a sovereign God, I used to put off the discovery, as what I could not bear. Once, I remember, a terrible pang of distress seized me, and the thoughts of renouncing myself, and standing naked before God, stripped of all goodness, were so dreadful to me, that I was ready to say to them, as Felix to Paul, "Go thy way for this time." Thus, though I daily longed for greater conviction of sin, supposing that I must see more of my dreadful state in order to a remedy; yet, when the discoveries of my vile, hellish heart were made to me, the sight was so dreadful, and showed me so plainly my exposedness to damnation, that I could not endure it. I constantly strove after whatever qualifications I imagined others obtained before the reception of Christ, in order to recommend me to His favour. Sometimes, I felt the power of a hard heart, and supposed it must be softened before Christ would accept of me: and when I felt any meltings of heart, I hoped now the work was almost done; and hence, when my distress still remained, I was wont to murmur at God's dealings with me; and thought when others felt their hearts softened, God showed them mercy; but my distress remained still.

Sometimes I grew remiss and sluggish, without any convictions of sin, for a considerable time together; but after such a season, convictions sometimes seized me more violently. One night I remember in particular, when I was walking solitarily abroad, I had opened to me such a view of my sin that I feared the ground would cleave asunder under my feet, and become my grave, and send my soul quick into hell before I could get home. And though I was forced to go to bed, lest my distress should be discovered by others, which I much feared, yet I scarce durst sleep at all: for I thought it would be a great wonder if I should be out of hell in the morning. And though my distress was sometimes thus great, yet I greatly dreaded the loss of convictions, and returning back to a state of carnal security, and to my former insensibility of impending wrath: which made me exceeding exact in my behaviour lest I should stifle the motions of God's Spirit. When at any time I took a view of my convictions of my own sinfulness, and thought the degree of them to be considerable, I was wont to trust in my convictions; but this confidence, and the hope that arose in me from it, of soon making some notable advances towards deliverance, would ease my mind, which soon became more senseless and remiss: but; then again, when I discerned my convictions to grow languid, and I thought them about to leave me, this immediately alarmed and distressed me; sometimes I expected to take a large step, and get very far towards conversion, by some particular opportunity or means I had in view.

The many disappointments, and great distresses, and perplexity I met with, put me into a most horrible frame of contesting with the Almighty; and my wicked heart often wished for some other way of salvation than by Jesus Christ; and being like the troubled sea, and my thoughts confused, I used to contrive to escape the wrath of God by some other means, and had strange projections full of atheism, contriving to disappoint God's decrees and designs concerning me, or to escape God's notice, and hide myself from Him. But when, upon reflection, I saw these projections were vain, and would not serve me, and that I could contrive nothing for my own relief, this would throw my mind into the most horrid frame to wish there was no God, or to wish there were some other God that would control Him. These thoughts and desires were the secret inclinations of my heart, and were frequently acting before I was aware: but alas! they were mine, although I was affrighted with them when I came to reflect on them: when I considered of it, it distressed me to think that my heart was so full of enmity against God; and it made me tremble lest God's vengeance should suddenly fall upon me. I used before to imagine my heart was not so bad as the Scriptures and some other books represented. Sometimes I used to take much pains to work up into a good frame, and humble submissive disposition, and hoped there was some goodness in me: but it may be on a sudden, the thoughts of the strictness of the law, or the sovereignty of God, would so irritate the corruption of my heart, which I hoped I had brought to a good frame, that it would break over all bounds, and burst forth on all sides, like floods of waters when they break down their dam. But being sensible of the necessity of a deep humiliation in order to a saving union with Christ, I used to set myself to work in my own heart those convictions that were requisite in such a humiliation; as a conviction that God would be just if He cast me off for ever; and that if ever God should bestow mercy on me, it would be mere grace, though I should be in distress many years first, and be ever so much engaged in duty; that God was not in the least obliged to pity me the more for past duties, cries, and tears. These things I strove to my utmost to bring myself to a firm belief of, and hearty assent to ; and hoped that now I was brought off from myself, and truly bowed to the Divine sovereignty ; and was wont to tell God in my prayers, that now I had those very dispositions of soul that He required, and on which He showed mercy to others, and thereupon to beg and plead for mercy to me. But when I found no relief, and was still oppressed with guilt and fears of wrath, my soul was in a tumult, and my heart rose against God, as dealing hardly with me. Yet then my conscience flew in my face, putting me in mind of my late confession to God of His justice in my condemnation. And this, giving me a sight of the badness of my heart, threw me again into distress; and I wished I had watched my heart more narrowly, to keep it from breaking out against God's dealings with me ; and I even wished I had not pleaded for mercy on account of my humiliation, because thereby I had lost all my seeming goodness.

Thus, scores of times, I vainly imagined myself humbled, and prepared for saving mercy.

While I was in this distressed, bewildered, and tumultuous state of mind, the corruption of my heart was especially irritated with these things following :—

1. The strictness of the Divine law. For I found it was impossible for me, after my utmost pains, to answer the demands of it. I often made new resolutions, and as often broke them. I imputed the whole to carelessness, and the want of being more watchful, and used to call myself a fool for my negligence. But when, upon a stronger resolution, and greater endeavours, and close application of myself to fasting and prayer, I found all attempts fail, then I quarreled with the law of God as unreasonably rigid. I thought if it extended only to my outward actions and behaviour, I could bear with it; but I found it condemned me for my evil thoughts, and the sins of my heart, which I could not possibly prevent. I was extremely loth to give up, and avow my helplessness in this matter; but after repeated disappointments, thought that, rather than perish I could do a little more still, especially if such and such circumstances might but attend my endeavours and strivings. I hoped that I should strive more earnestly than ever, if the matter came to extremity, though I never could find the time to do my utmost

in the manner I intended; and this hope of future more favourable circumstances, and of doing something great hereafter, kept me from utter despair in myself, and from seeing myself fallen into the hands of a sovereign God, and dependent on nothing but free and boundless grace.

2. Another grievance was, that faith alone was the condition of salvation; and that God would not come down to lower terms; that He would not promise life and salvation upon my sincere and hearty prayers and endeavours. That word, Mark xvi, 16, "He that believeth not shall be damned," cut off all hope there; and I found that faith was the sovereign gift of God: that I could not get it as of myself, and could not oblige God to bestow it upon me by any of my performances, Eph. ii, 1—8. "This," I was ready to say, "is a hard saying, who can hear it?" I could not bear that all I had done should stand for mere nothing, who had been very conscientious in duty, and had been exceeding religious a great while, and had, as I thought, done much more than many others that had obtained mercy. I confessed indeed the vileness of my duties; but then what made them at that time seem vile, was my wandering thoughts in them, not because I was all over defiled like a devil, and the principle corrupt from whence they flowed, so that I could not possibly do anything that was good. And therefore I called what I did, by the name of honest, faithful endeavours, and could not bear that God had made no promises of salvation to them.

3. Another thing was, that I could not find out what faith was; or what it was to believe, and come to Christ. I read the calls of Christ made to the weary and heavy laden, but could find no way that He directed them to come in; I thought I would gladly come if I knew how, though the path of duty directed to were ever so difficult. I read Mr. Stoddart's "Guide to Christ," which I trust was, in the hand of God, the happy means of my conversion, and my heart rose against the author, for though he told me my very heart all along under convictions, and seemed to be very beneficial to me in his instructions, yet here he failed, he did not tell me anything I could do that would bring me to Christ, but left me, as it were, with a great gulf between me and Christ, without any direction to get through. For I was not yet effectually and experimentally taught, that there

could be no way prescribed whereby a natural man could, of his own strength, obtain that which is supernatural, and which the highest angel cannot give.

4. Another thing that I found a great inward opposition to, was the sovereignty of God. I could not bear that it should be wholly at God's pleasure, to save or damn me just as He would. That passage, Rom. ix, 11—23, was a constant vexation to me, especially verse 21. The reading or meditating on this always destroyed my seeming good frames; when I thought I was almost humbled, and almost resigned to God's sovereignty, the reading or thinking on this passage would make my enmity against the sovereignty of God appear. And when I came to reflect on my inward enmity and blasphemy, that arose on this occasion, I was the more afraid of God, and driven further from any hopes of reconciliation with Him; and it gave me such a dreadful view of myself, that I dreaded more than ever to see myself in God's hands, and at His sovereign disposal, and it made me more opposite than ever to submit to His sovereignty; for I thought God designed my damnation.

All this time the Spirit of God was powerfully at work with me; and I was inwardly pressed to relinquish all self-confidence, all hopes of ever helping myself by any means whatsoever; and the conviction of my lost estate was sometimes so clear and manifest before my eyes, that it was as if it had been declared to me in so many words, "It is done, it is done; it is for ever impossible to deliver yourself." For about three or four days my soul was thus distressed, especially at some turns, where for a few moments I seemed to myself lost and undone; but then would shrink back immediately from the sight, because I dared not venture myself into the hands of God as wholly helpless, and at the disposal of His sovereign pleasure. I dared not see that important truth concerning myself, that I was "dead in trespasses and sins." But when I had, as it were, thrust away these views of myself at any time, I felt desirous to have the same discoveries of myself again; for I greatly feared being given over of God to final stupidity. When I thought of putting it off to a more convenient season, the conviction was so close and powerful with regard to the present time, that it was the best time, and probably the only time, that I dare not put it off. It was the sight of truth concerning myself, truth respecting my state, as a creature fallen and alienated from God, and that consequently could make no demands on God for mercy, from which my soul shrank away, and trembled to think of beholding. And though some time before I had taken much pains, as I thought, to submit to the sovereignty of God, yet I mistook the thing; and did not once imagine, that seeing and being made experimentally sensible of this truth, which my soul now so much dreaded and trembled at a sense of, was the frame of soul that I had been so earnest in pursuit of heretofore: for I had ever hoped, that when I had attained to that humiliation which I supposed necessary to go before faith, then it would not be fair for God to cast me off: but now I saw it was so far from any goodness in me to own myself spiritually dead, and destitute of all goodness, that on the contrary my mouth would be for ever stopped by it; and it looked as dreadful to me, to see myself, and the relation I stood in to God, as a sinner and a criminal, and He a great Judge and Sovereign, as it would be to a poor trembling creature to venture off some high precipice. And hence I put it off for a minute or two, and tried for better circumstances to do it in; either I must read a passage or two, or pray first, or something of the like nature; or else put off my submission to God's sovereignty with an objection, that I did not know how to submit. But the truth was, I could see no safety in owning myself in the hands of a sovereign God, and confessing that I could lay no claim to anything better than damnation.

But after a considerable time spent in such like exercises and distresses, one morning, while I was walking in a solitary place, as usual; I at once saw that all my contrivances and projections to effect or procure deliverance and salvation for myself, were utterly in vain. I was brought quite to a stand, at finding myself totally lost. I had thought many times before, that the difficulties in my way were very great; but now I saw, in another and very different light, that it was for ever impossible for me to do anything towards helping or delivering myself. I then thought of blaming myself, that I had not done more, and been more engaged, while I had opportunity; for it seemed now as if the season of doing

was for ever over and gone; but I instantly saw, that let me
have done what I would, it would not more have tended to
my helping myself, than what I had done; that I had made
all the pleas I ever could have made to all eternity; and
that all my pleas were vain. The tumult that had been
before in my mind was now quieted; and I was something
eased of that distress which I felt, whilst struggling against a
sight of myself, and of the divine sovereignty. I had the
greatest certainty that my state was for ever miserable, for all
that I could do; and wondered, and was almost astonished,
that I had never been sensible of it before. In the time
while I remained in this state, my notions respecting my
duties were quite different from what I had ever entertained
in times past. Before this, the more I did in duty the more
I thought God was obliged to me, or at least the more hard I
thought it would be for God to cast me off; though at the
same time I confessed, and thought I saw that there was no
goodness or merit in my duties: but now, the more I did in
prayer, or any other duty, the more I saw I was indebted to
God for allowing me to ask for mercy; for I saw it was self-
interest that led me to pray; and that I had never once
prayed from any respect to the glory of God. Now I saw
there was no necessary connection between my prayers and
the bestowment of Divine mercy: that they laid not the least
obligation upon God to bestow His grace upon me; and that
there was no more virtue or goodness in them, than there
would be in my paddling with my hand in the water, which
was the comparison I had then in my mind; and this because
they were not performed from any love or regard to God. I
saw that I had been heaping up my devotions before God,
fasting, praying, &c., pretending, and indeed really thinking
at some times, that I was aiming at the glory of God;
whereas I never once truly intended it, but only my own
happiness. I saw that as I had never done anything for God,
I had no claim to lay to anything from Him but perdition, on
account of my hypocrisy and mockery. O how difficult did
my duties now appear from what they used to do! I used to
charge them with sin and imperfection; but this was only on
account of the wanderings and vain thoughts attending them,
and not because I had no regard to God in them—for this I
thought I had; but when I saw evidently that I had regard

to nothing but self-interest, then they appeared vile mockery of God, self-worship, and a continual course of lies; so that I saw now, there was something worse had attended my duties than barely a few wanderings: for the whole was nothing but self-worship and a horrid abuse of God.

I continued, as I remember, in this state of mind from Friday morning till the sabbath evening following, July 12th, 1739, when I was walking again in the same solitary place, where I was brought to see myself lost and helpless as was before mentioned; and here, in a mournful melancholy state, was attempting to pray, but found no heart to engage in that or any other duty; my prime concern and exercise, and religious affections, were now gone. I thought the Spirit of God had quite left me, but still was not distressed: yet disconsolate, as if there was nothing in heaven or earth could make me happy.

And having been thus endeavouring to pray, though being as I thought, very stupid and senseless for near half an hour, then, as I was walking in a dark thick grove, unspeakable glory seemed to open to the view and apprehension of my soul; I do not mean any external brightness, for I saw no such thing; nor do I intend any imagination of a body of light, somewhere away in the third heaven; nor anything of that nature; but it was a new inward apprehension or view that I had of God, such as I never had before, nor anything which had the least resemblance of it. I stood still, and wondered and admired; I knew that I never had seen before anything comparable to it for excellency and beauty; it was widely different from all the conceptions that ever I had had of God, or things Divine. I had no particular apprehension of any one person in the Trinity, either the Father, the Son, or the Holy Ghost; but it appeared to be Divine glory that I there beheld; and my soul rejoiced with joy unspeakable, to see such a God, such a glorious Divine being; and I was inwardly pleased and satisfied that He should be God over all for ever and ever. My soul was so captivated and delighted with the excellency, loveliness, greatness, and other perfections of God, that I was even swallowed up in Him; at least to that degree, that I had no thought, as I remember, at first about my own salvation, and scarce reflected there was such a creature as myself.

I continued in this state of inward joy and peace, yet astonishment, till near dark, without any sensible abatement; and then began to think and examine what I had seen, and felt sweetly composed in my mind all the evening following. I felt myself in a new world, and every thing about me appeared with a different aspect from what it was wont to do.

At this time, the way of salvation opened to me with such infinite wisdom, suitableness, and excellency, that I wondered I should ever think of any other way of salvation; and was amazed that I had not dropped my own contrivances, and complied with this blessed and excellent way before. If I could have been saved by my own duties, or any other way that I had formerly contrived, my whole soul would now have refused. I wondered that all the world did not see and comply with this way of salvation entirely by the righteousness of Christ.

The sweet relish of what I then felt continued with me for several days, almost constantly, in a greater or less degree; I could not but sweetly rejoice in God lying down and rising up.

LEPROSY IN MEN.

THIS disease affects the skin, and sometimes increases in such a manner as to produce scurf, scabs, and violent itchings, and to corrupt the whole mass of blood. At other times it is only a deformity. The Jews regarded the leprosy as a disease sent from God; and Moses prescribes no natural remedy for the cure of it. He requires only that the diseased person should show himself to the priest, and that the priest should judge of his leprosy; if it appeared to be a real leprosy, capable of being communicated to others, he separated the leper from the company of mankind. He appoints certain sacrifices and particular ceremonies already mentioned for the purification of a leper, and for restoring him to society. The marks which Moses gives for the better distinguishing a leprosy, are signs of the increase of this disease.

An outward swelling, a pimple, a white spot, bright, and somewhat reddish, created just suspicions of a man's being attacked with it. When a bright spot, something reddish or whitish, appeared ; and the hair of that place was of a pale red ; and the place itself something deeper than the rest of the of the skin ; this was a certain mark of leprosy. Those who have treated of this disease, have made the same remarks, but have distinguished a recent leprosy from one already formed and become inveterate.

A recent leprosy may be healed, but an inveterate one is incurable. Travellers, who have seen lepers in the East, say, that the disease attacks principally the feet. Maundrell, who had seen lepers in Palestine, says, that their feet are swelled like those of elephants, or horses' feet, swelled with the farcy. The common marks by which, as physicians tell us, an inveterate leprosy may be discerned are these. The voice becomes hoarse, like that of a dog which has been long barking, and comes through the nose rather than the mouth ; the pulse is small and heavy, slow and disordered ; the blood abounds with white and bright corpuscles, like millet-seeds ; is, in fact, all a scurfy serum, without due mixture; so that salt put into it does not melt, and is so dry, that vinegar mixed with it bubbles up ; the face is like a coal half extinguished, unctuous, bloated, full of very hard pimples, with small kernels round the bottom of them ; the eyes are red and inflamed, and project out of the head, but cannot be moved either to the right or left ; the ears are swelled and red, corroded with ulcers about the root of them, and encompassed with small kernels ; the nose sinks, because the cartilage rots; the nostrils are open, and the passages stopped with ulcers at the bottom ; the tongue is dry, black, swelled, ulcerated, shortened, divided in ridges, and beset with little white pimples ; the skin of it is uneven, hard, and insensible ; even if a hole be made in it, or it be cut, a putrified sanies issues from it instead of blood. Leprosy is very easily communicated ; and hence Moses has taken so much precaution to prevent lepers from communication with persons in health. His care extended even to dead bodies thus infected, which he directed should not be buried with others."—*Calmet's Dictionary of the Bible.*

THE END.